W9-BXG-673

Other books by Godfrey Hodgson include:

America in Our Time (1976)

An American Melodrama (1969)
(with Lewis Chester and Bruce Page)

by Godfrey Hodgson

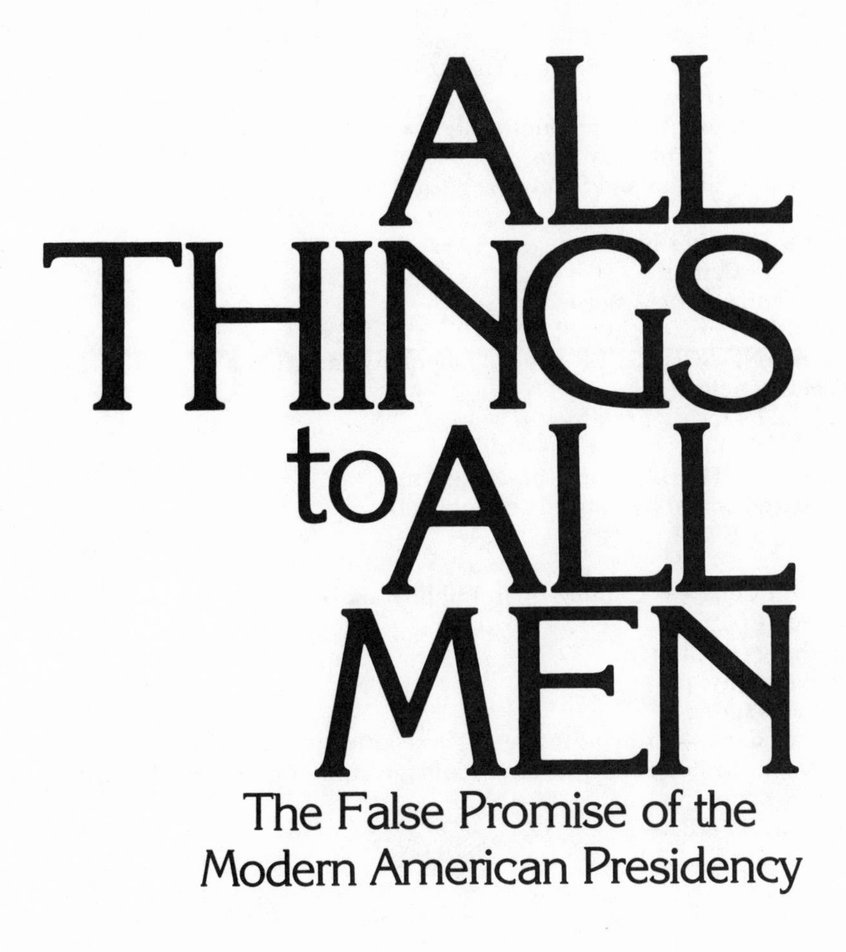

ALL THINGS to ALL MEN

The False Promise of the Modern American Presidency

Simon and Schuster New York

Published by Simon and Schuster
A Division of Gulf & Western Corporation
Simon & Schuster Building
Rockefeller Center
1230 Avenue of the Americas
New York, New York 10020
SIMON AND SCHUSTER and colophon are trademarks of
Simon & Schuster
Designed by Irving Perkins

Manufactured in the United States of America
Printed and bound by Fairfield Graphics Inc.
1 2 3 4 5 6 7 8 9 10

Library of Congress Cataloging in Publication Data
Hodgson, Godfrey.
All things to all men.
Bibliography: p.
Includes index.
1. Presidents—United States. 2. Executive power—United
States. 3. United States—Politics and government—1945- I. Title.
JK516.H62 353.03'1 80-15871
ISBN 0-671-24782-4

For Hilary

Acknowledgments

I could not possibly name, let alone adequately thank, all those who have helped me to write this book. In a sense, after all, it has been eighteen years in the making. It was in the spring of 1962 that I first used to haunt the West Wing of the White House. My thanks, therefore, are due collectively to all those who worked in the White House in the Kennedy, Johnson, Nixon, Ford and Carter administrations and who gave so generously of their time and knowledge to contribute to my education. I am especially grateful to those who agreed to be interviewed for a television documentary I made on the White House in 1976.

I would also like to thank the editors who encouraged me to keep up my education in Washington: David Astor of *The London Observer,* Harold Evans of *The London Sunday Times,* Bruce Page of *The New Statesman,* and, among television producers, Jeremy Isaacs, Gus MacDonald and Nick Elliott.

Thanks, too, to those who helped me while I was in Washington doing research specifically for this book, and especially to Beverly Cohen, Roderick MacLeish, Elizabeth Drew, Fred and Nancy Dutton, and the late Laurence M. Stern.

Finally, I would like to thank my friends and agents Michael Sissons and Peter Matson, and everyone at Simon and Schuster who helped to publish it, but most especially Alice Mayhew, who had the courage to let me attempt it.

Chilson, Oxfordshire
March 1980

Contents

I The Paradox of Presidential Power

Neither Genghis Khan, nor Alexander the Great, nor Napoleon, nor Louis XIV of France, had as much power as the President of the United States, whose acts or utterances might affect as many as one and one half billion people.

—Harry S. Truman, in an interview with *The New York Times*, 1952

The principal power that the President has is to bring them in and try to persuade them to do what they ought to do without persuasion. That's what I spend most of my time doing. That's what the powers of the President amount to.

—Harry S. Truman, in a speech on the national railroad strike, May 1948.

1

THE PARADOX of the presidency is simply stated—if hard to resolve. Never has any one office had so much power as the President of the United States possesses. Never has so powerful a leader been so impotent to do what he wants to do, what he is pledged to do, what he is expected to do, and what he knows he must do.

The disparity is not new. More than forty years ago Franklin Roosevelt heaved with a giant's strength against the bonds of the office and could not break them. The most even he could do was wriggle free a little some of the time. The tragedy of the presidency, he concluded, was the impotence of the President, and this was the man they accused of making himself into a dictator. All the strongest of his successors, Truman and Kennedy, Johnson and Nixon, have felt the same frustration and despair at the contrast between what people expect the President to be able to do and what he can actually achieve.

Over the years, the paradox—or apparent paradox—becomes more acute. The President still holds legitimate title to incomparable resources of power. Yet it is truer today than when Harry Truman left office that much of the time he is powerless to use that power.

His acts and utterances can still affect several billions of human beings. The economic resources, the technological creativity, the political influence, and the sheer military might of the United States are still superior to those of any rival power center. Yet the man who wields supreme authority over this unimaginably great complex of power still has to grab, as the political scientist Richard Neustadt once wrote of John F. Kennedy, "for just enough power to get by the next day's problems." Increasingly, it seems, his successors have been grabbing, and finding that their hands have closed on air; increasingly, they have simply failed to get through the next day's problems.

"The only power I've got is nuclear," Lyndon Johnson growled, "and I can't use that!" He understood that the power Presidents do have, to alarming extent, is the power to do things that no one in his right mind would have them do: to declare martial law, to throw the world's currencies into chaos, to invade Cuba, blow up the Middle East oil fields, incinerate the Northern Hemisphere. The power that eludes them is the power to do the very things people expect them to do: to end inflation, to ensure law and order, to negotiate disarmament without endangering the United States, to end the energy crisis.

This frustrating contrast arises partly because the relative strength of the United States in the world has declined faster than Americans' perception of their strength. As a result, for all their arsenal of thunderbolts, Presidents find it harder and harder to induce foreigners to behave as Americans want them to behave. The President cannot prevent the rise in the price of oil, the fall of Saigon, the revolution in Iran, the invasion of Czechoslovakia or Afghanistan, or any of a dozen other unwelcome shifts in the political situation, here, there, or anywhere in Africa, Asia, or Latin America. He cannot persuade the Japanese to buy more American goods or the Europeans to sell fewer arms or nuclear power plants. Gone are the days when he could impose American standards or values even on friendly countries. He cannot be sure of persuading his European allies to do what he wants. And he must stand by while the Soviet Union implacably builds up its military strength and fishes in every troubled water from Afghanistan to Angola.

But his position in international affairs is almost enviable compared to his situation at home: so much so that a President in deadlock at home almost reflexively turns to what seem the easier problems of finding peace in the Middle East or redefining the

West's relations with China. At home, the President cannot seriously hope to persuade Congress to pass more than a wretched fragment of his legislative program, itself carefully tailored down from what he would have liked to see voted into law in a perfect world. He cannot hope to carry out more than a fraction of the program he campaigned and was elected on. Broad strategies of reform, liberal or conservative, are unthinkable. He will be lucky if he can cope with some of the most urgent items on the national agenda. He will do his best to manage the economy, though Congress can make fine tuning impossible and can rewrite legislation so as to give presidential initiatives the opposite effect to the one they were intended to have. He cannot end inflation. He cannot bring about a serious reduction in energy consumption or make more than a token start on the search for alternative energy sources. Still less can he hope to attack structural social or economic problems. Whether he is liberal or conservative, or even if —as seems increasingly inevitable—he is both at once, he is unlikely to be able to achieve his goals or to fulfill his promises. The more urgent a social or economic malady, the less reasonable has it become to imagine that the President will be able to reduce it, either with surgery or with medication, within his first term.

Yet that is more and more likely to be all the time he will have. There is no more striking evidence of the problem of the presidency than the fact that Presidents find it increasingly hard to achieve even their own most urgent goal: to be reelected. Only Nixon, in the past twenty years, has been elected to two whole terms, and in order to win his second term, Nixon was constrained to do the things that led to its being cut short. If Jimmy Carter should still be President in January 1985, he will be the first incumbent in twenty-four years to survive two whole terms.

It would be a mistake to expend too much concern on the paradox of presidential power in itself. Like most paradoxes, it can be made to vanish into thin air if its terms are analyzed with sufficient clarity. If the President has so much power, how can he be powerless? Is it not rather that his power is an illusion? Or that the power, alternatively, is real enough but does not really lie within the President's control? In part, the seeming paradox can be explained away by drawing a distinction between presidential powers and presidential power: the President may have vast powers in theory yet find them useless unless he can persuade others to execute them. In part, too, the paradox arises because people confuse the power of the United States with the power of the

President, failing to realize that he has only limited possibilities of harnessing and commanding the nation's resources.

What demands our urgent attention, in any case, is not the apparent paradox between the theory of presidential power and the reality of the President's impotence, but the impotence itself. What matters is the practical problem. The presidency as an institution does not work. It does not enable the President to do what he wants to do or what the American people expect him to do. That is a dangerous state of affairs for the United States and for the world.

I have spoken of "the President." I mean any President. Jimmy Carter has failed to make the presidency work. But he has fared no worse than Eisenhower or Kennedy or Johnson, far better than Nixon, better than Ford. There is no reason to suppose that any successor will fare any better than he has done. If we are to begin to understand why that is so, we ought to take a look now, not at the grand theory of the institution, but at a flesh-and-blood President; not at a moment of high and solemn drama, nor at a crisis when he was fighting for his political life with his back to the wall. Instead, let us look carefully at a President setting about a routine, though certainly not unimportant, piece of business at a time when things were going neither exceptionally well nor exceptionally badly for him. Let us try to analyze what his resources are for getting others to do what he wants them to do. The same realities have constrained all recent Presidents. Still, by way of example, let us take a close if slightly impressionistic look at Jimmy Carter in the White House, just before the midpoint of his first term, on the afternoon of Tuesday, September 26, 1978.

2

The East Room is the largest and most impressive room in the White House. It was formerly known as the "Public Audience room," and even if you happen to know that the John Adamses used it to hang up their washing, and that Franklin and Eleanor Roosevelt's boisterous children used it for roller skating, it still comes closer than any other room in the mansion to monarchical splendor. With something truly regal in the gracious sweep of his arm, George Washington bids the visitor welcome in the portrait by Gilbert Stuart which Dolley Madison personally rescued from the marauding Redcoats in 1814. A parquet floor, white Corinthian pilasters, gold damask curtains, and three brilliant chandeliers make it, as a nineteenth-century New England clergyman put it, "a seat worthy of the people's idol." Seven dead Presidents have lain in state here, including Lincoln and John Kennedy. On happier occasions, First Ladies have used it for their levées, receptions, concerts, and balls. And in recent times it has usually been from the East Room that Presidents have addressed the nation on television.

On this particular Tuesday afternoon, however, the East Room was being put to a more prosaic purpose: not pomp, but politics. Some three hundred guests, mostly middle-aged, predominantly male, and all unmistakably prosperous, were being shepherded to rows of elegant gilt chairs by military aides of both genders in crisply pressed white uniforms. In the pillared hall that leads into the East Room, three high officials who were scheduled to address the afternoon's meeting were chatting to pass the time until the meeting was due to begin. "Remember," said one of them, "about twenty percent of these people are against us!"

This not-wholly-reliable audience was made up, as it happened, of hospital administrators. They had been dragooned to Washington from forty states at the suggestion of Anne Wexler, one of the President's political assistants. The purpose of this exercise of the presidential power to persuade was to try to convince a potentially influential group of opinion formers that the President was right and Congress wrong about the need for legislation to contain the rise of hospital bills. As a tactic, it bore a certain resemblance to the use of troop-carrying helicopters in what the military calls "vertical enfilade." Unable to make headway frontally against congressional resistance—in this as in many, many other matters—the President and his advisers were driven to try to leapfrog the congressional positions and take them in the rear.

The first speaker that afternoon was the Vice President, Walter F. Mondale. He went smoothly into a practiced routine of persuasion. Inflation was the nation's number one problem, he argued, and the inflation of hospital costs an important component cause of the general inflation rate. He appealed openly to the guests to go home and work on their congressmen. In effect, he was appealing over the heads of Congress to local opinion formers: to the director of the Baptist Medical Center of Little Rock, Arkansas, to the county commissioner of Summit County, Ohio, to the president of Blue Cross of Southern California, and all the others, in the hope of persuading them to go home and create a climate of opinion which congressmen, due to run for reelection only six weeks later, would not dare to ignore. After a few minutes of earnest admonition along these lines, the Vice President left to go to another meeting, trailing a small cloud of aides with him and shaking a surprising number of hands on his path to the door. "Nice to see *you*, sir," he was heard to say to one handshaker as he passed.

Mondale's place was taken by the President's top economic adviser, Charles L. Schultze. The cost of health care was rising at 15 percent each year, he began. "Think of the magic of exponential numbers!" Inflation was poisoning America. "You can only plan the future with dollars, and how do you plan the future with a yardstick that changes?" As an example, Schultze said that the increase in medical costs paid by an automobile manufacturer now added more to the price of a new car than the rise in the price of steel.

The third speaker was the under secretary of Health, Education, and Welfare, a plump, jovial Californian called Hale Champion. He came primed with flip charts and began attacking the counterarguments that would be made against the administration's case. The audience began to answer back. A lady from Florida said that controls were inflationary in themselves. Another woman, from Arizona, claimed that the Justice Department said that if the hospitals imposed voluntary restraints they could have antitrust problems. Champion was getting visibly annoyed and answered sharply that the Justice Department had said nothing of the kind.

The meeting did not seem to be going entirely according to plan.

A group of young men had gradually gathered outside the entrance to the East Room. White House staffers. I recognized Frank Moore, the President's top aide for congressional liaison, and then the President's closest aide, Hamilton Jordan himself, appeared. He was clowning a little, practicing putting shots in the air, and was surrounded by a respectful crowd of younger staffers.

Suddenly the chattering stopped.

A knot of men appeared at the opposite end of the corridor, walking fast toward the crowd of White House staff. Several were Secret Service agents, identifiable by their dark suits and lapel pins. Some of them muttered self-importantly into walkie-talkies.

In the middle of them was a smallish, slim man with close-cropped gray hair, pale-blue eyes, and a nervous smile. He nodded absentmindedly to left and right as he hurried toward the rostrum.

A white-jacketed military aide, his hair shorn to the scalp, had just enough time to call out: "Ladies and gentlemen, the President of the United States!"

The atmosphere in the East Room changed subtly, as the atmosphere always changes when the President enters any room, even one filled with men and women he has known for years and sees every day.

A charge of emotional current passed.

The President spoke briefly, quietly, and to the point. He had mastered his brief, and he marshaled the arguments for holding down hospital costs as if there were nothing in the world dearer to his heart than that his hearers should go back to Little Rock, and Akron, and Los Angeles, and preach the gospel of cheaper health care.

His guests—even those who had voted for his opponent two years before and who, only a moment earlier, had been quite ready to heckle a high official of his administration—now listened respectfully, in silence, some even with a faint flush of excitement on their faces.

It was not that they were hearing from the President any arguments they had not already heard from the previous speakers. Most of them, certainly, were painfully familiar with all the arguments about hospital costs long before they were contacted by Anne Wexler's office and invited to the White House.

No: they were excited, almost deferential, because the man who was talking to them, who in a minute would find the time to stand in a receiving line in the state dining room, shake their hands, and murmur a perfunctory courtesy to each of them was the President.

What was taking place and in an infinitesimal way reproducing the essential reality of presidential power was a kind of trade.

This, really, was what they had flown to Washington for: to see the President in the knowledge that the encounter would be, as people say, "something to tell their grandchildren," a certain badge of social status, a small ratification of professional success. And in return the President expected them to go home and exert on his behalf their small quantum of influence on only one of the dozens of issues that he must be concerned with, to call their congressmen, or write a letter to the local paper, or at the very least to speak favorably in influential circles in their home city of what the President was trying to achieve. The President, in short, was seeking to exchange a small scintilla of the radiance of his office against the tiny parcel of influence each of his guests could bring him.

The President's fifteen-minute appearance at that particular meeting was somewhat casually billed on his schedule that day as a "drop-by briefing" on hospital cost containment, the last of nine official and many unofficial items on a schedule that kicked off with a briefing by the President's national security adviser, Zbigniew Brzezinski, at 7:15 A.M. There was nothing casual about it. The previous day a neatly typed, seventeen-page memorandum landed on the President's desk, initialed by Anne Wexler, by Frank Moore, and by his chief domestic policy adviser, Stuart Eizenstat. The memo spelled out to the President precisely why he was going to be at the meeting, who the other participants were and why they had been chosen, and what press arrangements had been made. Only a pool of White House correspondents would be at the meeting, but the President was warned that some reporters from hometown papers and health-trade-paper writers would stay for the whole meeting.

The President was provided with a complete list of all the participants and with a head count, four days old, on the position of all members of the U.S. Senate on the hospital costs issue, broken down into those who were "right," meaning in sympathy with the administration's position, "wrong," "leaning right," "leaning wrong," and undecided. He was also given a two-page paper summarizing "talking points" his staff wanted him to bring out at the meeting. Nor did that exhaust the staff work that went into that single fifteen-minute appearance. Experts at the Council of Economic Advisers and the Department of Health, Education, and Welfare had briefed Schultze, Mondale, and Champion. The Vice President's staff had got in on the act. Three or four subunits in the White House, including Eizenstat's, Wexler's, and Moore's, had worked on the papers. And this, as we have seen, was only one of the President's multitude of concerns on that particular afternoon.

That same morning, at a meeting with members of the Black Caucus of the House of Representatives, Congressman John Conyers had stormed out because he didn't like the way the Vice President, in the President's presence, had dismissed Conyers's suggestion for a Camp David summit to talk about black unemployment. And the President had no time to brood about that either. The congressman had not been soothed down before the President had to plunge into another meeting on sensitive intelligence problems with national security adviser Brzezinski and CIA deputy director Frank Carlucci. Then, after a hurried private lunch with Mrs. Carter, on to two more meetings—one on the budget, one on export policy—before hurrying to the East Room to meet the hospital administrators.

Even in such a routine presidential appearance, we can glimpse in microcosm some of the conflicting realities that underlie the pardox of presidential power.

The President, for one thing, is indeed "institutionalized." He is programmed. His least political act is the result of strategic and tactical deliberations, planning, staff work, preparation. Even his most casual words will have been suggested by committees; his speeches will be the product of weeks of drafting, argument, redrafting. And this President is a model of informality compared to some of his predecessors—a Nixon, say, or an Eisenhower.

At the same time we can see how inextricably intertwined are the ceremonial and the political aspects of his office. His authority as head of state is reinforced by the knowledge that he is also the executive head of government. His ceremonial glamour also enhances his political effectiveness. His arguments are listened to more respectfully because his presence is always accompanied by an imaginary roll of drums, a silent fanfare of trumpets.

Both the ceremonial prestige of the office and its institutional resources must be pressed into the service of what is an act of persuasion, not an act of imperative command. The President attempts to barter a part of his prestige and his authority in return for the sum of the microscopic quantities of indirect power which hospital administrators, for example, have to lend him. He is constrained to rely on personal persuasion, and indirect persuasion at that, because he has no other way of ensuring that the decisions he has taken are translated into political or executive action. If he wants to keep hospital costs down, he cannot order the hospital administrators to freeze charges, as he could as chief executive in many countries. Nor can he procure the passage of legislation to freeze those charges, as he could in many other countries where the chief executive is so by virtue of his control of the legislature. No great national bureaucracy can be relied on to carry his intentions to the remotest corners of the country. There is no great political party to generate political support for his plans. Painfully, precariously, and with infinite effort he must construct his own coalitions on each separate issue out of whatever sticks and string he finds to hand.

Above all, he must trade. A dozen times a day the President must routinely reinvest his stock of power and prestige—both the resources of the office on which he has a four-year lease and what he has accumulated by his own efforts. In return he hopes to win the support he will need to respond to other appeals for help. If he is successful, that will add to his reputation and lend him a further bonus of new power to stake. The ultimate rationale of all this merchant adventuring in the commodity of political credibility is the President's reelection: a renewed lease on the stock-in-trade and goodwill of the presidency for another four years' enterprise in the Washington marketplace.

3

At that particular moment in September 1978 when we focused on him in action, Jimmy Carter was busy reinvesting the windfall political profits he had earned by his courageous venture in bringing President Anwar Sadat of Egypt and Prime Minister Menachem Begin of Israel to Camp David to negotiate a "framework of peace" for the Middle East. For the time being, he stood on a high pinnacle of success. But it had been a sharp turnaround. In the spring and throughout the early summer of 1978 his administration had languished in the doldrums. All summer long, from April to September, his rating in the Gallup poll had bumped along around a wretched 40 percent, and the Harris poll marked him even lower, at times at near-impeachment levels. His popularity in Iowa—scene of his first and crucial triumph in the 1976 campaign—had collapsed from 88 percent to barely half that figure in a year. Even more ominously, other polls showed him running well behind Senator Edward M. Kennedy of Massachusetts for the Democratic nomination. People in Washington were talking and writing about the possibility that Kennedy, Governor Jerry Brown of California, and perhaps other Democratic candidates would be in the ring against Carter in 1980.

Congress balked at passing the President's legislative program.

"We had an overly optimistic impression," Carter himself told *The New York Times* later, "that I could present a bill to Congress that seemed patently in the best interests of the country and the Congress would take it and pretty well pass it. I have been disabused of that expectation." Certainly Congress was showing Carter no favors. But the majority opinion in Washington was that Carter and his administration were not doing themselves any good either. They had ridden into Washington as outsiders and proud of it. They had found that to get anything done in Washington, you have to know your way around. They had proved slow to learn and were not especially adept at operating the levers even when they had found them. People were talking about the "competence factor" and the "eptness issue."

A group of powerful Washington lawyers, all veterans of previous Democratic administrations, took the unusual step of approaching Carter's White House staff, so concerned were they at the government's drift and demoralization. At two private meetings, they lectured key members of the administration about the mistakes the President was making. The President himself seemed to be aware of his problems. He brought in one or two old Washington hands to stiffen his Georgian irregulars. In mid-April, he took his whole inner circle up to Camp David for an earnest session of collective self-criticism. But little seemed to change and little went right. By midsummer, influential people in Washington were saying, and influential columnists writing, that Carter could be a one-term President. When the American Political Science Association met in New York early in September, the most authoritative pundits in America made up a unison chorus of disparagement. Indeed even the President himself on more than one occasion broke the elementary rule of self-protection and speculated out loud about the possibility that he might not enjoy a second term.

In the circumstances Carter's willingness to involve himself so directly in the search for a Middle East peace settlement was not merely courageous to the point of foolhardiness: it was a losing gambler's desperate last throw. And the gamble came off. It was on Sunday night, September 17, that Carter broke into network schedules to announce that the "framework" for agreement had been agreed, and to produce Begin and Sadat, embracing one another in full view of a hundred million Americans.

Suddenly it seemed that the President's problems were all over. The very next day the respected Washington syndicated columnist Joseph Kraft sat down to write a column that concluded that at Camp David Carter had taken "a first, big step toward realizing the promise of his presidency." With his "brilliant success" and "inspired leadership," wrote *The Wall Street Journal*'s Washington bureau chief a few days later, "Carter has reestablished his presidency in fundamental terms." By the end of the month both *Time* and *Newsweek,* the Tweedledum and Tweedledee of the instant opinion industry, had hit on the same accolade for Carter's presidency: "Born again!" In the *National Journal,* one of the shrewdest observers of the White House, Dom Bonafede, concluded that the summit had been more than a tonic for the President; it was a tonic for the presidency. "In a single, dramatic stroke," he wrote, "he showed that the President can achieve feats denied to the 535 members of Congress, who are primarily concerned with their own small constituencies."

In a single month, Carter's standing in the leading polls jumped by fifteen points or more. And there was one lesson none of the commentators failed to point out. Success could be counted on to breed success. The sudden accretion of popularity and acclaim would prove to be a negotiable commodity which the President could trade for further political profits in the future. Now Congress would have to treat him with a new respect. It might even pass a substantial part of his legislation. Now political rivals might hesitate to challenge him for the Democratic nomination. Foreign nations, friendly or adversary, would surely have to pay greater heed now to the President's wishes. Democratic candidates for Congress in the midterm elections, many of whom had noticeably avoided Carter's endorsement before Camp David, would now be eager for it. Suddenly summits were in fashion. Within weeks half a dozen interest groups had called on the President to invite them and their opponents to Camp David to apply a touch of his newfound magic to their problems.

Carter moved swiftly to try to cash in some of these potential political dividends from Camp David. On the Wednesday after his Camp David triumph, he flew to New Jersey where, as the veteran Republican Senator Clifford Case wryly put it, it was wonderful how many new friends he had made in a few days. On the Friday he made a quick foray into the Carolinas. On the Saturday he flew to western Pennsylvania and Ohio. In each of the five states he was speaking for Democratic candidates. In each case, of course, the trips had been planned before Camp David. But now Carter was doing his best to put his new-minted hoard of political prestige at the disposal of candidates who no longer showed any disposition to refuse the loan. If Camp David could be turned into solid gains for the Democrats in November, then Carter would not only face less obstruction in the dying weeks of the Ninety-fifth Congress. He could look forward to more cooperation from the Ninety-sixth.

At a fundraiser at Biltmore Estates, the former Vanderbilt château in the foothills of western North Carolina, the President doggedly shook hands for three-quarters of an hour with such local citizens as had been persuaded to contribute $500 to the somewhat forlorn-hope campaign of John Ingram for the Senate, and thus helped to raise $80,000 to pit against the $6 million Ingram's opponent, the conservative Senator Jesse Helms, was rumored to have received with the good offices of the conservative fundraiser Richard Viguery. In Columbia, South Carolina, at another fundraiser held under floodlights later the same evening on the lawn of a local heavy equipment millionaire's home, Carter spoke again on behalf of Charles ("Pug") Ravenel, who was challenging the even more conservative Republican incumbent, Senator Strom Thurmond.

Carter had scarcely taken a moment's rest since the tense, long-drawn-out poker sessions with Begin and Sadat at Camp David. Under the lights in the warm Southern dusk, he looked drained with exhaustion. Ingeniously, he related the remote problems of the Middle East to his Southern listeners: he quoted Anwar Sadat as having said that perhaps Southerners, whose ancestors had known what it was to lose a war and live under military occupation, might have an understanding for the Middle East that other Americans did not have. It was an impressive performance as stump political speeches go—impressive in its seriousness and its freedom from common political cynicism. But the President ad-libbed one aside that sounded even more from the heart than the rest of the speech, even if his hearers did take it as a joke. The presidency is a lonely job, Carter said, "except for prayer." And then he added: "When things go bad, you get entirely too much blame. And I have to admit that when things go good, you get entirely too much credit."

Perhaps in that moment at the end of a long day and a long week, Carter already had some premonition of how short-lived a political respite he had won at Camp David. True, in the closing weeks of the Ninety-fifth Congress the administration did win an impressive enough string of victories, or what passed for victories, on Capitol Hill. Congress did pass an energy bill and a tax bill. It did sustain a couple of controversial presidential vetoes, one on the funding for a new nuclear-powered aircraft carrier and the other on a particularly egregious pork-barrel water projects bill.

But neither the energy bill nor the tax bill bore more than a remote resemblance to the measures the President had recommended. Both were mutilated beyond recognition. Congress did finally pass the Humphrey-Hawkins full employment bill—but only after deleting the crucial enforcement provisions. Other important administration proposals failed altogether: welfare reform, labor law reform, a bill to set up a separate Department of Education, and another to establish a consumer protection agency. The President's urban policy passed, or rather some two-thirds of the bills involved passed: not those containing the major financial provision that would have been needed to make it effective. In short, Congress had failed to give the President in recognizable form any of the major programs he had asked for, or any of the major reforms he had proposed, with the single exception of civil service reform, and that legislation, though valuable in itself, was in truth no more than a pale shadow of the sweeping reform of the bureaucracy Carter had promised in the campaign and would have liked to carry through.

Nor were Carter's efforts to use his Camp David triumph to improve the complexion of Congress any more successful than his relations with the existing Congress. In November the Republicans gained three seats in the Senate and a dozen in the House. In terms of support for the President's most cherished policies, the losses were even more serious than those raw figures suggest. The defeat of Senator Dick Clark in Iowa, for example, the chairman of the Africa subcommittee of the Senate Foreign Relations Committee, was to have a grave effect on support for the President's southern Africa policy. Worse still, after November 1978 the President's support in the Senate on the Strategic Arms Limitations Treaty, which already loomed ahead as the most difficult and dangerous foreign policy test for the administration on Capitol Hill, was weakened by at least four votes.

Among other bills that failed to pass, in spite of all Anne Wexler's efforts, was the hospital cost containment bill. Among the candidates defeated for the Senate were the two the President had flown south to speak for in September, John Ingram of North Carolina and Pug Ravenel of South Carolina.

Two months after his triumph at Camp David, the President was no nearer to fulfilling his campaign promises. Indeed, some of those promises, like the commitment to cut back the federal bureaucracy drastically, increasingly looked irrelevant or naive. And the President was no nearer to tackling fundamental long-term problems: inflation, welfare reform, national health insurance, or energy.

What seemed to have happened was that, frustrated in his efforts to carry out what he took to be his electoral mandate and impotent to tackle major domestic problems, Carter had turned to foreign policy, seeking to establish a prestige and authority with a few swift foreign "spectaculars" that could be traded for domestic successes. He achieved just such a success at Camp David in September. But as it became clear that the "framework of peace" would not in itself encompass any substantial progress toward a settlement of the essential problem in the Middle East, that of the Palestinians, Carter turned aside toward another spectacular: a new relationship with China, leading to the opening of diplomatic relations. By late December, when reporters asked presidential press secretary Jody Powell why the President did not become personally involved in efforts to unsnarl a tangle that had developed in the Middle East peace negotiations, Powell replied that the President was too involved in the negotiations with the Chinese!

The China diversion in turn had an immediate and very damaging impact on the foreign operation from which Carter still at that time hoped for the greatest dividends of all: the SALT negotiations. A few days before Christmas, Secretary of State Cyrus Vance flew to meet Soviet Foreign Minister Andrei Gromyko in Geneva, in the full expectation that Gromyko would agree to name an early date for a summit meeting at which the President and Soviet President Leonid Brezhnev would sign a SALT treaty. To the surprise of the American delegation, the Russians were in no hurry to set a date. Gradually it became apparent that they were both annoyed and alarmed by the President's opening toward China and especially by his invitation to the Chinese leader, Deng Xiaoping, to visit the United States. They felt that delaying the SALT treaty was the only leverage they had to prevent the Americans and the Chinese ganging up on them. The summit was finally set for Vienna in mid-June, and the treaty duly signed there. But by that time the damage had been done. Some three or four months had been lost. As a result the process of Senate ratification of the treaty had become even more inextricably entangled with the opening moves of the 1980 presidential election than it was before. And over those same months, while the President's attention was engaged by the Chinese, the Soviets, and the Middle East, the Iranian revolution exploded. The immediate result was a renewal of the energy crisis. Less predictably, the seizure of the U.S. embassy staff as hostages led to an international crisis that dwarfed the fate of the SALT treaty and made even the Soviet invasion of Afghanistan seem secondary by comparison.

In the end, a peace treaty was signed between Egypt and Israel, though not before the President had risked a last-minute visit to the Middle East to prevent a breakdown in the talks. The treaty was a significant achievement for Carter's good offices, even if the problem of the Palestinian Arabs on the West Bank of the Jordan is no nearer solution now than it was before the Camp David meeting in 1978. In the end, the President and Leonid Brezhnev did sign a Strategic Arms Limitation Treaty in Vienna on June 18, 1979, though twelve months later it was further than ever from ratification by the United States Senate. Throughout 1979, the President's political reputation and strength in Washington continued to bob up and down in the most volatile way in response to the changes and chances of foreign crises.

At the beginning of July, Carter's fortunes seemed to have reached their nadir. Gas lines and incipient panic about energy supplies made him hurry back from a world economic summit in Tokyo, only to cancel an emergency television appearance at the last moment. For a week, the political world held its breath while the President communed with a somewhat oddly chosen assortment of counselors on the mountaintop at Camp David. On July 15 he descended at last to make his long-awaited speech. He duly announced that he would seek congressional approval for a massive new program intended to make the United States once again self-sufficient in energy. At the same time he diagnosed a national malaise, a crisis of confidence "that strikes at the very heart and soul and spirit of our national will . . . threatening to destroy the social and political fabric of America." Cynics and sophisticates wondered whether any amount of national malaise could be blamed for the high level of oil imports. But in general the speech was well received. It might have gone far to restore Carter's political fortunes had he not astonished political Washington two days later by abruptly demanding the resignation of his entire staff and cabinet, and finally firing four cabinet members. The bloodbath blurred the favorable impact of his speech and raised renewed doubts about his political competence. By August, the President's support in the opinion polls had slumped to within a point or two of the lowest ratings ever recorded. The prevailing opinion among the cognoscenti in Washington was that he was through, destined at best to limp through his time as a single-term President. In early September, Senator Kennedy began to move closer and closer into the open as a rival candidate.

In the meantime the Carter administration proceeded to administer what the *Washington Post* called "a self-inflicted technical knockout" to itself on another foreign policy issue, the presence and disputed significance of a Soviet "brigade" in Cuba. Both the President's performance and his prospects looked wretched when, on November 4, a group of "students" invaded the U.S. embassy compound in Teheran and took the embassy staff prisoner. The subsequent recovery in the President's fortunes could not be wholly attributed to the Iranian crisis. Nor was it certain even that affairs in Iran would not ultimately backfire on Carter if it began to appear that he had not acted forcefully enough. But by the end of that year the seesaw had swung wildly once again. Kennedy was down again, and Carter, at least for the time being, was up. On July 4, 1979, the President seemed powerless to do his job. He seemed becalmed, without even steerageway. Six months later, having made little or no impact on substantive national problems at home or abroad, Carter had soared to a twenty-point lead over Kennedy. It cannot really be said that the attempt to recruit strength and prestige for the Carter presidency through dramatic action in foreign affairs was any more effective than the attempt to recruit greater support in Congress. It was not the special manifestation of presidential charisma nor the second descent from the mountaintop with new tablets of redemptive law that kept presidential authority alive and sustained the hope of the President's reelection. Merely to "grab for just enough power to get by the next day's problems," the President had thrown the whole authority of his office onto the gambling table, not once but repeatedly: in September 1978 at Camp David, in March 1979 in the Middle East, in July 1979 at Camp David again. What saved him then was as close as you get in the great affairs of the world to sheer blind luck: the instinctive rallying round of public opinion in response to an unprovoked act of insanity in Iran and the Soviet invasion of Afghanistan, plus the President's dignity and self-restraint in the testing time.

Carter has been sorely, but not uniquely, tested. All modern Presidents have been frustrated by their inability to do anything about fundamental problems. Some have been tempted to improve their position by winning easy victories in foreign affairs. Often those victories have proved costly in the long run—as Carter's commitments in the Middle East may yet prove costly. Several have sought to free themselves from their shackles by calling for a metaphysical rededication of the national will. All have been disappointed.

"About this time, almost halfway through his first term," wrote James Reston in *The New York Times* before the Camp David summit of 1978, "most recent Presidents have found themselves in a slump between the end of the honeymoon and the struggle of the next election, and have had to decide whether to fight or compromise. Truman, Kennedy, Johnson, Nixon and even Eisenhower faced the same problem, and dealt with it in different ways. Now Carter has come to the same fork in the road."

But there is not just one single fork in the road for all Presidents. All face the same choices because all seek to operate a system that does not work, in the sense that it does not allow Presidents to do what is expected of them.

4

The appalling Washington summer weather has one particularly tormenting trick. For days, the humidity hangs over the city like a miasma, drenching shirts, draining energies, and souring tempers. Then overnight a sudden cloudburst fills the storm drains and clears the air. The next morning the city has a Mediterranean sparkle. Temperature, 72 degrees; humidity, 25 percent. Work becomes possible again and tennis, a pleasure. But over the next five days or so the heat builds up again remorselessly, sucking up the moisture from the Potomac and the Chesapeake. Once again the readings are: temperature, 95 degrees; humidity, 95 percent.

Some similar rhythm affects the city's political climate. The difficulties that hem in the President are too deep to be driven away for more than a few months by even the most brilliant successes. What is more, those who have worked in the White House and those who have studied it most closely have long been aware that these difficulties recur in a regular, cyclical pattern in the life of every administration. The pattern has been observable at least since the beginning of Eisenhower's presidency. In recent years it seems to have spiraled lower and lower, as longer periods of presidential frustration are relieved by briefer, more precarious periods of presidential success.

Lyndon Johnson was well aware of the limitations on presidential accomplishment set by this life cycle of a presidency—any presidency, even his own. "You've got to give it all you can that first year," he told his special counsel, Harry McPherson. Johnson saw the cycle primarily in terms of the degree of cooperation the President could expect from Congress:

> "Doesn't matter what kind of majority you come in with. You've got just one year when they treat you right, and before they start worrying about themselves. The third year, you lose votes . . . The fourth year's all politics. You can't put anything through when half of Congress is thinking how to beat you. So you've got one year. That's why I tried. Well, we gave it a hell of a lick, didn't we?"

Writing before Richard Nixon resigned, a political scientist, John H. Kessel, had already seen that the life cycle of the presidency did not solely depend on the matching cycle of the Congress. He elaborated this insight into the germ of a cyclical theory of the presidency:

> A newly elected president may expect a honeymoon period . . . The period of initial learning takes about eighteen months . . . The third year of an administration is the best time for accomplishment in the first term. . . . The fourth year, of course, is a time when partisanship becomes dominant . . . If he is returned to office by a sizeable vote, and if a congressional majority of his own party is elected at the same time, the fifth and sixth years provide the best opportunity for real accomplishment.

Kessel went further and detected a cyclical pattern in presidential concern with different kinds of issues. Thus, for example, he suggested, Presidents pay most attention to civil liberties immediately after they are elected, "presumably because of commitments made in the course of their campaigns." Their involvement in international affairs, he said, "builds during the first term, drops as re-election year comes around, and then becomes even more prominent during his second term." The distribution of social benefits, on the other hand, Kessel thought, "is primarily a first term phenomenon," and becomes "the most important concern during a President's fourth year in office."

An unidentified White House adviser, quoted by one of the most respected of the younger generation of political scientists, Thomas E. Cronin, in his 1975 book, *The State of the Presidency*, saw the cyclical constraints on presidential action in terms not of Congress but of the cabinet. "Everything depends," this man told Cronin,

> "on what you do in program formation during the first six or seven months. I have watched three presidencies and I am increasingly convinced of that. Time goes by so fast. During the first six months or so the White House staff is not hated by the cabinet, there is a period of friendship and cooperation and excitement. . . . So long as that exists you can get a lot done. You have only a year at most for new initiatives."

The most elaborate cyclical analysis of the presidency was worked out by Stephen Hess in a book called *Organizing the Presidency*. Hess is a distinguished political scientist who has had the advantage of working in the White House, not merely under two different Presidents, Eisenhower and Nixon, but also at the two opposite ends of their terms: at the beginning of the Nixon administration and for the last two years of the second Eisenhower administration. He could therefore see clearly that while some of the differences between those two presidencies were to be explained in terms of the different political philosophies and temperaments of the two Presidents, or by the different assumptions and circumstances of the times, others seemed simply the product of the stage that had been reached in the life cycle of their two administrations. Hess believes that the point could be demonstrated by a year-by-year study of all presidencies, at least as far back as 1953. He has spelled out in some detail what might be called the natural history of a presidency.

All Presidents, when they enter the White House, are confronted by certain opportunities and by certain dangers by virtue of the mere fact that they are new. All Presidents and their staffs share an understandable arrogance. For at least two years their whole endeavors have been concentrated on one end, winning the presidency, and they have won it. They have succeeded where others have failed. Moreover, in the last months of the campaign, as their man emerged as a possible winner, they have been exposed to not a little flattery by the media and by those who hope to get favors from them. At the same time, all administrations tend to react directly against their predecessors. After all, one of the chief reasons why they are now in the White House, and their predecessors out, is because they knew how to campaign against their predecessors, their policies, their style, their conduct and all their works, in a way that evoked a favorable response from the electorate. So it is natural that they start off by trying to do the opposite of what the previous administration has done.

In spite of or perhaps because of this, every new President is granted a honeymoon. His first few months, Hess says, pass in a state of "euphoria." Congress is respectful. The media are willing to give him the benefit of the doubt. The new President becomes a national institution. He may even become a superstar.

Then, as his first year wears on, he has to do things: make appointments, take stands, propose legislation, react to crises at home and abroad. Every time he does something, he offends someone. A "coalition of minorities" begins to form against him. His administration, sometime in that first year, "has its first foreign crisis and its first domestic scandal." And the President's poll ratings start to drop. (The poll ratings of all recent Presidents have dropped at an average rate of six percentage points a year, with the sole exception of Eisenhower's, which rose during his first term at the rate of two and a half points a year.) "By the end of his first year," Hess went on,

> the President should have learned two important lessons: first, that the unexpected is likely to happen; second, that his plans are unlikely to work out as he had hoped. The Soviet Union launches Sputnik. A U-2 is shot down. There is an uprising in Hungary, a riot in Watts, a demonstration at Berkeley. . . . The President finds that much of his time is spent reacting to events over which he has no control or trying to correct the errors of others.

So Presidents start to "turn inward." They become resentful of the media and suspicious of their own cabinet. They begin to feel that if things are going to be done, they will have to do them themselves. They come to rely more and more on the White House staff, whose members are trusted, familiar old friends and who possess no rival power base that could enable them to resist the President's wishes.

By now, the midterm congressional elections are approaching. "The President tries to restore his luster at the polls. He always fails." (The only modern President to win seats for his party in both the Senate and the House was Franklin Roosevelt in 1934: an exception that proves the rule if ever there was one.)

In the third year, the President turns to foreign affairs. Perhaps as much as two-thirds of his time in that year is spent on foreign policy, Hess calculated. In part, he does so because he has to: there are foreign policy issues that cannot be avoided. But, as Hess put it, "He also turns to foreign policy because it is the area in which he has most authority to act and, until recently, the least public and congressional restraint on his actions." Besides, foreign policy offers the elusive reward of a statesman's place in the history books. In the third year, too, the exodus from government begins, as able and ambitious men, having enjoyed an experience of government, drift away to secure their futures. Divisions and dissensions in the administration become deeper and more envenomed.

In the fourth year, with equal abruptness, "the President's attention snaps back to domestic considerations." Now everything the administration does is conditioned by the President's desire to be reelected. He puts off ambitious but dangerous projects for reforms which he himself, only a few months earlier, had been urging his subordinates to press ahead with. He becomes more cautious, more concerned with bread-and-butter economic issues. He finds more and more excuses to make "nonpolitical" speeches around the country. By the summer of his fourth year he is blatantly, unashamedly running for office.

Hess went on to argue that the second term is generally "downhill." It is a dubious proposition. Some would say, with John Kessel, that a President's chances for dramatic action are never better than in his fifth and sixth years. There are historical examples—the two Roosevelts and perhaps others—of Presidents who proved more effective in their second term than in the first. But the real reason why the second term must be left out of the argument is simply because there are so few examples to point to in recent years. Only Eisenhower and Nixon, since FDR, have been reelected to a second term in their own right (though it could be objected that Truman's first term "felt" like a second term because he succeeded Roosevelt so early in 1945). Eisenhower's second term was greatly affected by his poor health. And while Nixon appears to have planned to do great things in his second term, he in fact reentered the White House with a heavy mortgage to pay off for his reelection. Within three months of his second inauguration there was no longer any serious possibility that he would have the political strength for bold innovation.

If we restrict ourselves to looking at Hess's scenario for the first term alone, what is striking is how uncannily it predicts Jimmy Carter's experience in the White House, even though it was written long before Jimmy Carter even won the Democratic nomination. But the "life-cycle" theory of the presidency must not be pressed too far. There is nothing automatic or predestined about the cycle. Presidents can take arms against a sea of troubles and by opposing, end them. But the mere fact that someone writing in 1976 and drawing on the White House record of the five previous Presidents could so closely predict the sequence of events in a sixth presidency must establish a certain presumption in favor of at least the core of Hess's case: that to a significant extent all Presidents are now at the mercy of the same pressures and forces and needs so that there is an unmistakable chronological pattern to their experience of the White House.

5

That pattern has been one of frustration, disappointment, and failure. All Presidents enter the White House full of hope and honorable ambition. They have arrived there in large part because of their success in convincing the voters that they are capable of changing things. They want to improve the security and the standing of the United States in the world, to manage the economy and bring about greater prosperity, to "clean up the mess in Washington," to "get the country moving again," to "bring it together again," and to help it to "live up to its best ideals": in short, whatever the formula they have sold to the voters, they believe they can put right the wrongs left untouched by the ideological error or managerial incompetence of their predecessor. Conservative Presidents want to change things every bit as much as liberals, though of course they want to change different things. They find it equally hard to change anything. Some Presidents, naturally, have been more effective than others. Yet Jimmy Carter is not the first President to find himself baffled by the way the system works to prevent him doing what he wants to do and makes him impotent to carry out the policies he believes necessary. On the contrary, Carter is at least the fifth, and it can be argued the sixth, consecutive incumbent in the White House to fail to achieve his goals.

Unable, with rare exceptions, to bring about significant change, Presidents find themselves like a man in a nightmare whose limbs refuse to respond to the commands given by his head.

Even political survival has eluded them. President Eisenhower was the last President to survive two terms. He succeeded in this in part because his ambitions were so modest. He chose to reign rather than to rule.

President Kennedy was assassinated. The first instinct is to except him from the generalization of failure. Because of the "accident" of his assassination, it is tempting to say that we simply cannot know whether or not he would have successfully lasted for two whole terms. But even this apparently obvious assertion must be treated with some reserve. For one thing, we do not know for certain what was the motive of Kennedy's assassin, Lee Harvey Oswald. If, as seems at least possible, it was connected in some way with the acute tension between the United States and Cuba, it should be remembered that that tension was sharply exacerbated by the 1960 election campaign. Both candidates, Nixon even more than Kennedy, felt the need to take the strongest possible line against Fidel Castro. As a result, Kennedy organized an expeditionary force against Castro (as Nixon was committed to do if elected) and also connived at, if he did not order, attempts to assassinate him. Those attempts involved elements of organized crime that were deeply involved in Cuba and that, if the House of Representatives' assassination committee is to be believed, were also involved in the murder of the President. So no one can absolutely dismiss the connection between Oswald's motive and the need for presidential candidates, and Presidents, to strike spectacular stances in foreign policy.

Even if one totally rejects the "Cuban connection" among the possible explanations of Kennedy's assassination, the assassination cannot be regarded as pure accident. On the contrary, if Oswald's motive was buried in the purest private psychopathology, his decision to kill the President was plainly affected by the extraordinary charismatic elevation of Kennedy in the media. To win the nomination and then the election, Kennedy deliberately focused the most intense, dramatic emphasis on his success, his glamour, his youth, his style, his family's wealth, his wife's beauty, and in general the enviable splendor of his personal life: precisely the characteristics to inflame the envious fury of a solitary, inadequate, impoverished drifter like Oswald. So either Kennedy was killed as a result of a conspiracy related to actions he had taken for political reasons highly germane to his campaign for the presidency, or he was killed as a result of the style in which he had chosen to conduct himself in the presidency. This is not to predict future assassinations. Still less does it excuse them. Not every President who attempts to overthrow foreign rulers or who attempts to project himself as a figure of quasi-monarchical personal superiority must expect to be assassinated. Still, if such men are assassinated, it cannot be called wholly a matter of accident.

This dramatization of the presidency, this emphasis on the charismatic as opposed to the traditional or bureaucratic basis of its authority (to borrow a distinction from the German sociologist Max Weber which will be analyzed in more detail in a later chapter), is typical of the way the presidency has evolved since Franklin Roosevelt's time. In such an atmosphere, assassination may be an accident. It is, however, an accident which is not unexpected. The elaborate safety precautions, the size of the budget allotted to presidential protection, the fact that four Presidents have actually been assassinated and that attempts have been made to kill several other Presidents and presidential candidates: these pieces of evidence suggest that the problem of presidential survival is, among other things, a problem of physical survival.

The assassination, in any case, heralded a crisis of legitimacy for the presidency. This was a matter not of logic but of instinctive public feeling. The Warren Commission, to Lyndon Johnson's relief, rushed to the judgment that Oswald had acted alone and irrationally. But whatever Oswald's motives, and we are still a long way from understanding everything about the chain of causation that led to his act, people instinctively *felt* that the assassination could not have been an accident. Many felt at first, and especially because the assassination took place in Dallas, that Kennedy must have been killed on behalf of the extreme Right, perhaps in retribution for his civil rights policy. Later, when Oswald's Communist associations were known, others thought that the international Left was responsible. Others again surreptitiously wondered whether Lyndon Johnson himself were not implicated.

Johnson felt this problem of legitimacy acutely, in terms of what he thought of as the Eastern elitist prejudices of "the Kennedy people" but could be accurately called a tradition of interventionist, "internationalist" foreign policy that ran back through Kennedy to Truman and Franklin Roosevelt, Wilson and Teddy Roosevelt.

Another factor, unrelated to Johnson's individual personality, intensified the crisis of legitimacy brought on by his succession to the presidency. Precisely because the modern President is legitimized not by a slow process of emergence in political leadership but by the sudden laying on of hands in a sort of plebiscite, his legitimacy is diminished in the popular mind when he is not "an elected President." Never mind that he has succeeded exactly as the Constitution prescribes. Never mind that he may have brought a considerable addition to the voting strength of the ticket, and that his reputation may have been high for many years before the winning presidential candidate became known. He still lacks the charismatic legitimation of popular election. Whoever had succeeded an assassinated President in 1963, therefore, and whatever his personal political background, he would have had to establish his own legitimacy. And certainly, among the reasons for the present crisis of the presidency, one should not altogether omit the fact that for something like seven and a half out of the last twenty years, the White House has been occupied by two men—first Johnson, then Ford—who not only were not originally elected President in their own right, but also came to the presidency in circumstances of national tragedy and shame.

Lyndon Johnson was acutely aware of the fact that he had stepped into another man's shoes. He was explicit on the point in his memoirs:

> Every President has to establish with the various sectors of the country what I call "the right to govern" . . . For me that presented special problems . . . since I had come to the presidency not through the

> collective will of the people but in the wake of tragedy . . . I eventually developed my own programs and policies, but I never lost sight of the fact that I was the trustee and custodian of the Kennedy administration.

It can be argued that it was precisely because of his anxiety to remain faithful to the spirit of the Kennedy administration that he committed himself so wholeheartedly to the war in Vietnam. The argument is dubious, since if anything Johnson believed even more passionately and with less skepticism in America's duty to contain Communism than Kennedy had done. More narrowly, though, it is clear that it was Johnson's desire to remain loyal to the Kennedy policies—and so incidentally retain the loyalty of the Kennedy followers—that caused him to miss the opportunity for a change of policy presented by the fall of the Diem brothers shortly before Kennedy's death.

In any case, Lyndon Johnson strove to reestablish the tarnished legitimacy of the presidential office. But he failed. His policies eventually divided the country so bitterly that he was unable to appear in public except on the rarest occasions, and then in carefully chosen locations and with a shield of security arrangements so elaborate it seemed more appropriate to a dictatorship than to a democracy. For a while Johnson succeeded in being one of the most effective Presidents of the century. But that effort, too, ran out of steam. By the beginning of his fourth year as a President elected in his own right, Johnson had to admit defeat. He announced that he would not run for reelection. His motives were mixed. He seems to have thought, quite wrongly, that if his own personality were removed from the account it would be easier to negotiate peace in Vietnam. Less creditably, it was clear that he was in danger of a thrashing from his hated rival, Robert Kennedy, in at least some primaries. He threw in the towel, and once he had made that announcement, both the authority and the effectiveness of his presidency were at an end. The two significant achievements of his last year were taken from him: the chance of a negotiated peace in Vietnam because the South Vietnamese preferred to see whether they could get a better deal from his successor, and the credit for the nuclear nonproliferation treaty, because his successor was able to hold it up in the Senate long enough to get the credit for himself.

In short, public confidence in the legitimacy of the presidential office, gravely damaged by the assassination of Kennedy and the succession of Johnson, had not yet been fully reestablished when Richard Nixon was inaugurated in 1969. In retrospect, it is clear that the crisis of legitimacy in the presidency was not solely occasioned by the assassination or by Lyndon Johnson's succession. It was part of a more general crisis of authority in society. But by 1969 the desire for order and stability was reasserting itself. There was an excellent opportunity for reestablishing legitimacy. Johnson's unexpected withdrawal, the spectacular events of the campaign, including the murders of Dr. Martin Luther King, Jr., and of Robert Kennedy, the narrow margin of Nixon's victory, and the general sense of excitement and crisis that characterized the year 1968, all made it a high priority for the new administration to calm the nation's nerves and to restore the authority and dignity of the presidency. And that was what a majority of Americans wanted.

Many of Nixon's actions and attitudes in the first term gravely disturbed important sections of public opinion, and not just for partisan reasons. Many lawyers, for example, were appalled by his intervention in the case of Lieutenant William Calley, on trial for his part in the Mylai massacre. Still, in a superficial view, Nixon had by the time of his second inauguration succeeded to a very great extent in rebuilding the country's faith in the presidency. His foreign policy achievements in particular, whatever their real significance, corresponded with the picture many Americans had of how they expected a President to act. Nixon himself believed passionately, according to his lights, in the dignity of the office. For a while he appeared to be successful in his efforts to restore its prestige and authority. By 1972 more Americans than ever before were preparing to vote for a President's reelection. And more Americans than ever before were visiting the White House. Meanwhile Nixon was preparing, with a great deal of success, to wrap himself in red, white, and blue as he presided over the Bicentennial celebrations in 1976.

The portrait of Nixon the pacifier, the restorer of normality and of the legitimacy of the presidential office is, however, a very superficial one. As what Nixon's friend and attorney general, John Mitchell, called "the White House horrors" began to unfold in 1973, it became clear that the high view Nixon and his circle took of the presidential prerogative was only exceeded by the low view they took both of the spirit and of the letter of the Constitution. The convenient use of the word "Watergate" as shorthand for the administration's transgressions can obscure the gravity of what Nixon did. It tends to suggest that he was driven to resign because a team of burglars working for the committee to reelect him was found inside the Democratic National Committee's offices. That was, in the end, the least of it.

As the Watergate hearings, the media's investigations, the courts, the grand jury, the Freedom of Information Act and the President's own tapes flayed away one protective skin of secrecy after another, it became apparent how deeply falsehood and manipulation were part of the very essence of the Nixon administration. Its foreign policy was actually founded on a gigantic lie. In order to reconcile their (certainly accurate) perception that the war could not be won with their (doubtful) conviction that the American people would not forgive an administration which admitted that fact, they hit upon a simple solution: they would tell the American people that the war was being won when in fact it was being lost. That one big lie led to countless smaller deceptions, some of them big enough in themselves in all conscience. The fundamental falsehood of the administration's stance on Vietnam, the greatest political issue of the time, made necessary the deception of Congress and the American people about the bombing of North Vietnam and Cambodia, and about the betrayal of the South Vietnamese government. With the passage of time, deception became not so much a tactic to be used at need as a strategy and a habit, until no prudent man, anywhere in the world, wholly believed anything that either the President or his alter ego Henry Kissinger said. This strategy of deception abroad could not be prevented from filtering back into the administration's practice at home. It was in order to prevent leaks about its foreign policy, in the first instance, that the "plumbers unit" was set up, and the rest of the apparatus of spying and bullying used not only against an avowed opponent like Daniel Ellsberg, but also against the media and even against more scrupulous members of the administration itself like Dr. Morton Halperin.

Even before the crisis of conscience occasioned by the invasion of Cambodia in 1970, the administration was embroiled in the domestic intrigues and infringements of civil liberties that led to the "Huston plan" and that must surely have ended, had the exposure occasioned by Watergate not intervened, in the setting up of something not very far from a secret political police. The campaign to reelect the President, too, was similarly steeped in systematic falsehood. This extended far beyond the financial sharp practices—the laundering and the bagmen and the wads of unreported cash that were used to circumvent all restrictions on campaign finance. It went deeper even than the "routine" dirty tricks of the campaign itself—routine, that is, in the sense that Nixon, in his 1962 campaign for the governorship of California, had already practiced most of them with the help of H. R. Haldeman and many of the others who worked in the White House and at the Committee to Re-elect the President. In a more fundamental sense, the campaign was based on a strategy of misrepresentation. Nixon and his men systematically misrepresented the specific positions of Democratic candidates—first Senator Edmund Muskie, during the primary and preprimary period, and then Senator George McGovern. They also misrepresented the issues. To an unprecedented extent, long before the 1972 campaign formally opened, they were diverting attention from substantive issues to scapegoats: from the war and the real condition of the nation's cities to radical blacks, rebellious students, drug addicts, and welfare mothers.

Quite apart from the relatively petty lawlessness of their attitude to electoral law, to income tax, and to civil liberties, in several major ways Nixon and his men played fast with the Constitution itself. This is not the place to analyze the unconstitutional acts and threats to constitutional practice perpetrated by the Nixon administration. Even a cursory list suggests how high a view Nixon took of the presidential prerogative, and in particular how far he was prepared to go to tilt the balance of power between the White House and the Congress in his direction. He did his best to pack the Supreme Court with partisan mediocrities. He used presidential power and influence to attack the freedom of the press in numerous ways; he intended to introduce a secrecy law which many authorities felt would contravene the spirit of the First Amendment. In several instances, notably the refusal to enforce Title VI of the Civil Rights Act of 1964 and in the dismantling of the Office of Economic Opportunity, his administration came close to flat defiance of statutes. He vastly extended the use of the "pocket veto" power. He asserted unprecedented claims for "executive privilege," attempting to withhold witnesses and documents not only from the Congress but even from a grand jury. His use of the dubious presidential privilege of "impounding" appropriated funds as a kind of unconstitutional veto for policy purposes struck at the heart of the constitutional grant of the money power to Congress.

In short, Nixon from time to time claimed powers and immunities for his office that, if successfully asserted, would have had the effect of radically upsetting the constitutional system of checks and balances and of replacing the constitutional President with a new style of chief executive whose virtually absolute power was justified by the supposed requirements of "national security" and qualified only by the need to win a "mandate" from the voters every four years.

When Nixon fell, in August 1974, this high-flying doctrine of the presidential prerogative was temporarily discredited. Public confidence in the presidency fell to a lower level, perhaps, than at any previous moment in American history, lower, certainly, than at any previous crisis in the history of the modern presidency. Gerald Ford did his best to restore a sense of legitimacy. He succeeded to the extent that his basic honesty was not in question. Nor could anyone easily call him an imperial president. But in terms of legitimacy he was handicapped by one catastrophic mistake: his decision to pardon Nixon. At the time it looked to some like a mere deal: the price of his accession to the presidency. Very few probably now believe that it was anything as crude as that. But that was what five years of Nixon in the White House had done; it made people imagine that nothing in politics was done for any but the most self-interested reasons. What Ford had done by pardoning Nixon was to leave enough doubt about the degree of Nixon's culpability so that it remained possible for him and his partisans to argue, timidly at first, but with the passing of time more brazenly, that he had been forced out of office not as a result of his own criminality but by the revenge of his political enemies.

After Watergate a great wave of shame and shock submerged the American people. It is important to be precise, however, about what the majority were shocked by. There was certainly an overwhelming consensus before the end that if Nixon would not go of his own accord, he would have to be impeached. Yet though the Constitution somewhat ambiguously specified "treason, bribery or other high crimes and misdemeanors," it seems likely that Nixon was driven to resign by public indignation about his low crimes rather than about his equally real high ones. Scarcely a voice could be found to defend Nixon, among Republicans and conservatives any more than among liberals and Democrats, on the pettier charges: the campaign dirty tricks, the income tax fiddles, the attempts to obstruct justice to cover up what his people had done on his behalf. There were also, certainly, those who pointed out in no uncertain language how fundamentally Nixon had betrayed the spirit and broken the letter of the Constitution. Yet this remained more in the nature of a partisan charge than a unanimous national conviction. The revulsion against Nixon was more ethical than constitutional. People were disgusted that there was a crook in the White House more than they were afraid that there was an embryonic dictator there.

6

The paradox of the presidency is that the office has at once too much power and too little. And so the crisis of the presidency over the past twenty years has been a crisis of effectiveness as well as a crisis of legitimacy.

In retrospect, President Eisenhower is judged more kindly than he was while in office. Looking back from the troubled years of the late 1960s and the 1970s, many Americans tended to see the Eisenhower years as a tranquil interval of normality. That was not how they seemed at the time. Eisenhower was much liked, even loved. He was remembered as the organizer of victory. He was not, however, greatly admired for his competence in the White House. He was admittedly not an "activist" President. That would have been contrary to his political philosophy. But at the time there was a great measure of agreement between his liberal opponents and his conservative supporters that he had failed to act where action was required. He had disappointed expectations that he compete more vigorously with the challenge of Soviet adventurism, that he stimulate the economy, and that he respond more vigorously to social needs, not least to the rising demand from blacks for equality and civil rights.

It is hardly too much to say that the modern conception of the presidency owes as much to what Eisenhower failed to do as to the achievement of any single incumbent since Franklin Roosevelt. For it was in Eisenhower's time that his critics put forward the activist model which Kennedy, Johnson, and—admittedly in the service of very different policies—Nixon all attempted to follow. At the time, few saw Eisenhower as *unable* to operate the presidency. (Though Richard Neustadt, in a famous passage, quoted Truman as foreseeing that this would be so: "He'll sit here," Truman would remark (tapping his desk for emphasis), "and he'll say, 'Do this! Do that!' And nothing will happen. Poor Ike—it won't be a bit like the Army.") At the time, his critics saw Eisenhower as simply unwilling to use his office as energetically as they wanted him to use it. But by the end of his term, popular though he still remained, there was a very general agreement among those who were aware of the challenges facing American government and society—including, for example, even the President's own advisers on "national goals"—that Eisenhower's vision of what was demanded of the presidency in terms of political action was pathetically inadequate.

John Kennedy won the presidency by saying just that. It was time, he said at every whistle stop and shopping center, to get the country moving again. But that was just what he proved unable to do. Symbolically, Kennedy was superbly endowed for the presidency. He fitted the nation's hunger for a new kind of leadership: dashing, youthful, imperial, glorious. When Kennedy spoke of getting the country moving again, he was thinking almost exclusively of foreign policy and in particular of the competition between the United States and the Soviet Union which he saw as the most pressing of the country's problems. When he thought of the need to strengthen the economy or even to work for greater social justice and equality, he thought of these things to a surprising extent as necessary in order to strengthen the country for its conflict with the Soviet Union. His famous inaugural address was almost entirely devoted to international affairs, and his most significant successes—the test ban treaty, the management of the Cuban missile crisis—were all international. Perhaps his most lasting legacies were the revision of U.S. strategy and the immense buildup of military strength carried through by Secretary of Defense Robert McNamara at the Pentagon while Kennedy was President.

At home, Kennedy's greatest success proved short-lived. He and his economic advisers adopted the Keynesian doctrine of government intervention in the economy, and for a few short years it looked as if they had indeed discovered the secret of eternal growth and thereby unlocked the "fiscal dividend" to provide a painless source of growing government revenues to be invested in welfare programs of all kinds as well as in military expenditures. The Kennedy economic policy made possible Lyndon Johnson's Great Society programs. But neither the economic doctrine nor the social programs have stood the test of time. With relatively trivial exceptions, the rest of Kennedy's domestic policy can be dismissed in a single phrase: he could not get Congress to pass it.

A week before Kennedy's death, James Reston summed up the judgment of those who knew what was happening in Washington and who wished Kennedy well:

> There is a vague feeling of doubt and disappointment about President Kennedy's first term . . . His problem is not how to get elected but how to govern . . . It is a far cry from the atmosphere he promised when he ran for the presidency in 1960.

The trauma of the assassination brought Kennedy a great surge of posthumous support. A National Opinion Research Center survey showed that after his death about two-thirds of the voters thought they had voted for Kennedy in 1960, when the fact was that less than half of them had done so. In much the same way, the Kennedy administration was remembered through rose-colored glasses. It had its moments of triumph. It had its real promise. But Kennedy himself had to admit that it was harder than he had anticipated to make the presidency *work*.

At first sight it might seem perverse even to discuss Lyndon Johnson in the context of a theory of the frustration of presidential power. He was a masterful man (even if one of the reasons for his masterfulness was a rather obvious need to hide a secret sense of inadequacy). In many ways he was amply equipped by temperament as well as by training for the wielding of presidential power.

He quickly persuaded Congress to pass most of Kennedy's legislative program, much of which was then hopelessly becalmed when he took office. Then he added an ambitious program of his own and got Congress to enact that, too. His historic achievement was to carry out most of what was left over of the agenda of the New Deal and Truman's Fair Deal. The list of legislation is impressive enough in itself: the Civil Rights Act of 1964, the Voting Rights Act of 1965, the elementary and secondary education act, the Economic Opportunity Act, Medicare and Medicaid, and the urban and conservationist programs of the Great Society. But there was far more to it than the mere ability to induce Congress to pass legislation—even if his technical ability in that department was an attribute most modern Presidents had reason to envy him for. Johnson had a strategy for government action that derived from an unusually coherent (though in some respects confused) political philosophy. He would use the "fiscal dividend" accruing to the federal government in taxes from a growing economy to build a society in which class and race conflict would be superseded and "the ancient enemies of mankind," foremost among them poverty, whose tooth Johnson himself had felt in his youth, would be banished. In pursuit of this grandiose but not contemptible goal he was able to choose from the welter of ideas thrown up for him by the exceptionally able staff and officials he had inherited from Kennedy (and to which he had added some highly talented followers of his own). He was ready to be bold. His imaginative understanding of the emotional sources of the black rebellion enabled him to take a stand in his Howard University speech of June 1965 that went beyond the goal of equality to accept the controversial principle of compensatory action: that is, that the government should positively discriminate to help blacks overcome their historical disadvantages.

In the whole of the twentieth century there have been only three relatively brief periods when the government of the United States overcame the handicaps imposed by the Constitution and worked sweetly to produce rapid and necessary change, only three periods when innovative and capable Presidents worked creatively with a cooperative majority in Congress to achieve a significant body of legislative reform and social action. The first was during Woodrow Wilson's first term. The second was in FDR's first term. And the third was initiated by Lyndon Johnson between 1964 and 1966.

Yet on a closer inspection Johnson's tenure of the White House does not disprove the thesis of a frustrated presidency finding it hard to fulfill the nation's needs and expectations. It certainly exemplified to the full the paradox of presidential power. For one thing, Johnson's period of spectacular achievement was very brief. By the middle of 1966, and in some respects as early as the spring of 1965, he was experiencing a growing resistance to his Great Society plans in Congress and a growing reaction against the pace of change in the country. This was the famous "backlash" which first George Wallace and later Nixon were able to turn to their electoral advantage. Indeed, Johnson himself first lost confidence in some of the most important of his domestic programs and ultimately lost interest in them. During his last three years in the White House, domestic problems and programs generally, and programs for social action and social reform in particular, received a diminishing share of the President's attention. The reasons were complex and have been much discussed. In part, his attention and energy were diverted by the war. In part, in spite of his genuine commitment to "civil rights," he found it increasingly difficult to relate to the new mood of angry rejection of society among blacks.

But that was not all. What happened was that even Johnson encountered the limitations of presidential power. He had been able to take advantage of the massive but fragile consensus generated by Kennedy's death. But it became steadily harder to put together congressional majorities for new legislation. What political scientists call the "coalition of minorities" was beginning to re-form and to brake presidential initiative.

The clearest case was in the realm of economic policy. The decisive mistake of Johnson's presidency—even more catastrophic than the decision to intensify U.S. involvement in Vietnam in the spring of 1965—was the failure to ask Congress for a tax increase in 1966. That compelled the President to choose between guns and butter, between spending money on the war and spending it at home. In turn, therefore, it doomed to failure Johnson's dreams of the Great Society and embittered the domestic strife of the late 1960s. It also led to a sharp rise in the rate of inflation, and so indirectly to the economic troubles of the late 1960s and the 1970s with their novel combination of inflation and relative stagnation. One of the reasons why Johnson did not go to Congress for a tax increase was because he had only just succeeded in getting Congress to give him a tax cut. The process had taken so long, and had demanded such prodigies of political persuasion from both the Johnson and the Kennedy administrations, that Johnson just didn't have the heart to go back and ask Congress to reverse it. But the other reason, as Johnson himself pointed out in his own defense later, was that he simply didn't have the votes. Long before he acknowledged defeat in the spring of 1968, even Lyndon Johnson had discovered that the President cannot count on support from Congress even for the most essential measures. It is worth underlining that there are few other countries in the world, if any, where the executive could find itself so powerless in a matter so central as the strategic judgment at the heart of its own budget.

Which brings us once again to Nixon and to the paradox of presidential power. Where even the strong and domineering Johnson found that the traditional powers of his office did not allow him to do what he considered vitally necessary, can we altogether blame Nixon for wanting to free himself from the trammels of the accepted constitutional constraints on presidential freedom of action (even if we object to the way he set about doing so)? Was he not justified in trying to swing the balance of power between President and Congress decisively in his favor? Watching the struggles of a President like Jimmy Carter, who has tried to keep his office scrupulously within its constitutional limits, are we certain that we like the resulting inability to act decisively and to effect?

Each of the last five Presidents, at least, and arguably each of the last six or even seven Presidents, has failed to operate the presidency in a way that preserved both the constitutional legitimacy of the office as a symbolic apex of American society and its political effectiveness at the center of American government. True, some have failed more totally than others. Some have failed in foreign policy as well as at home. Their failures have not taken identical forms—though as we have seen there is an ominous pattern to their difficulties—and have been due to different causes. But when five consecutive men—all of them, with the possible exception of Gerald Ford, men of very great political ability—all fail to operate an office, when their task seems to get progressively more and more difficult with the passing of time, then the fault can hardly be in the individuals. It must be in the institution. It is time to see where the causes of the trouble lie.

II The Isolated President

1

THE MODERN presidency was created by Franklin D. Roosevelt. For more than a generation he has been *the* model of what a President ought to be. That is what Americans have expected their President to be like. That is also what Presidents have tried, and on the whole failed, to be. None of Roosevelt's successors has been quite his equal in sheer personal political talent. But no other President since FDR has had the advantage of occupying the White House in times of such manifest danger. First because of the economic crisis, then because of the war, no one could deny that strong leadership was needed. It is conceivable that a weaker President than Roosevelt, without his astonishing flair for making the system work, might have insisted on radical changes in the system. If, instead of a Roosevelt, two or three men of lesser gifts had conspicuously failed to make the presidency match up to the demands of that desperate time, then it does seem likely that there would have been changes, perhaps abrupt ones. The point is theoretical. Roosevelt did not need to change the system; he could make it work for him. What does matter is that his very virtuosity at operating the system as he inherited it, that eighteenth-century system so little adapted to the direction of a complex nation of continental scale and global reach in the second half of the twentieth century, his ability to bend and stretch the constitutional system to meet the exceptional demands of a time of crisis, sowed the seeds of difficulties for his successors. Once the power of Roosevelt's legend and of his personality and his incomparable political skill had disappeared from the scene, none of his successors has been able to make the system work well enough—except, arguably, two or at most three of the strongest of them for brief periods—to meet the most urgent challenges of their time. Because he succeeded in making the system work without adapting it in other than superficial ways, in other words, Roosevelt left behind a presidency burdened with a legacy of expectations that have never been fulfilled.

He did not, of course, make up the institution out of whole cloth. His essentially pragmatic political genius—and he was a political genius, in the same sense that Mozart was a musical genius, or Einstein a mathematical and scientific genius—was not only made up of a rare mixture of idealism and worldly wisdom, flexibility and determination. To an unusual degree, even among politically creative men, he combined the willingness to innovate boldly with a sturdy faith in the intrinsic strength of the political tradition he had inherited.

That tradition certainly afforded plenty of precedents for strong executive leadership. It has been a double tradition. There is the Madisonian legacy of powers separated and balanced among the executive, the legislature, and the judiciary. But there has also always existed, side by side with that legacy, a sense of the legitimacy of strong executive action that traces its pedigree back far beyond Madison's rival Alexander Hamilton; back, in fact, to the "balanced constitution" favored by eighteenth-century writers like Locke, Blackstone, and Montesquieu who accepted, even if they sought to limit, the royal prerogative of European monarchy.

Periods of strong presidential leadership have alternated with periods of congressional assertiveness. Washington and Jefferson took, and acted upon, a high view of the powers of the presidency. They were succeeded from 1809 to 1829 by three Presidents who were substantially under the control of Congress. Then came the Jacksonian "revolution," continued by Andrew Jackson's lieutenant, Martin Van Buren. But after that, for another twenty years, until Lincoln's inauguration, Congress, and especially the Senate, became the focus of energy in American political life. Faced with the imperious dangers of civil war, Abraham Lincoln asserted and exerted almost unlimited powers. As soon as he was gone, however, Congress once again established a dominance that was both more absolute and longer lasting than ever before. In 1866 Thaddeus Stevens, the leader of the Radical Republicans in the House of Representatives, told President Andrew Johnson baldly that the President "is the servant of the people as they shall speak through Congress." And the Radicals were as good as their word. When Johnson showed some obstinacy in resisting their plans for congressional Reconstruction in the South, they impeached him, and he only escaped conviction by a single vote. Nearly twenty years later, Woodrow Wilson, then a history teacher at Johns Hopkins, stated with equal finality that "the actual form of our present government is simply a scheme of congressional supremacy." In 1888, Lord Bryce, who later was British ambassador in Washington as well as a constitutional scholar, observed that Congress "has succeeded in occupying nearly all the ground which the Constitution left debatable between the President and itself." From the assassination of Lincoln in 1865 to that of William McKinley in 1901, the supremacy of Congress was as real in practice as it was absolute in contemporary theory. The President was little more than the servant who carried out the will of his master, Congress.

Just at the end of that long period the first signs of change began to appear. The turning point was the Spanish-American War of 1898. Although McKinley had a general authorization to use force against the Spaniards in Cuba, the war started, on presidential orders, several days before Congress acknowledged it. Once the war had started, the President was able to bring it to a triumphant (and highly popular) conclusion before Congress had time to object. In 1898, a Pittsburgh editor called Henry Jones Ford extolled the presidency (greatly exaggerating its historical powers and achievement) in a book which the great constitutional authority, E. S. Corwin of Princeton, called "the real herald of the twentieth century presidency." In 1900 Woodrow Wilson himself, in a new preface written for the fifteenth printing of his 1885 book, began to modify his theory of congressional dominance, and he saw that the change was a result of the war. "When foreign affairs play a prominent part in the politics and policy of a nation," he wrote, "its Executive must of necessity be its guide."

The modern presidency was not solely the product of the Spanish-American War or of the sudden plunge of the United States into imperial adventures. And its real herald, its Saint John the Baptist, was the man who succeeded McKinley in 1901: Theodore Roosevelt. In an almost uncanny way, his presidency anticipated in most of its chief themes that of his kinsman Franklin. There was the same appetite for power, the same aristocratic disdain for the humdrum politics of self-interest as practiced in Congress. There was the same sense of America's global responsibilities and opportunities, and the same conviction that there were economic and social problems in the country that only the President could tackle. The key to this whole new conception of the powers and duties of the presidency was Teddy Roosevelt's rediscovery of the old idea—it had been understood and used by Andrew Jackson and by Lincoln before him—that whereas no senator or congressman represented more than a fraction of the electorate, the President alone was "President of all the people."

Carrying this old idea one stage further, Teddy Roosevelt saw himself and presented himself as the people's tribune and advocate. It was in his time that the presidency first began to appear as the modern, the activist, the democratic branch of government, consciously contrasted by the incumbent and his supporters with the standpat, conservative Congress, sluggishly representing the old politics of the established interests. Even before his final break with the Republican party, Roosevelt was not a strong party man. He was one of the first Presidents to pay special attention to the press, which he consciously used to reach the people, of whatever party, direct. "I made up my mind," he wrote of his tactics as governor of New York, "that the only way I could beat the bosses . . . was . . . by making my appeal as directly and emphatically as I knew how to the mass of voters themselves."

Above all, Teddy Roosevelt was a nationalist. He meant to use the presidential office to make America felt in the world. He also meant to make himself felt as the champion of the people against the monopolists of economic power at home. He fought "the bosses." Yet he was no radical. He was a centrist who instinctively sought consensus even when his manner was at its most abrasive. "Crisis, leadership, the people," were key words in his conception of the presidency, a perceptive historian, Marcus Cunliffe, has written: "so were nation and nationalism." Every one of these same themes and these same key words was to reappear not only in the presidency of Franklin Roosevelt, but also in the mature doctrine of the modern presidency as it was to be expounded by the liberal professors. John Kennedy was the very model of the modern President; yet his political style was almost a carbon copy of the Rough Rider's nationalism and vigor.

In 1908 Woodrow Wilson was president of Princeton and still two years away from his first executive experience in public office as governor of New Jersey. Influenced by the ideas and the example of Roosevelt, who was then approaching the end of his time in the White House, Wilson gave a series of lectures in which he finally adopted the new, activist model of the presidency. "He is the representative," Wilson said, taking over Teddy Roosevelt's master slogan, "of no constituency, but of the whole people." And he added a famous phrase that has echoed in the heads of Presidents and their advisers ever since. "The President is at liberty, both in law and conscience, to be as big a man as he can. His is the vital place of action in the system, whether he accepts it as such or not, and the office is the measure of the man—of his wisdom as well as of his force."

When he became President himself, less than five years later, Wilson did his utmost to live up to that new conception of the scope of the office. In the end, he was unsuccessful. Because of his own stubbornness, the peace treaty he had personally negotiated at Versailles, setting up the League of Nations, was repudiated by the Senate. The event was catastrophic. The whole structure of international relations that had been Wilson's dream, and which in his unrealistic way he had worked so hard to turn into reality, came crashing down in ruins.

The debacle may have helped to delay the arrival of the modern presidency by fourteen years. For until that final disaster, Wilson had acted in the White House—admittedly in a very different personal style—much on the lines pioneered by Theodore Roosevelt. In many ways, too, Wilson's presidency foreshadowed the presidency of the second half of the twentieth century. He was a nationalist as well as an internationalist. He was a vigorous leader, who put the President for the first time in the role of a leader of Congress. He always saw consensus rather than partisan victory as the ultimate goal. He was activist in his conception of the office, interventionist both in economic matters and in foreign policy. He even relied, like modern Presidents, on personal advisers like Colonel Edward M. House, in preference to men with an independent standing in his party like his first secretary of state, William Jennings Bryan.

Any President in the first twenty years of the century would probably have developed the office to some extent in the directions set by Roosevelt and Wilson. It was quite plain, not only to "strong Presidents" like them, but also, for example, to William Howard Taft, that changed times might require changes in the interpretation of the President's duty. A newly urban, industrialized nation on a continental scale faced economic and social problems that were national in scope, and faced them, moreover, with a new, national consciousness. Only the presidency could respond on an appropriately national scale. The new international status of the United States reinforced the same lesson. Whether Americans liked it or not—and in the first twenty years of this century on the whole they were well enough pleased about it—the United States was now one of the Powers; indeed, for a time after World War I, as after World War II, it was the only power to have emerged from the conflict with its resources enhanced.

Yet for all the rather striking parallels between the first two decades of the century and its fourth and fifth decades, Theodore Roosevelt and Woodrow Wilson were the heralds of the modern presidency, not its builders. Neither, in the end, was notably successful. Their respective failures reflected the fact that while some of the trends of their time encouraged the evolution of a strong, activist presidency, in other respects the country was not quite ready for it. After 1919, in the inscrutable yet unmistakable way in which the mood of a whole society can suddenly change, the United States turned away from the vision these pioneers had offered. It turned back toward the traditional values of business and the small town, and their conservative ideology; away from the international role it had so brilliantly claimed, and away from the social doctrines of the Progressive age. It turned, in short, to Harding, and Coolidge, and Hoover, and all they stood for.

2

Republican leaders in the House of Representatives are not generally known as excitable people, least of all if they come from upstate New York. Nor, certainly, are they known for their prejudice in favor of Democratic Presidents. Yet in March 1933, when President Roosevelt's emergency banking bill was before the House, Minority Leader Bertrand H. Snell appealed to his Republican colleagues to vote for it in terms of stark despair. "The house is burning down," he said, "and the President of the United States says this is the way to put out the fire."

Franklin D. Roosevelt became the first modern President, because in a time of acute yet prolonged emergency, the American people, having nowhere else to turn, looked to their President for salvation. When he took office, most of the banks in the country had closed their doors, and it seemed only a matter of hours before Wall Street, too, would collapse irreparably. "The people of the United States want direct, vigorous action," FDR said in his inaugural address. He was right, and that was what he gave them. He succeeded in stopping the panic. He gave the nation hope. But he did not end the Depression. In 1929, the last year of the boom, the gross national product had stood at $103 billion. In 1933, it had fallen by almost 50 percent, to $55 billion: an almost unimaginable drop when we think that today any drop in the GNP, even by a single percentage point, is regarded as a disaster. And the Depression lasted for more than a decade. A sharp new recession in 1937 and 1938 wiped out all the gains achieved in the New Deal. As late as 1940 there were still more than ten million unemployed, or one American breadwinner out of every four. It was not until 1941 that the gross national product finally hoisted itself painfully back up above the 1929 level. And one should reflect upon the human cost and social implications of those simple statistical statements: the reality of "one third of a nation, ill-nourished, ill-clad, ill-housed," with no certainty that this would not be their permanent condition. As late as 1938 and 1939 some of the President's closest advisers—men like Harry Hopkins, Adolf Berle, and Paul Hoffman—believed that unless something dramatic were done swiftly, the unalleviated misery and demoralization of unemployment and stagnation must lead to a collapse of democracy itself and to its replacement by some authoritarian revolution, either of the Left or of the Right.

When the Depression was finally ended, it was by rearmament and the war, not as a result of the success of the government's policies. The nation plunged from the gravest economic crisis in its history straight into an international crisis that was a matter of survival. Victory led to a world in which the United States was confronted by an implacable and formidable antagonist in Stalin's Soviet Union. The entire twelve years that Franklin Roosevelt spent in the White House were a time of crisis. It was in those years and in response to that double crisis, first in the economy and then in international affairs, that the modern presidency evolved.

Franklin Roosevelt was by temperament a leader. But he was able to develop stronger leadership in the White House than any President since, briefly, Lincoln, because he knew that the call for leadership was more urgent and more unanimous than at any time since the Civil War. That was why he could put himself at the center of the national political stage and dominate it for twelve years with no real rival. And that, too, was why he was able to transcend certain of the constitutional and customary limitations on the power of the presidency in the system, *without,* however—and this is crucial—bringing about any overt or fundamental change in the system itself. The presidency eclipsed its rivals and emerged as the dominant element, effectively abolishing the constitutional balance of powers, because for twelve years the presidency was occupied by a political genius at a time of undeniable economic and international crisis.

There were four grand instruments of leadership in the Rooseveltian presidency: the control of the bureaucracy, the leadership of Congress, the mastery of communications, and the welding together of a great coalition of popular support. Significantly, it has been the inability of his successors to wield precisely these same instruments that has led to their frustration and failure.

First, FDR greatly extended the reach of the federal government and its capacity to affect the life of the country: it built dams, set prices, subsidized farmers and electrified farms, hired the unemployed, lent money, wrote guidebooks, guaranteed consumer standards, intervened in a myriad of ways between lender and borrower, manufacturer and consumer, employer and employee. At the same time he put the President more firmly in charge of the federal government than ever before. He did this—in spite of a strong temperamental aversion to bureaucratic ways—both by strengthening the federal bureaucracy and by inventing new devices for the President to control it.

His cabinet was both more energetic and more dependent on himself than most previous cabinets. Instead of the semi-independent potentates, like so many ambassadors from the various estates of the nation, whom previous Presidents had tended to choose as their cabinet members, FDR chose able, ambitious men, and one woman, who had in most cases neither independent political ambitions—at least not before FDR chose them!—nor an independent power base.

At the same time, FDR felt no compulsion to fit the new agencies Congress was creating at his urging neatly into the jurisdictions of the existing cabinet departments. Roosevelt was the first President to indulge in the bad habit of all subsequent Presidents; that is, when a new problem required attention, to set up a new agency to deal with it, leaving the existing bureaucracy that had been nominally responsible demoralized. There was always an ad hoc, not to say an ad hominem flavor about the New Deal. Roosevelt's way was to set up a new agency to administer every new piece of legislation and to cope with each perceived problem until people in Washington, bemused by all the new three-letter agencies whose names they had to remember, began to talk about "alphabet soup."

At the same time, it is important to notice what FDR did *not* do. He did not systematically reorganize the federal civil service, equipping it with a new professional education, with grades and ranks and esprit de corps, on the model of the most successful of the foreign bureaucracies of the time in Berlin and Paris and London and New Delhi. He vastly increased the sheer size, the complexity, the scope and power of the government. Yet he did nothing to strengthen the status, or the morale, or the training of the bureaucrats who were to run it. Instead he relied on "in-and-outers," "dollar-a-year-men," talented amateurs recruited from law firms or universities or other corners of the private sector to which, in most cases sooner rather than later, they eventually returned. In this, too, Roosevelt set a precedent (though he did not originate the tradition). In so doing, he procured gifted and energetic men and women to run the government in a time of emergency and expansion. He also enriched the government permanently by endowing it with a tradition of drawing widely on the talents available and not sticking rigidly to a caste of professional administrators. But on balance I believe the failure to create such a body of professional administrators, with the highest possible standards of training, discipline, and dedication, as the permanent national civil service was a disaster.

That was not the only unfortunate precedent set in the Roosevelt years. The essence of bureaucracy is rational organization, established procedures, a clear hierarchy of subordination, resulting, not in predictable outcomes, but in predictable process. From the start of the New Deal, Americans grumbled about the growth of the bureaucracy in Washington. Yet properly speaking what Roosevelt created was not a bureaucracy at all, but an inspired mishmash of programs, agencies, bureaux, and free-lance troubleshooters slapped together with knowing carelessness precisely so that they would not display the systematic tenacity of a true bureaucracy. The whole shambling mess was ingeniously arranged in such a way that the frontiers of every agency's jurisdiction would overlap, so that each was in constant competition with its neighbors. The result, which was by no means accidental, was that the White House could retain day-to-day control of a machine which, if it had been more logically constructed, must have developed a momentum of its own. The political skill of this behavior has been much praised; the administrative chaos it caused has been less noticed. It would have been wiser if more of the President's political astuteness had been channeled into devising ways of allowing the bureaucracy to perform its gigantic tasks without constant prodding, vetting, and initiative from the White House.

Inevitably, especially from his second term on, as he became aware both of the intractable nature of the problems a President must face in the real world and also as he wrestled with the artificial complexity he had himself introduced into the New Deal, Roosevelt became more and more conscious that, as the Brownlow committee on administrative management put it in 1939, "the President needs help." He set about building up an inner, parallel bureaucracy in the executive office which not only helped the President to perform his own inescapable duties, but also acted as his intelligence service. It informed him about what was going on in what was, after all, nominally "his" executive branch of the government. It rode herd on the departments. From time to time it even indulged in a little bureaucratic covert action.

What political scientists call the "institutionalized presidency," in other words, began under FDR. It may be objected that this was inevitable: that the growing complexity of government and the vastly increased demands made of it in the mid-twentieth century left no alternative. But this is not so. A vast expansion of the federal bureaucracy may well have been inevitable. Given Roosevelt's policy of government intervention, it was certain. What was not inevitable, what was Roosevelt's choice, was that it should have developed as it did, not as a unified, carefully subordinated hierarchy, whose authority was guaranteed as carefully as its powers were limited, but as an ill-organized flock of agencies, with the sheep dogs in the White House snapping at their heels as the President whistled the signals. None of Roosevelt's successors, not even General Eisenhower, the organizer of victory in World War II, has succeeded more than intermittently in controlling or giving direction to the bureaucracy Roosevelt left behind. Sometimes the flock has grazed in too lush pastures. Sometimes the sheep dogs have been too fierce. In either case, it is no surprise, for Roosevelt took great care *not* to build a true bureaucracy.

The second instrument of Roosevelt's power was a transformed relationship between the President and Congress. "As for Congress," President Kennedy told his friend Benjamin Bradlee as they were sitting around in the family living room in the White House, "they're impossible. Ever since Roosevelt's day all the laws have been pretty much written downtown," meaning in the executive departments. That was rough-and-ready history. But it wasn't altogether wrong. Some scholars, like Clinton Rossiter, have spoken in this connection of a "revolution," initiated by Teddy Roosevelt and Woodrow Wilson and carried forward by FDR's successors, but in which the decisive steps were taken by FDR himself. This is going too far. It was not a revolution, not least because FDR was so careful to respect the forms of the separation of powers and the sensibilities of congressional leaders. Even as late as the end of his second term, he did not appoint a formal congressional aide, though of course he did have aides whose job it was to work with the Congress.

It might have been better, indeed, if Roosevelt *had* adopted a more revolutionary approach, if he had restructured the relationship between the White House and Capitol Hill in a more formal way. He might have appointed key cabinet officers from among sitting members of the Senate and House. He might have set up a regular machinery of consultation between congressional and executive leadership. Or he might have adopted any of the many other reforms that have been advocated recently to bridge the gap of rivalry and misunderstanding between the executive and the legislature. He did none of these things. What he did do, while respecting the constitutional forms and traditional amenities, was to transform the power ratio between Congress and the President.

The decisive change came right at the start, in the Hundred Days of emergency session in the spring of 1933, when Congress did not so much debate the bills it passed, as some wit said, as salute them as they went sailing by. It is true that many of those bills did not originate in the White House. Yet never before had a President taken it upon himself to act to such effect as the leader of Congress. The pattern of expectations between President and Congress would never be the same again.

Roosevelt's dealing with Congress can be roughly divided into five phases. The Hundred Days were the first phase. Senators and congressmen were so stunned by the state of the country that they hardly dared to question the President's proposals. It was this exceptional set of circumstances, more than any deliberate act of will on Roosevelt's part, that irreversibly transformed the President's relations with Capitol Hill. Yet Roosevelt was willing to seize the opportunity presented by exceptional circumstances.

The circumstances themselves were quite short-lived. Already by the time the Seventy-fourth Congress assembled in January 1935, its members were in a new frame of mind, no longer inclined to go along with whatever the President proposed. Yet in terms of sheer virtuosity this second phase was the high point of Roosevelt's performance as a legislative leader. Congress wanted to go home early, leaving the President without a dozen bills he thought he needed. Working with the Democratic leadership, he maneuvered Congress out of an adjournment until ten of the twelve bills were passed. Then, in 1937, he went to the opposite extreme. Lulled into overconfidence—not to say arrogance—by the huge margin of his electoral victory the previous November, he seemed to have forgotten all he knew about handling legislators. Instead of wooing them, he tried to bully them. A phase of bitter confrontation ended in bitter defeat. After the attempt to pack the Supreme Court failed in 1937, half a dozen major pieces of New Deal legislation stuck, becalmed, on Capitol Hill. The old, mainly Southern conservative leadership in Congress seemed to have triumphed over Roosevelt and the 1936 class of New Deal congressmen he had helped elect. Then, after 1939, during his long campaign against the isolationists, something of his old skill and restraint came back. And in the last phase, as in the first, Congress could hardly do too much for him. It was wartime, and congressmen vied with one another in their patriotism to vote the money the President wanted for the national defense.

Again, some considerable part of the reasons for Roosevelt's emergence as the unofficial leader of Congress must be set down to the exceptional circumstances of his presidency. In the early months of the New Deal, the American people were desperate for any ray of hope. Again, in World War II, individual senators and congressmen virtually abdicated any power to resist the Commander in Chief's dictates. Throughout the period, Congress as a whole looked for leadership, and Roosevelt gave them what they were looking for. But there was another reason for Roosevelt's success, and that was his sheer skill in playing members of Congress at their own game. Judge Sam Rosenman, who worked closely with FDR in the White House, recalled his "many varieties of persuasion" with members of Congress: "flattery, diplomacy, implied threats, promises, horse trading, intellectual arguments, charm, arguments of party loyalty, or a combination" of all these. Another aide remembered how much the master enjoyed the game:

> [He] caught a glimpse of the President after he had succeeded in calming down an angry congressional delegation. Roosevelt, not aware that he was observed, leaned back, slowly picked out a cigarette, stuck it in his holder, lit a match, and took a long puff. "A smile of complete satisfaction spread over his face."

By the end of his twelve years in the White House, the temporary shift in the balance of power between the President and the Congress resulting from the dramatic initiatives of the Hundred Days had become the way Washington worked. Roosevelt had tipped the balance firmly toward the White House and made the President, in defiance of the theory of the separation of powers, the leader of Congress. He had established the principle that the major agenda for Congress in each session would be a program of important legislation proposed by the President. And, by his own highly personal methods, he had succeeded in getting six successive Congresses to pass a very high proportion of the legislation he sent up. But for all that he had done nothing to change the rules of the game. He had simply shown how it was possible to win most of the time. In so doing, he had greatly heightened expectations—both in Congress and in the nation—of what his successors would be able to accomplish. Yet after all he had done nothing, except by his example, to help them meet those expectations.

Roosevelt himself was perfectly well aware that he would never have been able to succeed as he did in his dealings with Congress had it not been for the third of his additions to the armory of the presidency: his grasp of the new possibilities of mass communication. He called in a new world of public opinion to redress the balance of the old world of politics. Or, to put it another way, he appealed over the heads of the professional politicians in Congress to their constituents and ultimate masters, the American people.

Here, again, he was following a trail roughly blazed by his two early twentieth-century precursors. If Franklin Roosevelt was what the veteran journalist Heywood Broun called him, the "finest newspaperman who has ever been President of the United States," Theodore Roosevelt ran him close. Throughout the nineteenth century, of course, politicians had been highly sensitive to the judgments passed on them in newspaper editorials. Teddy Roosevelt was the first President to understand the help a politician could get from news, as distinct from editorial opinion. That was why his first appointment after McKinley's funeral was not with powerful New York publishers, but with the heads of the three most important wire services of the day. Teddy Roosevelt, said his friend Archie Butt, "was his own press agent, and he had a splendid comprehension of news and its value." He appreciated instinctively the way news could influence the electorate, and therefore the need to manipulate the reporters so that the messages they transmitted were favorable to what he was trying to achieve.

It was McKinley who first allowed the reporters out of the rain and into the White House. Teddy Roosevelt first gave them working quarters inside the building and met them regularly for informal press conferences. He knew how to flatter them and bully them, and sometimes he would allow favored correspondents to chat with him while he was being shaved at the end of the afternoon. Wilson began the first formal press conferences and held them almost twice a week. He also had, in fact though not in name, the first presidential press secretary in Joseph P. Tumulty, his private secretary, who handled the press for him.

In the 1920s the press conference almost died out, and Hoover almost stifled it in formality; he refused to answer any questions of which he had not received notice in writing. But on only his fourth day in office FDR announced that he proposed to continue in the White House the "very delightful family conferences" he had held in Albany as governor of New York. Altogether, he held over one thousand press conferences in his twelve years in the White House, an average of almost two a week. He dominated the meetings with his warmth and wit from the start, and though he occasionally scolded a reporter who had written something he didn't like, on the whole the tone remained jovial as well as intimate, even though, over the years, as the President learned to make himself indispensable as a source of hard news, more and more reporters crammed into the Oval Office.

Roosevelt was greatly helped in his dealings with the press by the first official press secretary in the history of the presidency,

Steve Early, who had been with him since his campaign for the vice presidency in 1920. The President at his conferences and Early in between them made sure that the White House's point of view was never absent from the papers. The press conference was an invaluable tool of leadership. FDR knew not only how to charm and bamboozle the reporters, but also precisely how to use them, both to put his own version of events across to the country and to sound out public opinion and find out what the country would stand for. His admiring biographer, Arthur M. Schlesinger, Jr., goes so far as to speak of "the clandestine manipulation of the press." Certainly what Roosevelt learned to practice was a kind of "double vertical enfilade." He used the news values and the often more sympathetic political attitudes of the reporters and editors to outflank the hostility of the publishers, the great majority of them Republicans. So he was able to turn the flanks of his Republican and conservative opponents in Congress as well by virtue of the way he and his policies were presented in their hometown papers. Apart from any advantage this gave him in seizing the initiative, its importance as a defensive tactic was essential; given the hatred with which Roosevelt was held by the class that included most newspaper publishers, if he had not had this means of defending himself and his program, they would have been able to hoot him from the stage.

What put him at the center of the national stage, as no previous President had been, though, was his mastery of the new medium, radio. Even before he entered the White House he had grasped its potential. "Time after time," he wrote, "in meeting legislative opposition in my own state, I have taken the issue directly to the voters by radio, and invariably I have had a most heartening response." He was not the first President to speak to the nation over the radio from the White House. He was the first to understand that radio could do something more than merely transmit a political speech of the conventional kind. It could allow the President, and in practice *only* the President among politicians, to come into every home in the land as a trusted family friend at the fireside.

Roosevelt studied hard to perfect an intimate style for his "fireside chats," very different from the pompous buncombe of traditional political rhetoric. At the same time he was a gentleman of the old school, born in the Victorian century and educated by Dr. Endicott Peabody at Groton; there was no danger with him of intimacy degenerating into undignified overfamiliarity or the shameless hard sell. It was a long way from the way Roosevelt mentioned his dog, Fala, to the way Nixon used his dog, Checkers. Sometimes he used the fireside chat in an explicitly political way, to bring pressure on members of Congress in support of specific legislation. More often, the effect was indirect: he used the radio talks as a means of educating the public to see the problems of the nation and the world as he saw them. In the process those who heard him were then more likely to vote for representatives who shared at least the elements of the Rooseveltian philosophy.

Perhaps the most important change that Roosevelt brought to the presidency through his new ability to use radio was something more fundamental than an improved technique of political communication. More than any previous President, Roosevelt as President came to symbolize the nation as a familiar, everyday figure. He thus decisively enhanced that identification between the presidency and the nation that is one of the essential traits of the modern presidency. At the same time he personalized the presidency more than ever before, and so encouraged a double identification: of the President with the presidency, and of the presidency with the nation, so that the President became for most Americans the living symbol of the nation in a direct and personal and emotionally vivid way as not even Washington or Lincoln had ever been.

This vast projection of his own personality through the mass media helped Roosevelt to forge the fourth improved instrument of presidential leadership that he was to leave to his successors: a new conception of the function and nature of the political party as an agency of presidential power. (In the past, some Presidents had been little more than agents of their party. Now the relationship was decisively reversed.) "The President built a Grand Coalition," James MacGregor Burns put it succinctly, "but it was a coalition around himself, not a coalition organized within the Democratic party."

FDR's attitude toward the Democratic party had been ambiguous from the start. In his early days in New York politics, his stance as an upper-class reformer put him squarely in the tradition of his illustrious kinsman and the Bull Moose movement. When he became President many of the key members of his New Deal administration, like Harold Ickes, Hugh Johnson, and Donald Richberg, were recycled Bull Moose Republicans. In Albany,

Roosevelt had danced an elaborate quadrille with the reformers and their Tammany Hall opponents. He fought Tammany and machine politics courageously, but not unremittingly. He had a Puritan's and an aristocrat's disdain for the corruption that was the lifeblood of the machine. In New York City he helped Mayor Fiorello H. La Guardia build a microcosm of his national coalition. Yet overall he was too much the pragmatist to quarrel beyond redemption with the big-city bosses.

The same pragmatic ambiguity marked his relations with the Southern wing of the Democratic party. "First things come first," he once told his wife when she urged him to support antilynching and anti-poll-tax legislation. Some might have argued that to end lynching must be a first priority. Not Roosevelt. Arthur Schlesinger maintains in his biography that Roosevelt's lifelong ambition was to convert the Democratic party into a liberal front against conservatives, and there is some evidence to support the view that this was his intention. But what he left behind, after a dozen years at the head of the Democratic party, was something quite different: not a liberal party, but a coalition of liberals, labor, big-city machines, and Southern conservatives. It did use its combined strength to pass liberal reforms, some of lasting importance; but its overall thrust was not liberal, still less radical, and can best be described as centrist. The Roosevelt coalition gave the President the support he needed to take emergency measures to quell the panic and alleviate much of the most pressing distress of 1933. It enabled him to take the country into World War II, and to win it. But it did not succeed in ending the Depression. Still less did it break the power of entrenched institutions and interests or create new mechanisms of redistribution of wealth or popular power. No such all-under-one-big-tent coalition could have done those things. The legacy of the Roosevelt coalition was no profound remodeling of American society, or even of American political institutions, but what turned out to be a short-lived ideology of consensus and a new, dominant role for the President, as an individual, in the system.

The Roosevelt coalition was a formidable machine for reelecting Franklin Roosevelt. It was less reliable as a means of organizing support for radical change. It is no accident that it was in FDR's time that the dislocation between the presidential and the congressional parties recorded by James MacGregor Burns in a 1963 book, *The Deadlock of Democracy,* first became complete. To a certain extent, perhaps, some such split is inevitable in the

American system, simply because the individual members of Congress are elected in single-candidate constituencies, while the President is elected by the nation as a whole. But Roosevelt was brilliantly successful at mounting essentially personal campaigns, aimed at voters from either party or no party who liked his style and trusted his policies. In this way he severed the links that had once bound Presidents to their parties. At the time, and for long afterwards, few saw anything but good in this. How better by far that the President should soar free from the encumbering obligations, the hackneyed slogans, and obsolete prejudices of party, its sordid deals and closed coteries! Only a generation later did the suspicion dawn on some of the most astute observers of American politics that in cutting loose the spoiled cargo of party, Roosevelt also deprived his successors of ballast and tackle needed to steer the ship.

"My sword," said Mr. Valiant-for-Truth in the *Pilgrim's Progress,* before the trumpets finally sounded for him on the other side, "I give to him that shall succeed me in my pilgrimage, and my courage and skill to him that can get it." It is not that the seven Presidents who have occupied the White House since Roosevelt died have lacked courage or skill. Some have had the strength to wield his sword and the cunning to bend his bow. The trouble has been, rather, that the political legacy he left behind was so personal, so idiosyncratically devised to fit the instincts of his own wayward political genius, that few have been able to handle his weapons, except for brief intervals, as trenchantly as he did. Nor is this wholly a matter of mere personal attributes. The presidency Roosevelt left behind him worked well enough in the specific circumstances of his lifetime. The standard we must demand of political institutions, however, is not that with luck they can be made to work miracles by an occasional genius, but that they should enable able, honorable men of common clay to meet the more important demands that society makes on them.

Roosevelt cannot be blamed for his exceptional gifts, still less for not anticipating the different challenges a later generation would have to meet. Yet because he made little consistent effort to adapt the institutions he inherited to new circumstances, because in his time, if ever, there *was* an opportunity for modernizing the system, because instead he relied on pyrotechnic displays of his own virtuosity in making the unreformed system work: for all these reasons, Franklin Roosevelt must bear some share of the blame for his successors' failure to meet the overloaded expectations of the office which his very success did so much to arouse. But, just as generals fight the last war, so intellectuals recommend for the future the institutions they think worked in the past. If Roosevelt missed a historic opportunity to change the presidency in the 1930s, many of its problems forty years later stem from those who, after his death, sought to impose a Rooseveltian presidency on a different world.

3

The modern presidency may have been created by Franklin Roosevelt. The theory of the modern presidency is of more recent date. It was created, you could almost say, by Dwight Eisenhower unintentionally. The real power and size of the institution grew as a response to authentically desperate needs and mortal threats. But the aggrandizement of the theoretical claims made on behalf of the presidency was justified on more dubious grounds and sprang from motives that were not always so innocent as the wish to prevent sharecroppers' children going hungry or to make sure that Adolf Hitler did not rule the world. At best, the doctrine of presidential supremacy was brought to its height because of the frustration felt by liberal intellectuals who found the Eisenhower administration not activist enough for their liking. At worst, it owed a good deal to the impatience of Democratic politicians and their speechwriters to recapture power. The theory may not seem to matter in comparison with the reality. But "with words we rule men." The words of the Neustadts and Rossiters and Theodore Whites, who glorified the presidency and thought it ought to be more powerful and more active, helped to build the imperial presidency of Kennedy and Johnson and—though they did not foresee it—also that of Nixon. The idea of the presidency and the reality of the presidency have been tightly intertwined. The intellectuals' theories have been influenced by what Presidents were doing—or not doing; but Presidents also often acted as the intellectuals told them they ought to act.

There was little theoretical discussion of the presidency before the Eisenhower years. The study of the institution, like the institution itself, lay mainly dormant from Woodrow Wilson's time until Roosevelt's. In 1940 the British socialist Harold Laski published his learned study of *The American Presidency,* and eight years later Professor E. S. Corwin came out with his magisterial treatise *The President: Office and Powers.* Then came a spate of biographies of the strong Presidents of history, many of them admiring to the point of hagiography. Books like Douglas Southall Freeman's *George Washington,* Carl Sandburg's *Abraham Lincoln,* or Marquis James's *Andrew Jackson,* whatever their merits, all focused on the President as hero and savior. They treated the White House as the temple of a political religion.

It was not until the middle 1950s, however, that is, not until two strong, activist Democratic Presidents had been succeeded by a Republican who was arguably strong but certainly not activist, that books about the presidency as an institution began to proliferate. In 1954 Sidney Hyman published *The American President.* In the spring of 1966 Clinton Rossiter gave a series of lectures at the University of Chicago that were to become his *The American Presidency,* and that same year Richard Neustadt published the essay that was to develop into his *Presidential Power* (1960). Still in 1956, Corwin and Louis Koenig published *The Presidency Today,* and in 1960 Koenig's *The Chief Executive* appeared. In that year, Rexford G. Tugwell published *The Enlargement of the Presidency* and Herman Finer, *The Presidency: Crisis and Regeneration.* And that is only a sampling.

There are, of course, two separate questions about presidential power: How much power does the President have? And how much power should he have?

Almost without exception the writers who addressed themselves to the presidency in the second half of the Eisenhower administration agreed that the President ought to have very great powers indeed. The most significant division among them was that some thought he ought to have great power, and that he did have it; others thought he didn't have as much as he deserved, and needed.

All of them laid great emphasis on the idea, which we traced back to Theodore Roosevelt, and Woodrow Wilson, and beyond, that the President deserved to be the supreme actor within the constitutional system of checks and balances because he alone was "President of all the people." Harry Truman, like Teddy Roosevelt and Wilson before him, had gone on from the undoubted fact that only the President, unlike senators or congressmen or governors, was elected by the whole nation, to the idea that the

President was therefore the representative of "the people," in the Populist sense, as opposed to the representatives in Congress and elsewhere, of "the interests." (A moment's reflection on the career and beliefs of, say, McKinley, Harding, or Nixon is enough to show up the flaws in this argument.) Still, Truman used to say that the President was "the only lobbyist the whole people had in Washington," and most of the writers on the presidency we are talking about followed him without question in that view. Herman Finer went so far as to say that the President was "the incarnation of the American people in a sacrament resembling that in which the wafer and the wine are seen to be the body and blood of Christ."

A second idea that was a favorite with these writers was that of the President as the wearer of many "hats," the ubiquitous man in the American system. Harry Truman said there were six of these hats: those of the head of state, the chief of the executive branch, the Commander in Chief, the party leader, the legislative leader, and the director of foreign policy. Corwin had a similar list, while Rossiter went no fewer than five better and awarded the President eleven hats: chief of state, chief executive, Commander in Chief, chief diplomat, chief legislator, chief of party, "voice of the people"—traditionally a synonym for the voice of God!—protector of the peace, manager of prosperity, world leader, and "President of the West!" The list of titles sounds like the sort of thing that was dreamed up by courtiers to flatter the more immodest Byzantine emperors. But similar lists of the sacred attributes of the All-Highest found their way into public consciousness by way of college textbooks, high-school civics texts, and more or less serious journalists. A similar list of attributes, for example, turned up in a column by James Reston in 1956, while Theodore H. White's almost obsequiously deferential but immensely influential *The Making of the President 1960* was greatly influenced by Neustadt's and Rossiter's ideas. In the late Eisenhower years the social scientist Robert E. Lane, interviewing intensively a small sample in New Haven, Connecticut, found how deeply embedded were both the "President of all the people" notion and the "imperial" conception of the presidency.

> The President proposes [so Lane summarized the views he encountered], Congress disposes . . . Congress looks inward toward the nation; the President looks outward toward the world. Congressmen have their special duties to their home districts; they are the custo-

> dians of popular welfare. The President is the custodian of popular safety, national destiny, the conscience of the people. Congress expresses the immediate impulsive needs; the President has the longer view. Congress offers "secondary gain"; the President offers a chance to fulfill the life goals of the nation.

It would be wrong to impute all such exaggeratedly deferential attitudes to the presidency to the influence of a group of academic writers, of course. To some extent they represent the survival of very old American attitudes, like those inculcated in Parson Weems's *Life and Memorable Actions of George Washington.* In part, too, they represent a perfectly accurate and rational observation of the contrast between the goals and performance of the President on the one hand, and the Congress on the other, over the twenty-five years from 1933 to 1958.

Still, the school of writers who set about describing the powers and glories of the presidency in the late 1950s were certainly not modest in the claims they made. "We must cease wasting our energies in discussing whether the government of the United States is going to be powerful or not," wrote Clinton Rossiter, one of the deans of the school, and in the context what he meant by the government of the United States was the executive branch. "It is going to be powerful, or we are going to be obliterated." That was part of it, of course; the nuclear power of the President was reflected in his civilian persona. Again, Rossiter wrote in a more poetic vain:

> The President is not a Gulliver immobilized by ten thousand tiny cords, nor even a Prometheus chained to a rock of frustration. He is rather a kind of magnificent lion, who can roam widely and do great deeds, so long as he does not try to break loose from his broad reservation. . . . He will feel few checks upon his power if he uses that power as he should.

"The influence of the Crown," ran John Dunning's famous resolution in the eighteenth-century British House of Commons, "has increased, is increasing, and ought to be diminished." One of the main themes of the literature on the presidency that accumulated during the later years of the Eisenhower administration was almost exactly the opposite. The power of the presidency—so the liberal professors maintained—had increased, had temporarily stopped increasing, and ought to be increased again. "The

Presidency," Rossiter wrote, "is a standing reproach to those petty doctrinaires who think that executive power is inherently undemocratic . . . no less a reproach to those easy generalizers who think that Lord Acton had the last word on the corrupting effects of power."

At a casual reading, the most influential of all these books about the presidency might be taken as an exception. Richard Neustadt's view was subtler. Be clear about the difference between the President's *powers* and his effective *power*. The President has vast formal powers. But he does not obtain results by giving orders "—or at least," Neustadt added with characteristic scrupulousness, "not only by giving orders." Despite the undeniable power of the government of which he is the head, and despite the great powers he has, still, when it comes to the moment when he either gets what he wants or not, when push, as they say, comes to shove, then "presidential power is the power to persuade."

In a sense, all the writers I have been discussing were propagandists. Almost without exception they were liberals and they were Democrats. Most of them had worked either for Roosevelt or for Truman, or for both. Corwin was a special assistant of Roosevelt's. Tugwell was a member of the original Brain Trust. Louis Koenig and Neustadt himself worked for both Roosevelt and Truman. Neustadt's book was written almost as a primer for the next Democratic President, and in fact he advised both Kennedy and Johnson.

Yet their estimate of the presidency sprang from something more respectable than mere self-interested partisanship. The presidency, to them, stood for all that was best in America. It was not only the national, as opposed to the sectional, the international, as opposed to the isolationist, the efficient, as opposed to the stagnant, the modern, as opposed to the outdated branch of government, though as contrasted both with the Congress and with state government they did see it as all of those things. It was the great instrument of power to which they looked to carry out the liberal program of social reform and to enforce the liberal consensus. And so, understandably, if not perhaps altogether wisely, they called for more power to the President's elbow. There was a gap between the President's responsibility and his authority, Rossiter thought. Koenig called it "a chasm between the amount of power the President needs and what he has." "Even though the enlargement of the presidency has been enormous," thought Tugwell—who had acquired personal experience of the frustrations of executive power as the governor of Puerto Rico—"it may possibly not have been enough."

The essence of the liberal consensus that dominated American politics in the first half of the 1960s was a sort of vast deal that had been consummated many years before between the demands of foreign and domestic policy and the imperatives that motivated liberals and conservatives. By the terms of this deal, negotiated in effect by Roosevelt, conservatives accepted the two cardinal tenets of liberalism at home, namely an interventionist economic role for the federal government, and welfare programs, while liberals accepted the need for a strong military establishment and a firm anti-Communist stance in the interests of national security. The presidencies of John Kennedy and Lyndon Johnson were the children of that marriage. As long as the liberal program seemed to be working at home and the liberal policy seemed to be guaranteeing national security and national honor abroad, there was little disposition to challenge the powers of the President, certainly not among liberals.

In the end, the liberal consensus on domestic policy broke up. The Johnson administration's effort to follow a policy of civil rights for blacks in the South with a serious attempt to achieve economic and social equality for blacks all over the country produced a backlash, a reaction, call it what you like, and not only among hardhats and the white ethnic working class. The political will to press on with the liberal program fell apart.

The consensus in support of the liberal foreign policy collapsed first. President Kennedy's firm stand against the Soviet Union in the missile crisis of fall 1962 greatly strengthened his popularity. But Lyndon Johnson's Vietnam commitment, even though it was undertaken with the enthusiastic advocacy of the inner circle of Kennedy's advisers and out of conscious loyalty to what Johnson thought Kennedy would have done, soon began to provoke dissent that was both thoughtful and strong. The wave of feeling against the Vietnam War had many consequences for the Johnson presidency. It also had a perceptible effect on the theory of the presidency in general. For the first time, and as a direct result of the Vietnam War, the idea began to spread that if the presidency was not as strong as it needed to be in order to do what liberals wanted to do at home, it might be altogether too free to roam like a mighty lion and do great deeds abroad.

This distinction between the foreign and domestic presidencies was first drawn—so far as I have been able to discover—in an article by the political scientist Aaron Wildavsky called "The Two Presidencies," which appeared in December 1966:

> The United States has one President, but it has two presidencies; one presidency is for domestic affairs, and the other is concerned with defense and foreign policy. Since World War II, Presidents have had much greater success in controlling the nation's defense and foreign policies than in dominating its domestic policies.

Wildavsky does not appear to have been led to this observation by his feeling that the Vietnam War was a disaster. He does not mention the war in the article, and on the contrary argues that Presidents had been successful on the whole in running foreign and national security policy. Nevertheless, the idea of the two presidencies was to be picked up. It was a natural progression from the idea that the President had more power in foreign policy to the idea that he had too much. Both Tugwell and Koenig adopted this view, changing their original position that the President needed more power in general. "The President has too much power," wrote Tugwell in 1971, "and he has not enough power. He can send the armed forces into any part of the world, risking war on any scale" . . . yet he has too little power as "chief legislator and maker of foreign policy," and no time to "take care that the laws be faithfully executed." Many other writers came to similar conclusions in the late 1960s and the early 1970s: Saul K. Padover, for example, the biographer of Jefferson, called the President "for all practical purposes . . . a dictator in international affairs."

During the same period, the men who had forged the doctrine of presidential supremacy, and called for presidential power to enforce their liberal ideology, had not one shock but two. There was the impact of the Vietnam War, with all its shameful implications both for American power and for American honor. This was what Andrew Hacker called *The End of the American Era,* and Henry Steele Commager *The Defeat of America,* and there was no getting away from the fact that this was a defeat for which the responsibility lay squarely with the presidency. Not one President, but four consecutive Presidents and their advisers, almost without exceptions, had plunged on with the disastrous policy of commitment to victory in Vietnam. While Congress as a whole was certainly not opposed to the war until it was over, the responsibility could not be shifted to Congress. Defeat in a presidential war inexorably raised questions about unchallenged presidential supremacy on the issues of peace and war.

That was one cause of the revision that took place. There was another. The liberals had extolled presidential power, knowingly or not, because they took it for granted that the presidency would be "their" part of the government. (John Kennedy, as senator, had even argued against the abolition of the Electoral College explicitly on the ground that the Electoral College overrepresented the industrial North, thus offsetting the Southern strength in Congress. And liberalism was in large degree the doctrine of the industrial North, with its immigrants, its labor unions, and its urban problems.) One morning in 1968, to their horror, the liberals woke up to find that the White House, on which they had counted as the bastion of their power to do battle with the benighted doctrines entrenched in Congress and in statehouses, had fallen into the power of their archenemy. One does not need to share the prejudices and suspicions of men like President Nixon's former aides, Patrick Buchanan or Raymond Price, for example, to believe that, from the moment when Nixon was sworn in as President, enthusiasm for presidential power waned abruptly in such places as the political science departments of great Eastern graduate schools and in the editorial offices of *The New York Times* or the *Washington Post.*

An amusing vignette from 1970 illustrates the process. On May 7, 1970, thirteen influential Harvard professors, most of them with many years' experience in Washington as either appointed officials or consultants with the executive branch, flew down to Washington to see their former colleague, Henry Kissinger. The group included Richard Neustadt, advocate of presidential power; George Kistiakowsky, science adviser to the Eisenhower White House; Adam Yarmolinsky, special assistant to Robert McNamara at the Pentagon under Kennedy; Francis Bator, deputy to Walt Rostow on the Johnson National Security Council staff; and Thomas Schelling, Kissinger's former colleague at the Harvard Center for International Affairs. Their purpose was to protest about the invasion of Cambodia. They were given a dusty reception. Kissinger hardly seemed interested in their views, and other officials treated them almost contemptuously. It was humiliating, it was almost unthinkable, but these men, who had been at home in the executive branch of the United States government for a generation, were treated as strangers, worse, as unimportant! Schelling tried to put the best face on it. "We are in effect saying goodbye," he said afterward. And then he added: "We are going to look to the Hill." Another member of the group echoed him: "In the executive branch we've shot our bolt today. From now on, we'll just have to work with Congress."

Not all intellectuals, not even all Harvard intellectuals, despaired of getting a hearing at the Nixon White House. But the essential point remains. The rift between the intellectuals and the White House, firm allies since the days of the New Deal, had become visible well before Watergate. The liberal intellectuals who had collectively forged the doctrine of the strong presidency began to lose faith in it, not so much when the President was seen to be abusing his power as when he was no longer their ally. "Around 1960," the political scientist William G. Andrews wrote in a paper delivered in 1971, long before Watergate, "political scientists and historians burst forth with a veritable barrage of elaborate encomiums to the American presidency. . . . Ten years later this school was in wild disarray under furious assault from an army of outspoken critics of presidential power."

The ground was thoroughly prepared for the orgy of handwringing and lamentation that greeted the Watergate revelations in the spring and summer of 1973. Now the reversal was complete. The advocates of presidential power became the scourges of the imperial presidency. After working as a special assistant in the Kennedy White House, Arthur Schlesinger thought the problem was that the President needed more power. "The problem of moving forward," he wrote then, "seemed in great part the problem of making the permanent government responsive to the policies of the presidential government." That was in 1965. By 1974, Professor Schlesinger had discovered that the "revolutionary" imperial presidency had been growing right through the period he had been serving it in the White House, growing, too, at the expense of constitutional order, so that the presidency, "the pivotal institution" of the American government, "has got out of control and badly needs new definition and restraint." In 1975 Joseph A. Califano, who had served that most imperious of imperial Presidents, Lyndon B. Johnson, as loyally as any and more aggressively than most, discovered that "the forces now at play in our society will press towards a dangerous concentration of presidential power." Eighteen months later, Califano was back at work for another Democratic President. (Who was, indeed, to exercise presidential power at Califano's expense another two years later.) This was a time, Eisenhower's former speechwriter, Emmet John Hughes, shrewdly remarked at a conference called in Washington in late 1973 to debate the question "Has the President too much power?," when "liberal ideologues could be as tempted to shackle the Presidency as were conservative ideologues a generation ago."

Yet it was not simply a matter of whose ox was gored. The long and disastrous record of the exercise of presidential power in Southeast Asia, culminating in the revelation of ruthless, secret applications of military force by President Nixon and Henry Kissinger; the discovery that Nixon and his staff had operated what amounted to the rudiments of a secret political police in the White House; the uncovering of the general ethical sleaziness that had flourished behind the veil of secrecy there; finally, the tension and drama of Nixon's cover-up, exposure and fall: taken together the whole political history of the first half of the 1970s combined to strip the institution of the presidency of the aura of legitimate majesty that had clothed it since Roosevelt's day.

Majesty? More and more observers pointed out that the presidency had indeed taken on some of the characteristics of a monarchy. As early as 1970, in his thoughtful book, *The Twilight of the Presidency,* Lyndon Johnson's former press secretary, George Reedy, warned that the White House was becoming a court, and "the Presidency had taken on all the regalia of monarchy except ermine robes, a scepter, and a crown." "The Presidency has increasingly emerged as an imperial office, at home as well as abroad," concurred Walter Dean Burnham of MIT. Another respected academic, F. G. Hutchins, of Harvard and the Princeton Institute for Advanced Study, roundly proclaimed that "the American presidency has become the tyranny that Jefferson foresaw." Others predicted that presidential supremacy was in danger of degenerating into presidential dictatorship. "It can happen," Reedy wrote:

> A highly irrational personality, who under other circumstances might be medically certifiable for treatment, could take over the White House, and the event never be known with any degree of assurance. . . . where presidents are concerned, the tolerance level for irrationality extends almost to the point of gibbering idiocy or delusions of identity.

In 1970, it was assumed that Reedy was exaggerating. By 1974, no such assumption could be made.

Immediately after Watergate, even those who did not go so far were clear on the central point. The problem of presidential power was not that the President had too little power, it was that he had too much. Or, as political scientist Thomas E. Cronin put it in a book published in 1975, "the problem becomes one of controlling the great power that has been vested in a single institution."

One should beware of deforming the positions of writers by selective quotation. Arthur Schlesinger, for example, made it plain in the foreword to his *The Imperial Presidency* that he was doubly concerned both by "inordinate theories of presidential power" and by the danger of "an inordinate swing against the presidency." Cronin, too, was careful to warn that the presidency must be made more effective and also "safe for democracy." Nonetheless, on balance the shift in the primary concern of those who studied the presidency between the early 1960s and the middle 1970s was unmistakable. In the aftermath of Watergate, presidential accountability, not presidential effectiveness, was seen as the first priority.

In that same mood, there was a certain tendency among academics and journalists to feel, as Henry Kissinger's Harvard colleagues had felt in 1970, that the future must lie with Congress. Some felt that Congress ought to recapture territory at the expense of the presidency, as a safeguard against the danger of excessive presidential power. Others felt that, desirable or not, it was in any case inevitable that Congress's position would grow stronger in relation to the White House as a result of Nixon's disgrace and fall. And, as we shall see, as a result both of Vietnam and of Watergate, that is to some extent what did actually happen.

As the immediate trauma of Watergate faded, however, there were widespread second thoughts about the whole dilemma of presidential power. Was the question of power truly the important one? people began to ask. Wasn't it based on a confusion, indeed on a whole set of confusions, between military and political power, between power and powers, between legitimate authority and breaches of constitutional legality? Was the power relationship between President and Congress really, as the pendulum image seemed to presuppose, that of the "zero-sum game" of the theory of games, so that if one gained, the other player automatically lost? Wasn't it more a question of fitting both President and Congress to perform their respective roles better within the framework of the constitutional balance of powers?

Once again the connection between the reality and the theory of the presidency remained close. These new questions replaced the former concern with the paradox of power as the reality of Gerald Ford and then Jimmy Carter in the White House began to efface the memory of Richard Nixon and Lyndon Johnson. Few could seriously envisage Ford as a dictator or suspect Carter even of harboring such an evil thought in his heart.

Yet, in the changed mood and circumstances of the late 1970s, the paradox of presidential power remained unresolved. The President seemed more impotent than ever to tackle the country's problems. Still, he remained so central to the system that no one could seriously imagine that they could be tackled by anyone else without him.

The question of the presidency is more urgent now than ever. But the emphasis of the inquiry has shifted again. It is no longer on the potential of the President himself, roaming far and wide like Rossiter's "magnificent lion." It is not on the danger of presidential dictatorship nor on the prospect of presidential eclipse in a period of revived congressional dominance. Increasingly the interest of those who study the presidency has shifted to the *connections* between the President and the rest of the political and social systems he presides over. What ought to be his relations with Congress? With his cabinet? With the federal bureaucracy? The states and local government? With American society as a whole? How should he find out what the American people truly want? How to get through to them what he feels must be done? Through what intermediate institutions, or relationships, or connecting rods, or gears can he transmit the drive of presidential power to the wheels of the system?

How, in short, can he overcome what is now often seen as the essential problem: the isolation of the President? Reedy had described the President's psychological isolation: "from the President's standpoint, the great staff problem is that of maintaining his contact with the world's reality that lies outside the White House walls. Very few have succeeded in doing so." Benjamin V. Cohen, who worked for Roosevelt in the White House and had watched Presidents closely and shrewdly for almost another forty years in Washington, also emphasized the dangers of isolation in a notable lecture to the University of California in 1974, in which he proposed giving the President a supercabinet executive council to help him. But serious as is the President's psychological isolation from reliable information about the outside world, it is less dangerous than his isolation from effective means of acting upon the outside world.

"In the aftermath of Watergate," wrote the political scientist Richard M. Pious as long ago as 1974," the *interactions* between the departments, the President and Congress need more attention." Robustly, too, in a 1975 article Aaron Wildavsky brushed aside fashionable talk about the weakening of the presidency:

> Not so. Does anyone imagine fewer groups will be interested in influencing a President's position in their own behalf or that his actions will matter less to people in the future? The question answers itself. The weakening of the presidency is about as likely as the withering away of the state.

Instead, Wildavsky, too, focused his powerful analysis on the relationship between the President and the people's expectations of the presidency, and on the relationships between the President and those "institutional competitors," as Wildavsky called them, who are also his chief means of carrying out his job. He discussed four of them in particular. We met them before, when we were looking at the techniques Franklin Roosevelt developed to create the new presidency. The federal bureaucracy. The Congress. The communications media, especially press and television. And the political parties. The list gives us a convenient agenda for looking at the President's hopes of overcoming his isolation and tackling the problems of the United States at home and abroad.

III Effete Bureaucrats and Macho Staff

For I also am a man set in authority, having under me soldiers; and I say unto one, Go, and he goeth.

—The Gospel according to Luke 7:8

"Yes, but you don't go!"

—Major-General Stanley to the chorus of policemen who have just proclaimed that they go to fight the foe, in *The Pirates of Penzance*, by W. S. Gilbert and Sir Arthur Sullivan

1

OF ALL the themes Jimmy Carter sounded in his campaign for the presidency in 1976, none was more insistently repeated, and none was more effective, than his promise to do something about the bureaucracy in Washington. He would reorganize the government, he told countless audiences, and give it back to the people. He would cut back the number of individual agencies from nearly two thousand to two hundred, as he had slashed the number of state agencies in Georgia when he was governor. The implication —though Carter was careful never to spell it out too precisely— was that by reorganizing the government he would be able to simplify procedures, eliminate duplication, increase efficiency, cut back payrolls and save dollars, all while maintaining or improving the government's service to the citizen.

It was easier said than done. The whole sad story of Jimmy Carter's efforts to reorganize the federal bureaucracy is instructive. Even the story of the President's efforts to move a single subcabinet agency, the Forest Service, from one cabinet department to another, is a sobering lesson in the real limits on presidential power.

On March 1, 1979, *The New York Times* reported that the President had announced that he intended to create a new cabinet-level Department of Natural Resources. The main element would be the transfer to the new department from the Department of Agriculture of the 22,000 employees of the Forest Service, with jurisdiction over some 187 million acres of forest. Eleven weeks later, on May 15, administration officials quietly announced that they were dropping their plans for a Department of Natural Resources. In so doing, observed one close observer of the lethal lobbying that had forced the President to back off, "they did more than merely kill the last of President Carter's grand reorganization schemes. They also signaled the sputtering conclusion of one of Carter's chief campaign themes."

Neither the need for reorganizing the federal bureaucracy nor the specific idea of creating a new Department of Natural Resources originated with Jimmy Carter. In 1949 a commission under former President Herbert Hoover looked at the tangle of new federal agencies and recommended that some of them should be fitted into a new cabinet-level department of Health, Education, and Welfare. It was not until Eisenhower's time that it was done, however. Lyndon Johnson succeeded in creating two new cabinet offices, a Department of Housing and Urban Development and a Department of Transportation. More than one task force told Johnson that he should create several more new cabinet departments; the last of these, chaired by the retired railroad executive Ben Heineman, proposed a new Department of Economic Affairs, a Department of Social Services, and a Department of Natural Resources and Development. Almost the first thing President Nixon did when he became President was to set up an advisory council on executive reorganization under his friend, the chief executive of Litton Industries, Roy L. Ash. The Ash Council, too, came out for reorganization, and among the four new domestic cabinet departments into which the existing departments and agencies were to be regrouped was a Department of Natural Resources and Development. One of the first things Jimmy Carter did when he got to the White House was to set up a reorganization team in the Office of Management and Budget (the former Budget Bureau, which serves the White House as an in-house staff agency). After two years' work, it came up with a number of plans for creating new agencies and regrouping existing ones. Sure enough, one of these was a proposal for a Department of Natural Resources. It would brigade together some surviving functions of a slimmed-down Department of the Interior and the Forest Service.

The Forest Service, to the sophisticated ears of Washington, sounds dull and apolitical. Yet it has it within its power to affect the whole economy of large parts of the United States. Its bureaucratic status has been the symbol and the prize of a contest between two competing philosophies of land management for three-quarters of a century.

Jimmy Carter gave no indication of knowing it, but when Theodore Roosevelt, in 1905, wanted to show that he was serious about conserving the national heritage, he removed the national forests from the control of the Department of the Interior and gave them to Gifford Pinchot, one of the founding fathers of the conservation movement, who was Chief Forester under the Department of Agriculture. In the 1920s, Albert B. Fall, Harding's secretary of the interior and the villain of the Teapot Dome scandal, after selling off as much of the nation's oil reserves as he could, did his best to prize the forest lands away from Agriculture so that he could sell them off, too. By the time of the New Deal, the Department of Agriculture and the Forest Service had become symbols of honest management of the nation's patrimony; Interior stood for the pillage of the public domain by private interests and their friends in government. Franklin D. Roosevelt appointed as Secretary of the Interior a man of a very different kind: Gifford Pinchot's friend, Harold Ickes. No need to protect the national forest from him, Ickes thought, and set out to recapture the Forest Service for Interior from Agriculture. The battle reached levels of startling intensity, with savage insults exchanged between Ickes and Roosevelt's Agriculture Secretary, Henry Wallace. But in the main it drearied on almost unnoticed outside the agencies concerned, "a depressing feature," one historian wrote, "of the Washington landscape," and in the end Ickes failed.

It would be the greatest mistake, however, to imagine that this obscure dispute was only of interest to the Washington bureaucrats affected. It was a dispute about power and about very large amounts of money. There are some 500 million acres of commercially usable forest in the United States. About one-fifth of this, or 107 million acres, is controlled by the federal government, the great majority of it by the Forest Service, and this includes a disproportionate share of the softwood used by the construction industry.

Over the years, while the professional expertise of the Forest Service has been greatly admired, a cozily symbiotic relationship grew up between the service and private forest industry. In 1975 this relationship was thrown into turmoil by the decision of a federal court of appeals in the so-called Monongahela case. For many years, the Forest Service had fallen into the habit of allowing the logging companies to "clear-cut"; that is, to harvest all the trees, young as well as old, in a given swath of forest. The practice is economical. It is also, as the environmentalists and conservationists began to point out with increasing indignation, highly damaging. It not only destroys future timber. It leaves scars on the land that testify eloquently to the ruthlessness of those who have left no tree standing for many square miles.

Anyone who followed the congressional fight over clear-cutting in 1976 (when Jimmy Carter and his future aides were otherwise engaged) could have been in no doubt that shifting the Forest Service from Agriculture to a new department was no mere bureaucratic tidy-up. The forest industry, backed by its customers in the construction business, wanted production. The Forest Service had come to share its attitudes. Both had drawn together for the common defense against the rising environmentalist movement. A Forest Service left where it had been for more than seventy years, in the Department of Agriculture, had come to seem the guarantee of a status quo the loggers had learned to thrive under. Moving the service to a new department, on the other hand, would be the signal for a renewed assault by the environmental lobby which, the loggers assumed, would dominate the new bureaucracy.

The President and his men were left in no doubt about the forest industry's feelings. The National Forest Products Association wired the President that the proposed reorganization would "reduce standard of living and U.S. world economic power." Home builders and other wood-using groups joined the lumber interests in their lobbying efforts. The loggers' friends in Congress stood by them in their hour of danger. Within an hour of Carter's announcement that he proposed to move the Forest Service to a new department, the chairmen of the two main congressional committees with jurisdiction turned their thumbs down. "I intend to do everything I can to persuade my colleagues in the House to vote down the reorganization plans," said Congressman Thomas Foley, Democrat of Washington, a state in which lumber interests bulk big. Senator Herman E. Talmadge, chairman of the Senate Committee on Agriculture and Forestry, was even more contemptuous. "This is a classic case of bureaucratic box shuffling," he said, "by naive planners, academic theorists, and other assorted dreamers."

The loggers held the high cards, and both sides knew it. The President was forced to drop his original intention of carrying out the reorganization without legislation. Even friendly senators and congressmen warned that if he persisted in reorganizing the Forest Service his Strategic Arms Limitation Treaty might be endangered! It was becoming hard to hold the bureaucrats themselves in line. There were resignations, and rumors of resignations, among key people not only in the Forest Service, but also at Interior. In mid-May, the President gave in, so dropping what was among the last remaining substantial relics of his once ambitious plans for reorganizing the federal bureaucracy: "his" branch of the government, according to traditional theory.

There are quite a few lessons to be drawn from the case of the Forest Service. The first is that the permanent government in Washington is more resilient, and the ways of Washington more devious, than might appear—even to some presidential candidates. Certainly many staff members of any of the last half-dozen administrations would echo the sad admission of one of Carter's aides, who told Elizabeth Drew of *The New Yorker* the lessons he had learned in the White House:

> "We learned that you can't pick that many fights. No one has that much time for it, and the Cabinet agencies won't stick with you. The Secretary will at first, and then will walk away from our position under questioning by a congressional committee. The assistant secretaries will stay farther away, and the bureau chiefs will pull the rug out from under you."

The fate of this particular corner of President Carter's reorganization plan certainly suggests the degree of gear slippage that now occurs between the presidential operation as a whole—including the campaign, the "mandate of heaven," the President's program, White House policy, and staff implementation—and what the French call "the real country." It illustrates just how far the presidential politics of the campaign for election every four years, and also of that other perpetual campaign for reelection that preoccupies the inhabitants of the White House, have slipped out of contact with the "real world," with its industries, its interests, its centers of power and influence. It reminds us of something that no President since Roosevelt has understood before he entered the White House, and every President since has learned there: that, as Professor Hugh Heclo of Harvard has put it, "between the politicians' intentions and the government's final action passes the shadow of the bureaucrat."

Why are the President and his men so powerless when it comes to carrying out their policies, even within their "own" government? The question goes to the heart of this whole inquiry into the problems of the modern presidency. But it is worth suggesting one partial answer even at this stage. It is that the executive branch is not really the President's branch. It is not effectively controlled by him. It marches to other drums.

For whatever reasons—and we shall have to examine more closely later just why this is so—the President cannot *order* his own men, not even the cabinet secretaries or the subcabinet officials he has appointed himself, to do what he wants. Or at least he cannot always order, on all subjects, and be sure that he will be obeyed. Poor Jimmy Carter, like "poor Ike," learns that it is indeed not a bit like the Army or the Navy. Since he cannot order, the President must do his best to persuade. And when wisdom and eloquence and charm and political charisma are all exhausted, as they will be when great issues are at stake, and determined rivals are in the field, then the President must trade. All too often he finds that when it comes to swapping wampum and glass beads, even within his "own" executive branch, others have more desirable trade goods than he has.

The former Nixon aide John Ehrlichman put it pungently in Key Biscayne, Florida, late in 1972. The administration appointed men to high posts, he complained; they had their picture taken with the President, and then "we only see them at the annual White House Christmas party. They go off and marry the natives." Reduced to bargaining with his own subordinates to carry out his policies, the President finds he has too few sticks and others have more enticing carrots.

Ehrlichman and his boss Nixon made the mistake of supposing the trouble was that the permanent government was staffed by Democrats and liberals, and that good Republican conservatives were swallowed by these ideological ambushes in the departments. Nixon "thought all those people were out to sabotage him," the political scientist James L. Sundquist told me in an interview, "and there was just enough truth in it" for the illusion to do profound damage to his presidency. But the case of the Forest Service does illustrate one of the abiding reasons why Presidents have less influence with the executive bureaucracy than they expect to have, and less influence than the country expects them to have.

The official in the executive branch is only one pole in a triangle of power. You can call it a "subgovernment," or a "triple alliance," or an "unholy trinity," or an "iron triangle." Power in Washington is split three ways. In each triangle, there is an interest group. It may be, in the judgment of a particular observer, legitimate or illegitimate. It may be patriotic or frankly rapacious. But it is there. It disposes of a certain quantum of power. Second, there is that part of the federal bureaucracy that is supposed to administer matters of interest to the interest group. And at the third pole there are the congressional committees, their chairmen and staff, who are supposed to oversee and legislate for those interests. Some of these triangles are as tiny and sheltered as rock pools: others, like the military-industrial complex or the galaxy of lobbies that protect the interests of automobile manufacturers, represent awesome agglomerations of power. In either case, the relationships within a "subgovernment" are not necessarily always cozy or collusive; the point is that the public officials involved look not upward to a hierarchy of power with the President at its apex but sideways, to their constituency in the world outside government, and to their opposite numbers in Congress.

Numerous former players in this three-sided game have described the interests and the forces that govern it. Not every American, for example, perhaps realizes that there is a school lunch lobby, but there is, according to an executive in the Department of Agriculture, who explained it to Hugh Heclo:

> "We can't end the pilot school milk program, even though we now have the school lunch program, because of the school lunch lobby, equipment manufacturers, milk lobby, and our own Nutrition Service. Each program also has a certain congressman's stamp on it. Eliminate it, and it is an affront to him, the clients and the bureaucrats delivering it to them."

This particular example is a reminder that many such "triangles" are in reality pentangles or even more complex polyhedrons; school milk programs, like school textbook programs and the infinitely vaster health care delivery and highway lobbies, involve state and local governments as well as both executive and legislative branches at the federal level. Again, the point is that in practice the bureaucrat at the decision-making level is not always, or even often, responsive to policy as transmitted downward by a rational chain of command from the President. Joseph Califano's testimony is eloquent, because he has climbed to the tip of each of the three points of the iron triangle as President Johnson's top aide for domestic policy, as a highly successful Washington lawyer-lobbyist, and as cabinet secretary of Health, Education, and Welfare (HEW) under President Carter. Presidents face a "problem of loyalties," says Califano. Middle-level bureau chiefs and regional administrators in the big government departments are often "predominantly concerned about the attitudes of the substantive or geographical constituencies they serve and the senators and congressmen with whom they must work." In practice, he concludes, many smaller federal agencies are simply not accountable to the President.

Kermit Gordon, director of the Bureau of the Budget under Presidents Kennedy and Johnson, observed the process at work from close enough to enable him to see the world through the bureaucrat's eyes:

> He lives at the center of a special world inhabited by persons and groups in the private sector who stand to gain or lose by what he does, certain members of Congress . . . and a specialized press to which he is a figure of central importance. The approbation which is most meaningful to him is likely to be the approbation of the other inhabitants of this special world. . . . the President will loom as a distant and shadowy figure who will, in any case, be succeeded by someone else in a few years.

Nor do all the subgovernments in Washington operate only at the middle level. On each scale, the pattern is repeated. In sheltered rock pools, in broad lakes, and in mighty oceans, the same triangular power relationship is the rule. The forest industry has its protectors and its regulators in Congress and in the Forest Service. A similar triad links the water resources lobby, from Passamaquoddy, Maine, to the Hoover Dam, with the engineers in the Bureau of Reclamation for the West and in the Army Corps of Engineers east of the Mississippi River, and with the Public Works and Appropriations committees of Congress. Harry McPherson, who once presided over the Corps of Engineers as a civilian official in the Pentagon, had no illusions about the nature of that relationship.

> The Corps, like all other uniformed military organizations, was under civilian control. But in its case the controlling civilians were on the Hill. . . ."We are the Congress's Engineers," a general of the Corps once told me, as the doorman of a men's club might say to a stranger, "Members Only."

Dozens of congressmen are helped to keep their seats by the water projects built in their district: fortunes are made by entrepreneurs of many kinds once the water, at great public expense, has been dammed. The cotton growers farm the corridors of Washington, as a planter in the Mississippi Delta once told me. The medical research lobby knows how to operate there, in a triangular relationship with the bureaucracy at HEW and at the National Institutes of Health and with the appropriations subcommittees. The insurance industry has its iron triangle, and so do the drug companies, and the savings and loan people, and Hollywood and Wall Street and Detroit, the bankers and the steelmakers, television, airlines and aerospace.

Mightiest of all these trinities of power, of course, is the great military-industrial complex which, as President Eisenhower warned in his parting speech, makes its influence felt "in every city, every statehouse, every office of the federal government." Once it was fashionable to denounce the military-industrial complex. Now it is becoming at least respectable to pretend that it does not exist. But it does exist, so long as hundreds of uniformed Pentagon liaison officers are at work stroking dozens of senators and congressmen who sit on the committees that authorize and appropriate tens of billions of dollars for weapons systems, and so long as the contracts to build those systems can make the fortune of major corporations and mean ruin or prosperity for whole sections of the country. Literally hundreds of billions have traveled this three-cornered route in the past thirty years. Presidents and their secretaries of defense have sought to impose their authority on the process. They have rarely succeeded for long.

The fate of the TFX (later called the F-111), the pet project of perhaps the strongest secretary of defense since the office was created, reveals the limitations of presidential authority when it comes up against the defense in depth organized by service traditions, giant industries, and powerful congressional committees. In 1961, with President Kennedy's full support, Defense Secretary Robert S. McNamara decided that the same basic fighter aircraft must serve the needs of both Air Force and Navy. Almost seven years and many determined congressional maneuvers later, McNamara gave in and agreed to drop the Navy version in deference to the power of the admirals and their friends on Capitol Hill. "The Navy is one service McNamara never really brought under control," said one man in his own office. "They have enormous power on Capitol Hill. Even if they were to testify in favor of the F-111, it's what they say to senators over drinks later on that counts." The military-industrial complex itself, on closer inspection, is made up of a honeycomb of smaller three-cornered relationships, each linking congressmen, defense contractors, and subsections of the sprawling defense bureaucracy.

In themselves, these relationships are morally neutral. The special interests involved may be those of the Boeing Company and the State of Washington, or those of General Dynamics and the State of Texas. They may be those of General Motors, or the Sierra Club, or indeed of a labor union, a church, or ethnic group. It makes no difference from the point of view of the President. To the extent that vital decisions are taken within the walls of the iron triangles, they are outside the President's effective authority. And to that extent he is not master in his own house.

2

Once again we come up against the paradox of presidential power.

It is true that the President is incomparably the most powerful single figure in the executive branch, that his authority is imposing and his real power felt in every corner of the bureaucracy. He is not just one of the actors in the Washington comedy; he is perpetually at the middle of the stage. He can give instant publicity to any issue that attracts his attention. Even his stubbornest opponents in the Congress treat him with respect. Even the most recalcitrant member of the permanent government knows that the President can fire him if he steps too far out of line. Few interests in the country are unaware of the advantages of presidential favor and the dangers of presidential enmity. Only the President can give a sense of direction and a set of priorities to the executive bureaucracy. In normal times and on most issues, the bureaucracy is happy enough to accept presidential leadership, always provided that it does not trespass on the cherished interests of the constituency that any particular part of the bureaucracy serves over the long term.

It is even true that the President has too much power in the executive branch, in the sense that there are too few others to share his load. Only he and his White House staff can initiate innovations in policy, draw the permanent government's attention to new needs, rush its sandbags to new breaches in the seawalls of society. Only presidential initiative can respond to new circumstances like the unemployment of the 1930s, the black rebellion of the 1950s, the urban problems of the 1960s, or the energy crisis of the 1970s. The departmental bureaucracies can do little positive on their own. They have to peddle new ideas suggested by their knowledge and experience either to the officials appointed by the President or to their friends in the Congress. They can only hope to find a patron.

There is no smoothly working system for lifting inputs of information and feedback from the lowest levels of the governmental system. It will be years before Washington becomes aware that the same welfare mother may have to deal with half a dozen federal offices in the extreme opposite corners of Philadelphia or Los Angeles, years more before anyone can overcome the obstacles to rationalizing the provision of services. There is no smooth mechanism for the transmission of ideas, decisions, authority, and leadership from the top.

Despite George Reedy's sly reminder that "no president ever died of overwork," the overload is undeniable. It shows itself not so much in the things that Presidents do as in the things they cannot hope to get around to doing. Presidential leadership is needed at more points in the system than any one man can hope to visit more than occasionally, on, as it were, random tours of inspection to make sure that the sentries are not asleep at their posts. Or alternatively the system should be more autonomous, so that it could respond more, innovate more, without specific presidential initiative. In this sense, the presidency bears the burden of too much power. It bulks too large in the governmental system. Neither Lyndon Johnson, an insomniac with demonic energy, nor Richard Nixon, covering yellow pad after yellow pad behind the protective screen of his "German shepherds," nor Jimmy Carter meticulously checking multiple options far into the night has been able to master the sheer quantity of work routed into the Oval Office by the centralization of power in the person of the President.

Yet Presidents since Franklin Roosevelt have railed in their frustration and impotence under "the shadow of the bureaucrat."

The Treasury was so "large and far-flung and ingrained in its practices," Roosevelt complained when it was considerably smaller and less far-flung than it is today, that he found it almost impossible to get the results he wanted. And the Treasury was not to be compared with the State Department. But the Treasury and the State Department put together were nothing as compared with the Navy.

"To change anything in the Na-a-v-y," he drawled, "is like punching a feather bed. You punch it with your right, and you punch it with your left, until you are finally exhausted, and then you find the damn bed just as it was before you started punching."

"I thought I was the President," Harry Truman told David Brinkley, "but when it comes to these bureaucracies, I can't make them do a damn thing."

President Eisenhower recalled in his memoirs that when he met President Kennedy during the transition period in 1960, he was "amazed" to discover that Kennedy "seemed unaware of the limitations on presidential power to enforce decisions." Kennedy had raised with Eisenhower some thoughts about the need for a sweeping reorganization of the Pentagon. Eisenhower was appalled because Kennedy seemed to think the only question was whether the reorganization was a good idea; Eisenhower, a former five-star general who knew his way around the politics of the military bureaucracy perhaps better than any man alive, had with the greatest difficulty, after years of effort, finally succeeded in pushing through a far more limited reorganization.

Lyndon Johnson claimed to his biographer Doris Kearns that he had no problem with bureaucracy with a capital B, but only with individual bureaucrats. Yet once the prestige of his triumphs began to wear off and—to borrow the vivid metaphor he used himself—"the wolves were tearing away at every joint," he experienced just the same difficulty as other modern Presidents in getting the bureaucrats to push the policies he wanted pushed.

As for Richard Nixon, he was all but paranoiac on the subject of the Washington bureaucracy. He believed that it was made up of New Dealers, liberals, and Kennedy Democrats who were deliberately sabotaging his programs, and in that he was not wholly wrong, if only for the understandable reason that men who had spent years devising programs were naturally less than enthusiastic about dismantling them, and quite a few bureaucrats in Nixon's administration were called upon to do that. Whether it was justified or not, there is no doubt about the depth of Nixon's frustration. It burst out to Ehrlichman one day in the Oval Office in the spring of 1973: "We have no discipline in this bureaucracy!" he barked. "We never fire anybody. We never reprimand anybody. We never demote anybody. We always promote the sons-of-bitches that kick us in the ass!"

Presidents do not exaggerate when they complain that they cannot get the government to do what they want.

This is equally true of the most routine acts of domestic management and of the most solemn moments of international crisis, when the nation's existence is literally at stake.

In 1977, to take a relatively routine example first—though, even so, one that could be a matter of life and death, not to mention many millions of dollars of federal liabilities—President Carter issued a directive to seventy-five different federal agencies, ordering them to use whatever authority they had to discourage developers from building in low-lying areas where there was a danger of flooding. Twenty-five months later the federal bureaucracy had virtually ignored this plain order from the President. Of the seventy-five agencies that received it, only fifteen agencies, one in five, had so much as proceeded to the preliminary step of drawing up regulations to show how they might, for example, deny federal funds to local governments that persisted in building in flood-prone areas. Forty-six of the recipient agencies, or almost two-thirds, had in more than two years simply done nothing at all in compliance.

What is far more serious is that two separate careful studies of the Cuban missile crisis of 1962 by the Harvard scholar Graham T. Allison and by Morton H. Halperin have shown that during perhaps the most dangerous period in relations between the United States and the Soviet Union since the beginning of the Cold War, the bureaucracies of the U.S. military services repeatedly ignored orders, including direct, face-to-face orders by the President himself, with results which actually led to military action contrary to the President's expressed intentions.

In spite of an explicit presidential order, the Air Force left aircraft lined up wing tip to wing tip, and therefore vulnerable to enemy attack, on airfields in the southeastern United States. This appears to have been sheer incompetence, though it may have been bravado. In defiance of a presidential order to avoid provocative intelligence operations during the crisis, U.S. reconnaissance aircraft strayed over the Soviet Union at least once during the crisis. Just how dangerous this disobedience could have been is suggested by the language of one of Soviet leader Nikita Khrushchev's letters to President Kennedy during the crisis: "Is it not a fact that an intruding American plane could easily be taken for a nuclear bomber, which might push us to a fateful step?"

A tentative decision was taken by the President at one point that if a U-2 reconnaissance plane were to be shot down over Cuba, he would authorize the bombing of Cuba. When a U-2 was attacked, the incident was taken by the U.S. Air Force as authority to go ahead with the bombing, even though the President had issued no such order and had in fact decided by then against bombing: only by chance was the bombing forestalled. Although the President gave no orders to attack Soviet submarines, the U.S. Navy continued to force Soviet submarines in the Caribbean to surface throughout the crisis. In spite of an explicit order from the President's mouth to the chief of naval operations to move the line of the blockade five hundred miles or so closer to Cuba, the Navy left the blockade where it was, with the result that the President was constrained to allow several Soviet ships through the blockade. Less flagrant, but perhaps most serious of all, the Air Force, asked by the White House whether it could mount a "surgical" air strike on the Soviet missile sites, persisted in maintaining that the only operation possible would be one that had been prepared for the utterly different contingency of an invasion, with the result that the President was effectively deprived of the option of an air strike—the exact opposite, one would have thought, of what the Air Force would have wanted.

The experience of the Cuban missile crisis is not unique. Major unauthorized operations took place on more than one occasion in the Vietnam War, sometimes with potentially grave political consequences. It is enough to raise serious doubt whether, if the President "pushed the button," he could be sure that the intended consequences would take place, and even more serious doubt whether, in a situation where nuclear war was a possibility and he decided *not* to take a certain course of action, he could be sure that the military bureaucracy would obey.

3

In the early Middle Ages, when by no means all kings and very few of their subjects could read or write, they lent their authority to documents with the mark of their seal pressed into lead or wax. Soon it became necessary for the king to have a clerk to look after his seal and to keep records of the grants of land, patents of nobility, pardons, charters, and all the other royal acts that had been sealed with it. This clerk evolved into the chancellor, one of the most important officials in any medieval king's retinue, and it was not long before his office, the chancery, became a busy place, with dozens of clerks at work and many thousands of records on file. The king began to need some more personal and mobile way of certifying his will on documents, and so in England he began to use what was called his "privy seal." Something similar happened in every other medieval kingdom and in the Papal Curia. It was only a matter of time, however, before the keeper of the privy seal, too, set up a small bureaucracy of his own, and so the king started using the signet ring on his own finger to seal documents done under his personal authority. By the end of the Middle Ages, this third method of signifying the royal will had become bureaucratized in its turn. Finally the Tudor monarchs—who could read and write very well in several languages—began to sign documents with what was called the "sign manual." The man who organized the flow of paper for the royal sign manual was addressed as "Mr. Secretary," and it was from this fourth level of bureaucracy that the whole of the modern British civil service developed.

In medieval Europe, in other words, over a period of some five hundred years, the rulers wrestled against the constant tendency of bureaucracies, originally created to serve the king's own will, to develop a logic and traditions of their own and so gradually float outside the king's personal control: to "go off and marry the natives." Again and again the kings tried to create a new inner bureaucracy, responsive to their own direction, only to see the process repeat itself. Something very similar has happened in Washington. Presidents have wrestled to keep their personal grip on the bureaucracy, and by and large they have failed. So they have set about building up a new inner bureaucracy of their own. There, too, they have failed. The result is that the modern President and his staff operate at the apex of what ought to be "his" branch of the government a little like a band of raiders, watched by the sullen inhabitants of a city they have stormed, desperately trying to find the switches and connections to make the city's life support systems function.

It was in the last quarter of the nineteenth century, in reaction against the corruption of the Grant administration and the excesses of the robber barons of the Gilded Age, that mainly upper-class reformers succeeded in replacing the "spoils system" with "civil service." The initiative did not come from Presidents. But Presidents like Grover Cleveland, Theodore Roosevelt, and Woodrow Wilson recognized that the spread of civil service would help them to establish their authority as against that of the potentates of the Congress.

By the middle 1960s, the civil service system had triumphed, to the point that 85 percent of all federal jobs were covered by it, probably as high a proportion as would ever be covered. Yet at the same time—except to a limited extent in such specialized bureaux as the Forest Service, the Bureau of Reclamation, the Bureau of the Mint, or the Bureau of Indian Affairs, and in some organizations that people do not immediately think of as belonging to the bureaucracy, such as the Federal Bureau of Investigation or the Central Intelligence Agency—the United States bureaucracy never developed an ethos or an esprit de corps like those of the great civil services of Europe. The civil service ideal in America remained largely negative. It aspired to protect the public against graft, nepotism, and incompetence. It scarcely offered a coherent ideal of the public service. Still less did it lay any claim to being a governing elite. Nor did it acquire any widely diffused philosophy of the service of the state, such as animated the discipline and professional standards of the great Prussian civil servants in the nineteenth century, or still gives to the graduates of the Ecole Nationale d'Administration in France or the officials of the British Treasury their collective self-confidence and sense of purpose.

During the long period while this somewhat limited civil service concept was spreading over the federal employees in Washington, another event of immense importance in the history of American government was taking place: the vast expansion in the sheer size of the federal government and in its impact on virtually every corner of American life. That process of growth began before the New Deal, and it has not finished yet. Professor Samuel Beer of Harvard has pointed out that if you express public expenditure as a proportion of the gross national product, the figure rises from 6.5 percent in 1902 to 19.1 percent in 1938, after all the innovations of the New Deal, and by 1976 had reached 34.2 percent. A particularly sharp surge in public expenditure that lasted through the Nixon years was caused by the Great Society programs started by President Johnson.

Contrary to much often repeated mythology, however, the growth of the federal government took place in two distinct phases. In the first, the number of government employees increased sharply. In the second, their number remained roughly constant, while the work they did, as measured by the amount of money they spent and the number of regulations they wrote, grew rapidly. To be specific, the number of federal civilian employees rose between 1933 and 1950 from a few hundred thousand to just over two million. Since then, while conservative rhetoric about the swollen federal bureaucracy has become part of the national subconscious, the federal bureaucracy has scarcely grown at all. Since 1955, the number of federal civilian employees has grown by less than one-fifth, and has hovered around the two-and-a-half million mark for many years, while the number of employees of state and local government has multiplied by two and a half times, from fewer than five to more than twelve million. In that same period, both the number of federal regulations written, and the size of the federal budget, have risen sixfold.

While this spectacular growth was taking place, first in the numbers and then in the activity of the federal bureaucracy, the civil service ideal was spreading in theory. But in practice something very different was happening. The bureaucracy was becoming politicized. This was not so much a matter of party politics, the original danger that civil service reform had been targeted against, though as late as the Eisenhower administration the Republican National Committee tried through the "Willis plan" to capture patronage in the federal government. It was more that, at the key levels of the bureaucracy where policy is formed, decisions are taken, and control is exercised, the lines between presidential appointees and career civil servants were becoming blurred. "For almost 7,000 people near the top of the government," wrote Hugh Heclo in the most authoritative study to date of the federal bureaucracy, "the formal demarcation between bureaucrat and political appointee is far from obvious." The same is true of another three thousand executives in separate provinces of the federal government such as the Foreign Service, the CIA, and the Atomic Energy Commission. On the one hand there is a tendency for political appointees, near the end of an administration, to be "blanketed in," or otherwise transformed into career civil servants with permanent tenure. On the other hand, it behooves career civil servants more and more to be aware of political considerations and above all to be constantly sensitive to the political needs and wishes of the White House.

The process has been going on a long time. The Bureau of the Budget, for example, is one of the absolutely crucial mechanisms of control over what the federal government is doing. It is not surprising that Franklin Roosevelt saw that it was therefore a priceless lever of presidential control. The bureau was founded in 1921. In 1939 it was moved into the President's executive office building, across West Executive Avenue from the West Wing of the White House. There, under the faceless but formidable Harold D. Smith, it began, as one historian has put it, "to serve presidential goals." The process of politicization continued under Kennedy and Johnson. It was not a matter of party patronage, but rather of appointing men and women who were thought to be personally loyal to the President, so that they would act as his eyes and ears and arms in what was seen as the indifferent if not actually hostile territory of the career civil service. Many of the political appointees put into the higher levels of the bureaucracy for this purpose were utterly ignorant of specialized issues such as space exploration, economic policy, or energy policy which they were called on to administer. Seven out of ten of them had less than two years' experience in government when they were appointed, and about half stayed in government less than two years after their appointment. The intention, insofar as it was consciously formulated, appears to have been to improve the quality of management and policy planning in the federal government by bringing in an elite of talented generalists from the private sector: from corporate business, law firms, and universities, where—it seems to have been assumed by almost everyone in the Kennedy administration—standards of talent were higher than in government. It is doubtful whether many of those recruited in the Kennedy and Johnson period contributed greatly to the technical level of government's performance. A half left before they had had time to have much impact. Many of the rest were either out of their depth in specialized work or were soon captured by the attitudes of the permanent government.

The real motive for the politicization of the bureaucracy lay in the attempt, the perfectly understandable desire, of Presidents to capture the bureaucracy, to shake it up and activate it as the instrument of an activist presidency. The result has been catastrophic in many ways. "Our career civil service has been virtually destroyed," said James L. Sundquist in an interview. In some agencies, such as Health, Education, and Welfare, he said, presidential appointees from previous administrations go five and six levels down, that is, three levels down in the bureaux, below secretaries, deputies and assistant secretaries. By 1952, after twenty years of the New Deal and Fair Deal, Sundquist said, there was a career management elite in the Bureau of the Budget and in key jobs, such as the assistant secretary for administration job, in each department. "All the best people left," he went on. "All the best administrators in town are now working as consultants." After eight years, the Democrats recaptured the White House. Or rather John F. Kennedy did. But the people he appointed to key executive jobs were not necessarily the best available career professionals. They were appointed because they had helped him in the campaign, or because they had been recommended in a national "talent search" conducted by three of his aides, or because for some other reason he thought he could count on them to be "his men" in a particular department or agency. And after another eight years the process was repeated by President Nixon: one might say with a vengeance.

As an indication of the degree to which the career civil service has become politicized, Sundquist said that in 1952 there were no presidential appointees in the Bureau of the Budget: there are now ten. The assistant secretaries for administration in almost all departments are now political appointees: so are the program associate directors in the Office of Management and Budget, as the Bureau of the Budget has been called since 1970. The process accelerated during the Nixon administration because of the intense suspicion shared by the President and his men toward the permanent civil service in Washington. During those years, Heclo comments, political intrusion in the operations of the bureaucracy was "more systematic and widespread than ever before"; there was "an unprecedented degree of White House centralization, a search for monolithic power that would tolerate [no] internal opposition."

4

Neither the power to appoint to a thousand-odd jobs at a significant executive level in the federal hierarchy nor the gradual, more subtle process of politicization of the career civil service has given Presidents the control they want and feel they need over the executive branch of the government. And so increasingly they have turned to the equivalent of the medieval king's signet ring. They have looked to their own men and women on the White House staff to ride herd on what too often seems, from the perspective of the Oval Office, the unreliable, unresponsive, inert bureaucracy.

The President's staff has been growing for a long time, but the decisive step, in this as in so many other aspects of the presidency, came in Franklin Roosevelt's time. In his first term, President Ulysses S. Grant was authorized by Congress to have $13,800 a year to pay the wages of one private secretary, one stenographer, two executive clerks, one steward, and one messenger. In 1937 FDR had thirty-seven employees in the White House office, and in 1938 he had forty-five. Two years before that, Roosevelt asked for help. The sheer volume of work threatened to swamp him. Roosevelt himself said that it had been common knowledge for twenty years that the President was overworked, that he was so overwhelmed with minor details that it had become "humanly impossible" for him to carry out his constitutional duties as chief executive. So FDR set up the Committee on Administrative Management, under Louis Brownlow of the University of Chicago.

The Brownlow committee's recommendations led directly to the first clear step in the direction of the modern expanded and institutionalized presidency. Since the growth of the White House staff has been much criticized, it is relevant that the Brownlow committee did not back into recommending an expansion of the President's staff by accident or with its eyes shut, even though its members might have been surprised by just how much the White House was going to grow over the next forty years. "Those who waver at the sight of needed power," the report said, "are false friends of modern democracy. Strong executive leadership is essential to democratic government today. Our choice is not between power and no power, but between responsible and capable popular government and irresponsible autocracy." It was in this robust spirit that the Brownlow committee's report came to its famous conclusion that "the President needs help."

The help it recommended, and which Franklin Roosevelt gracefully accepted with his Executive Order 8248, took the form of giving the President six administrative assistants; of setting up, in addition to his White House office, first listed as such in the Government Manual in October 1939, an Executive Office of the President; of transferring the Bureau of the Budget, originally established by Congress in 1921 inside the Treasury, to the new Executive Office; and of creating a number of minor offices which turned out to be short-lived.

The White House staff grew rapidly under Truman, from 48 in 1944 to over 250 in 1952. It was in Truman's time, too, that the staff first grew a second tier: important aides like Clark Clifford acquired assistants of their own under them. Two important statutory enactments helped to complete the structure of the institutional presidency. Together they gave practical shape to a new conception of the presidency that had been evolving under the stresses of the Depression and World War II. The underlying compact that made possible the consensus politics of the 1950s was the acceptance by conservatives of the liberal doctrine that the government must intervene to keep the economy prosperous, matched by the liberals' endorsement of the strong national security posture of the Cold War period. Each of these wings of the grand strategy of consensus, so to speak, was represented by an addition to the presidential inner bureaucracy. The Employment Act of 1946 provided the President with a Council of Economic Advisers, to assist him with the preparation of an annual economic report to the Congress every January. And the National Security Act, signed by President Truman in July 1947, besides unifying the armed services under the control of a civilian secretary of defense and establishing a Central Intelligence Agency, also equipped the President with a National Security Council to advise him. Almost from the start, the NSC began to acquire staff, though it was not until the appointment of McGeorge Bundy as his national security assistant by President Kennedy in 1961 that the head of the National Security Council staff in the White

House began to rival and at times to eclipse the cabinet secretaries of state and defense in terms of real power.

The very fact that President Eisenhower was relatively inactive seems to have fostered the development of the institutional presidency: there were things to be done which, if they were not going to be done at the express orders of the President, were going to have to be done by someone else, and presidential assistants in the neat, low-profile Eisenhower White House were quite ready to step into such partial vacuums. By 1956 James Reston was reporting to the readers of *The New York Times* that the White House office staff had grown by a half to almost 400 in the four years since Eisenhower took office. By the end of the second term the Executive Office, including the Budget Bureau, the Council of Economic Advisers, and other functions, had a payroll of nearly 3000. Already, when John F. Kennedy took office, the President had a skeleton parallel bureaucracy of his own which shadowed and could be used to control all the strategic points of the government: the Budget Bureau to put the President firmly in charge not only of the budget itself, but also, as a result, of fiscal strategy and domestic policy; the council to control economic reporting and analysis as well as policy; the national security staff as an elite to help give the President a handle on defense policy, diplomacy, and the vital issues of war, peace, and international relations.

Kennedy made one major institutional addition to the White House staff. He greatly increased the importance of the congressional liaison operation, which he put under a trusted lieutenant, Lawrence O'Brien. After attempting to discontinue the new practice introduced by Roosevelt and Truman, even Eisenhower was obliged to send a program of recommended legislation to the Hill every year. So Kennedy's development of the congressional liaison office in the White House merely gave administrative recognition to the reality that the President had evolved into the real leader of the Congress.

Kennedy also brought a new spirit to the White House staff: a spirit of activism, of intellectual confidence, not to say arrogance, and of an attitude toward the permanent bureaucracy not far short of contempt. But what was more important in the long run than the abrasive relations between the White House staff and the rest of the executive branch—and these were a constant throughout the Kennedy, Johnson, and Nixon years—was a change in the way Presidents were using their White House staff.

To sum it up, you could say that instead of using them as their eyes and ears, they were using them more and more as their strong right arm. Joseph Califano, who managed most of the domestic policy under Johnson, put it clearly, if polysyllabically:

> The dysfunctional organization of the executive departments and the congressional rejection of the several reorganization proposals of recent presidents . . . [have] encouraged presidents to establish ad hoc organizations and to deploy their personal staff as a superjurisdictional corps of executive vice presidents.

Bill Moyers, who worked in the White House under Johnson, too, put it more briefly: "The job of the White House assistant is to help the President impress his priorities on the Administration."

By 1976, after Nixon and his men had passed through the White House, political scientist Aaron Wildavsky was more acid:

> To the White House staff, the separation of powers is anathema. They have wonderful ideas, apparently, only to see them sabotaged in the bureaucratic labyrinth. How dare those bureaucrats get in the way! . . . It is as if the Presidency were *the* government. The President's men tend to see themselves not as part of a larger system, but as the system itself.

Actually, there were two stages to this extension of the role of the White House staff. Originally, they were to have been administrative assistants to the President; that, and inevitably his advisers. But certainly when the Brownlow committee recommended, and Roosevelt gladly welcomed, the creation of White House assistants, it was not intended that they should be "superjurisdictional vice presidents." At first their role was to help the President: to read, evaluate, and digest material for him; to help him draft speeches, messages, and other texts; to meet with the people he could not see and in general to share the physical burden of his office. Gradually they became not just an extension of the President's person, but an extension of his power. ("Always remember," Lyndon Johnson told a friend of mine when he went to work for him at the White House, "that when you pick up a phone and call someone from here, it's as if you had a *howitzer* trained on him!") Under Kennedy and Johnson, the White House staff developed from being the President's assistants to being his enforcers, following through to make sure that his intentions had actually been carried out. And of course the task of transmitting the President's wishes easily became a grant of power. Joseph Califano was not the first presidential assistant, or the last, to be widely suspected in the government of using "the President wants . . ." when the wish originated in his own head.

This honcho role in itself created strains and stresses in the line bureaucracy of the departments, and may well have been an unnecessarily duplicated and ultimately an inefficient way of running the government much of the time. Under Nixon the process went a whole stage further. In earlier administrations the staff, sometimes peremptorily, had overseen the rest of the bureaucracy's managerial function. Now under Nixion the staff itself began to manage, thus clearly reduplicating the activity of the rest of the government and almost paralyzing large parts of it.

The Nixon people often talked as if this take-over by the White House staff was made necessary by the infiltration of liberals, New Dealers, and Democrats into the bureaucratic ranks. Yet the take-over was at least as aggressive in the field of national security, where the military as well as the putatively soft-boiled State Department were losing power to the White House, as in the domestic departments. When the White House staff got back to their offices after watching their new boss inaugurated in January 1969, they found a batch of brand-new national security memorandums on their desks. The first two, the historian of Kissinger's arms control efforts has put it, "solemnly established nothing less than a completely new national security system." It amounted, Kissinger's aide Don McHenry, later U.S. ambassador to the United Nations, told me, to a "coup d'état." Kissinger deliberately set about redesigning the flow of information and responsibility so as to cut both the secretary of state and—for all but operational implementation—the secretary of defense out of the channels. By the time Kissinger himself was finally made secretary of state, he had reduced that office to merely ceremonial functions. He frequently conducted secret diplomacy in the White House that appeared to be hidden as much from the State Department as from foreign governments: indeed Kissinger seemed to treat the State Department as an adversary power, even if not one of quite the first rank. He would presumably justify this concentration of power over foreign and national security policy in the hands of the President and his national security assistant (helped by a staff of some seventy) as justified because of the unreliability of the State Department and to a lesser extent the Pentagon bureaucracies. A more convincing explanation is perhaps that Kissinger saw he could win a unique position for himself by ensuring that any activity in the international field that could confer glamour and statesmanship on the President must be personalized as presidential, so that the President's political position—not to mention the fame of his national security adviser—could get the greatest possible assistance from his prowess as a world leader.

One of the few attitudes Richard Nixon shared with the Washington Establishment was the firm prejudice that foreign policy was more "noble" than domestic administration. The White House tapes reveal that he dismissed the domestic side of the presidency as "building outhouses in Peoria." Still, in his first two years at least, Nixon was a creative domestic president, and while Henry Kissinger was conducting his surreptitious bureaucratic coup d'état in the basement of the West Wing, Nixon was making a serious effort to establish presidential control over the domestic departments.

As soon as he became President, Nixon appointed an advisory council on executive reorganization with such heavyweight members as former Texas governor John Connally, Frederick Keppel, former boss of AT&T, and George P. Baker, dean of the Harvard Business School. It was chaired by Roy Ash, of Litton Industries. The Ash Council took over many of the ideas that had been proposed by earlier task forces under Lyndon Johnson and which had become widely accepted among those who thought about such arcane subjects as how the federal government should be organized. It proposed regrouping the domestic cabinet agencies under four "supersecretaries." It recommended transforming the essentially career, nonpartisan Budget Bureau into a new Office of Management and Budget, firmly dedicated to serving the President's interests, and the President happily accepted that suggestion. Finally, as a counterpart to the National Security Council, it proposed the establishment of a Domestic Council, its members the cabinet secretaries, but its staff provided by the White House, and that suggestion, too, was adopted. The Domestic Council was set up on July 1, 1970.

During his first term, Nixon's strategy was to appoint what he considered strong, independent cabinet secretaries, and at the same time to have them closely monitored by an expanded, aggressive staff made up of unquestioning personal loyalists. Many of his first-term cabinet appointments went to men with substantial independent political positions and reputations: men like George Romney, Robert Finch, Elliot Richardson, John Volpe, and Walter Hickel. Almost all of them soon fell foul of the White House loyalists led by the head of the Domestic Council staff, John Ehrlichman. At the same time, Nixon was consciously trying to reverse what he regarded as thirty years of mistaken Democratic policy, imperfectly interrupted by the Eisenhower years. Since the New Deal, as Nixon saw it, the federal government had grown steadily at the expense of the state and local tiers (as we have seen that is not true in terms of sheer numbers), and as a consequence at the expense also of business's freedom of initiative and the citizens' freedom generally. The same Democratic policies, as he saw it—and there were plenty of voices, including those of some renegade liberals, to confirm him in this judgment—had involved the federal government in an endless tangle of ill-conceived programs, most of them essentially programs for handing out public money in one shape or another. Welfare programs as such were not wholly excluded from Nixon's political philosophy. It was, rather, that he believed they should be concentrated on those in the greatest need. The result was that Nixon's attempt to strengthen the President's administrative grip on the government, which was very much in line with what Presidents had been trying to do since Truman's time, coincided with two quite new elements. One was the plan for structural reform, which Nixon called the New Federalism. The purpose of that was to devolve decisions, and through "revenue sharing," also expenditure, downward and outward to the lower tiers of government. The other was a strategy, which whatever may be said for it can fairly be called ideologically reactionary, for dismantling most of the welfare and other interventionist programs set up by successive liberal administrations, culminating in Lyndon Johnson's Great Society.

This strategy was disappointing for Nixon. Ehrlichman and his White House lieutenants constantly found that the cabinet secretaries seemed to be captured by the traditional constituencies of their departments, and to rally to the defense of the departments' existing programs, instead of taking the sometimes ruthless line the President wanted them to take. That was not the only cause of frustration. A Republican President was faced with a Congress on which he could not count for legislation to change directions. And as one academic observer put it, to Nixon and his men it seemed that they faced "not only an opposition Congress, but an opposition executive." Two academics sympathetic to the Nixon philosophy who interviewed 126 top domestic civil servants in 1970 found that they were "ideologically hostile" to the Nixon administration's policies. It would have been truly surprising if it had been otherwise. After all, these were men who had spent their lives developing the policies and administering the programs that Nixon and his White House staff were openly deriding and setting out to destroy. Even so, there is no serious reason to believe that the bureaucracy disobeyed presidential orders or sabotaged presidential policy in an unacceptable manner: rather that departments and agencies did what they had always done in the competitive, bargaining Washington system, and fought for their corner.

Still, the President's frustration and that of his trusted lieutenants, especially John Ehrlichman, mounted into indignation. The landslide victory in the 1972 election seemed to provide the mandate for a radical new approach. Nixon was emboldened to take a tack so different from previous ways of running the government that its historian, Richard P. Nathan, called it "the plot that failed." In his words:

> Nixon unveiled his strategy for an "administrative presidency" on the morning after his reelection. At a hastily called meeting, he told cabinet members and their chief subordinates that they should submit their resignations immediately. The instruction was given in a spirit very different from the *pro forma* manner of the past; it was clear that an entirely new team would be named for the second term. One of their essential tasks would be to take charge of the domestic bureaucracies. Key members of Nixon's new team were James T. Lynn at Housing and Urban Development, Caspar W. Weinberger at HEW, Earl L. Butz at Agriculture, along with a second line of subcabinet officials primarily made up of former White House aides with close ties to Ehrlichman. The new team was to *take on* the Congress and *take over* the bureaucracy.

The experiment was short-lived, and indeed was hardly noticed in the surrounding hubbub. Only thirteen days after the inauguration, on February 2, 1973, Judge John Sirica, who had presided over the trial of the seven conspirators arrested for the Watergate break-in, announced that he was "not satisfied" that the full story was disclosed at the trial, and expressed a hope that a Senate committee would "get to the bottom of what happened in the case." The fuse was lit, and the explosion was not long delayed.

By April 30, John Ehrlichman, the man Nixon counted on to carry out his *coup de main* against the federal bureaucracy, had left the White House. It was not long before Nixon himself had no time to think of anything but his own political survival. In the circumstances, his ambitions of taking over the federal bureaucracy and restructuring the executive branch in strict subordination to the President were forgotten.

But the episode was important. It is hard not to feel that it represented a false end to a process that is still not complete: the rivalry between the traditional cabinet secretaries and the White House staff for control of the executive branch of government.

That struggle is still going on. By February 1978, after the Carter administration had been in office a little over a year, Jody Powell, one of the insiders of the Carter staff, was talking to Elizabeth Drew in a way that sounded just like John Ehrlichman with a Georgia accent:

> There's been a general feeling around the White House since about the turn of the year that it's time to tighten up around here a little bit . . . When I said "around here" I mean the executive branch. We were reluctant to be hard-assed at first because we were learning and we were making our mistakes. Now there's a feeling that people have had their chance and things should happen where they're supposed to happen or there should be a reason.

A year later, Carter's domestic adviser, Stuart Eizenstat, was at loggerheads with Health, Education, and Welfare Secretary Joseph Califano over the President's national health insurance policy in a way that uncannily echoed the Nixon White House's struggles with HEW under first Robert Finch and then Elliot Richardson. In both cases, it seemed to the White House, the HEW secretary had been converted by his bureaucrats to maximalist literal positions that would do the President harm politically.

In July 1979, faced with an acute crisis of confidence in his administration, President Carter retired to Camp David and came back with the same inspiration that had visited Nixon at Key Biscayne: cut the cabinet back to size and trust your own guys. Like Nixon in 1972, Carter demanded the resignation of his entire cabinet (and of his top White House staff). Eventually he fired Califano, James Schlesinger at the Department of Energy,

Brock Adams at Transportation, and W. Michael Blumenthal at the Treasury. As these four experienced public servants, each with a distinguished career behind him and an independent public position of his own, left the stage, the winner in the contest for power and influence in the Carter administration took his bow: Hamilton Jordan, thirty-four years old, with no professional qualifications, no career achievements, no administrative experience: only twelve years of intimate personal service to Jimmy Carter.

The cabinet has been losing ground to the White House staff for a long time now. The cabinet in the United States has never had the power it has in Britain, where in theory the prime minister is only the first among equals around the cabinet table, and the cabinet shares collective responsibility. The American President has been elected by the people: the members of his cabinet have been appointed by him, with the advice and consent of the Senate. It may be advantageous for him to consult them, as a group of shrewd and experienced men: he does not need to consult them as independent politicians with the power to deliver support for his policies. Richard Fenno, in his classic study, *The President's Cabinet,* published in 1959, concluded that "the President's power to use or not use it is complete and final. The cabinet is his to use when and if he wishes." And Harold Ickes said of the Roosevelt cabinet of which he was a member: "The cold fact is that on important matters we are seldom called upon for advice." Someone else who was present at Roosevelt's cabinet meetings called them "a solo performance by the President, interspersed with some questions and very few debates."

Of course not all the work of cabinet members, or even their most important work, is done around the cabinet table in the West Wing of the White House. They are advisers to the President, whether he chooses to take their advice collectively, or individually, or not at all. In the past, they were also chosen to bring him support. Cabinets used to be more carefully balanced, so that the South and the West, and such conflicting interests as Silver Republicans, Gold Democrats, or high and low tariff men would all be represented. Describing the incoming McKinley administration in the spring of 1897, a historian of the Republican party writes that appointments were distributed "with due regard for geography, seniority and standing in the party." Already by 1952, when Eisenhower sat at the cabinet table surrounded by "eight millionaires and a plumber," the concept of the cabinet as a balanced ticket, drawing support from different groups to the administration, lingered on mainly in the tradition that the secretary of labor must be a "labor stiff." And that tradition did not last much longer.

But first and foremost, cabinet members are the administrative heads of huge, heterogeneous bureaucracies. The most dangerous recent development in respect of the cabinet has not been that Presidents no longer treat the cabinet as a great council of state: they never did. Nor is it that Presidents take less notice of their cabinets' advice: for they never took that much notice of it. It is that Presidents increasingly do not trust their cabinet secretaries to run their departments without monitoring, second-guessing, and disciplining them through White House staffs whose sole loyalty is to the President, and whose only criterion of a department's performance tends to be whether it brings grist to the President's political mill. Both Roosevelt and Truman delegated more administrative independence to their cabinet secretaries than more recent Presidents have done. Dean Acheson, himself an exceptionally able and independent member of the Truman cabinet, has left a cogent account of their reasons for doing so: "The administrative tasks of the great departments of government," he wrote in his memoirs, "are beyond the capacity of even the President's large personal staff to assume. To attempt to do so impairs both the broad direction of national affairs and the specific administration of particular parts of the whole."

Eisenhower showed little interest in his cabinet as such, but followed the same policy of delegating administrative responsibility, leaving himself free to concentrate on what he considered major issues of policy. But what was regarded at the time as a low ebb for the cabinet, as Aaron Wildavsky has put it, seems in retrospect almost to have been its high tide. President Kennedy's postmaster general, J. Edward Day, has scathingly described Kennedy's "thinly disguised impatience" with his cabinet, and concluded that "what discussion there was [was] a waste of time." Lyndon Johnson's biographer, Doris Kearns, has graphically described both Johnson's feelings about the cabinet and his methods of dealing with its members.

> "When I looked out at the heads of my departments [Johnson told Kearns] I realized that while all of them had been appointed by me,

> not a single one was really mine. I could never fully depend on them to put my priorities first. . . . I was determined to turn those lordly men into good soldiers."

It is a telling revelation of Johnson's strange combination of egotism and insecurity. But, as Kearns points out, it would be wrong to attribute Johnson's way with his cabinet solely to his personality. On the contrary, it derived from the best liberal thinking of the time.

> Applauded by the liberal theory of his time, which saw the decline of the Cabinet and the rise of the White House staff as one aspect of a more general movement toward concentrating power in the hands of "the one institution that represented the public interest," Lyndon Johnson moved effectively to exploit his advantage. He used every tool at his disposal, most prominently his budget and his White House staff, to concentrate information, publicity, and decisions in the Oval Office. . . . He assumed personal control over decisions on the budget and on personnel, forcing his Cabinet to plead with him directly for money and staff. He refused to allow the findings of his commissions and task forces to be released to the public; the information and ideas they contained would be distributed when, and if, he wanted. He alternately encouraged and rejected requests for private meetings. In these, and other ways, Johnson made the members of his Cabinet act as courtiers.

At the beginning of his administration, Richard Nixon appears to have made a genuine effort to break with this high-handed Johnsonian way of treating the cabinet. Nixon took the novel step of going on television to introduce the members of his cabinet to the nation: "Every man in the cabinet," he said, "will be urged to speak out . . . on all the great issues." And Carter, too, started out with an effort to revive the cabinet. By the spring of 1978, when Carter had been in the White House a little over a year, *The New York Times* was reporting that Carter was departing in practice from "his oft-stated commitment to cabinet government," and an exceptionally shrewd observer of the White House, Dom Bonafede, confirmed that competition between the cabinet and the White House staff "becomes sharper." "At almost every chance he gets," Bonafede wrote, "Carter praises his cabinet—but the fact remains he is cutting back his weekly cabinet meetings to once every two weeks."

Where successive Presidents, starting with such different preconceptions, have all come to rely more and more on their own staff and less and less on their cabinet members, where, moreover, two such different Presidents as Richard Nixon and Jimmy Carter have both turned to their staff for help after an initial, apparently sincere effort to reverse the trend and give more authority to cabinet members, it is tempting to come to the conclusion that the decline of the cabinet is inevitable. Many White House aides certainly think so. James Fallows, for example, attributed Carter's initial attempt at "cabinet government" to mere naïveté and a "truncated historical view." If a President wants to allow cabinet secretaries full control, Fallows wrote after leaving the Carter White House, he must make almost daily efforts to find out how that control is being used. When the first serious calamity happens, the President will feel angry and frustrated. "If he cares about his policies and his own political future, he will feel compelled to act. He will send in his own people, good loyal people, to 'get the job done right.' " A similar view has been expressed in an interview by Richard Cheney, who acted as President Ford's chief of staff before becoming a congressman:

> Carter made a fundamental mistake . . . when he chose a strong cabinet and weak White House staff with no chief. In this day and age with 1700 people in the White House operation you have to have a strong, structured system. But Carter reacted to Watergate and denied himself the strong tools he needed.

It is tempting to make the rejoinder that it is Fallows and Cheney who are being naive. Nobody will disagree that the President needs a "strong, structured system," still less that it is a good thing to "get the job done right." The questions are, rather, whether the White House staff, as presently recruited and organized, are the right people to provide a strong structure, and whether loyalty to the President, to *his* politics, and *his* political future are all that is needed.

Key members of the White House staff are among the most powerful people in the whole of American government. Their responsibilities are immense. Yet the process whereby they are recruited is bizarre. It could have been designed to select people who not merely know nothing about the government in Washington, but start with a certain bias against the whole idea of government as such. It certainly tends to select very few people with any experience of government. Where one would look for the President to be surrounded by experienced, professional, expert, and independent-minded staff, the system has consistently tended to select young, inexperienced political amateurs whose careers and position are wholly dependent on the President's favor.

Essentially the trouble starts from the fact that the core of the President's staff is recruited from the people who have worked for the candidate in the campaign. This has been true for a long time. Quite a few of the men FDR brought to Washington as his Brain Trust had worked for him in political campaigns, some of them long before 1932. A surprising number of Eisenhower's staff, including Sherman Adams, his chief of staff, "moved right into the White House with the President from his campaign train," as *The New York Times* put it at the time. The custom has survived the passing of the campaign train. Altogether two-thirds of Eisenhower's and half of Kennedy's starting staff came to the White House from the campaign. And if anything those figures underestimate the influence of the campaign veterans in the White House. All Presidents surround themselves with an inner ring of trusted intimates, and the former campaign workers are even more highly represented in that circle than in the staff as a whole.

It is far from clear that the presidential campaign is an ideal field in which to recruit staff for the White House. The skills learned in political campaigns, whether the future staff man worked as an advance man, a press briefer, a travel scheduler, a speechwriter or coat holder, are not likely to equip him to run a large modern bureaucracy. If the candidate, like Carter in 1976, campaigns "against Washington," so that his staff members are kept away from the sinful city until the election has been won, the problem is merely aggravated. Besides, the modern campaign is not only an adventure, it is a long-drawn-out and rather risky adventure. To be in the inner ring of the candidate's oldest cronies, one has to have been in a position to give up eighteen months or even two years of one's life on the off chance that the adventure will end up in the White House. Those who can afford to invest two years of their life to accompanying the candidate on a marathon tour of the Holiday Inns in thirty-odd primary states may be admirably idealistic people: they are not necessarily the ablest or even the stablest of their generation. "One need only look at why they were in the campaign," comments Stephen Hess, twice a White House aide himself, of that group of his colleagues. "The chief motivation may have been the expectation of excitement, an excess of zeal or hero worship."

In short, recent Presidents, in choosing their staffs, have behaved almost as if they were deliberately minimizing their chances of hiring men with administrative experience or ability. To an extraordinary degree, given the mobility of this generation of Americans, they seem to have felt that they could only trust people from their own home state. And this has been true even when, as with John Kennedy or Richard Nixon, they have spent little of their adult life in that state themselves. Not only did Kennedy fill the White House with people from Massachusetts, and Richard Nixon with southern Californians, and Jimmy Carter with Georgians: several recent unsuccessful candidates have also threatened to staff the White House with their own home-state mafias, like Barry Goldwater's Arizonans, George Wallace's Alabamians, and Hubert Humphrey's friends from Minnesota. Some of the most effective staff members in the White House have been those who had experience of a congressional office beforehand, as did Theodore C. Sorensen on Kennedy's staff and George Reedy, Bill Moyers, and Harry C. McPherson on Johnson's. At least they had some practical experience of government in Washington. But in general the essential test for recruiting White House staff, during a period when Presidents have come to rely more and more on their staffs not merely to oversee the government, but actually to run it, has been unquestioning personal loyalty, like that of Kenny O'Donnell for Kennedy, Jack Valenti for Johnson, Bob Haldeman or Chuck Colson for Nixon, and Hamilton Jordan for Carter.

Loyalty is an admirable quality, but it is not enough. Some of those who have been recruited in this haphazard fashion have turned out to possess what Joseph Conrad called "ability in the abstract." (Though not as many as you would have gathered from reading the uniformly sycophantic profiles the Washington press corps prints about White House aides, depending as it does on these paragons for inside information about what is going on.) But where able people have been recruited, it has been in spite of the system, not because of it. And the type of ability that has been attracted is not necessarily the kind that is needed for the steady running of vast, complex bureaucracies. To make such systems work, something more is needed than youth, energy, self-confidence, blind loyalty and blind ambition. In their zeal to serve their boss, the President, rather than the chief executive, these devoted enthusiasts have not always served the presidency well.

5

What America needs, the political scientist and former Johnson administration official Robert C. Wood wrote a decade ago, is "a better bureaucracy, not less of one, disciplined bureaucracy, not amateurs run riot." It is not a popular view. Bureaucracy is not popular anywhere. It gets a specially bad press in America. Conservatives detest the bureaucrat as the enemy of freedom. Populists deride him as the pointy-headed elitist who doesn't know enough to park his bicycle straight. Radicals see him as the enemy of change. Businessmen see what he does as a nuisance, and intellectuals think it futile and boring. The bureaucrat's bad image goes deeper than ideology or fashion. Perhaps it has its roots in the universal suspicion of government, more intense in the United States than anywhere. If so, it seems illogical that the politician's staff aide should escape the bureaucrat's bad image, since both eat at the public trough. But he does. In Washington, bureaucrats never quite escape the stigma of being a little effete. Staff aides are undeniably macho. Why this should be so baffles me. The White House aide's job, for example, comes closer than the line bureaucrat's to personal service, which has traditionally been held in low esteem. But it is so. The President's man, lashing the toiling bureaucrats to produce ever shorter summaries of complicated issues ever more quickly, is seen as a go-getter, cutting through foolish trivia. He shares the charisma of the presidency as the bureaucrat does not.

It was the great German sociologist Max Weber who invented the contrast between bureaucratic (or "rational") and "charismatic" authority. (There was a third type of authority, "traditional" authority, in Weber's system. Americans rejected that, in theory, at the Revolution.) Weber took the term, "charisma," the gift of grace, from the vocabulary of the early Christian Church. He used it in a morally neutral way to mean any kind of authority that rests on the belief in the special goodness, or heroism, or power of an exceptional leader. Weber himself repeatedly insisted that pure types of authority are not to be found in the real world. But to a striking extent the modern presidency has developed as a charismatic form of leadership in Weber's terms: one that depends on the followers' belief in the exceptional personal qualities of the leader, rather than on rational, predictable, bureaucratic structures like those of a church, an army, a bureaucracy, or a political party.

Weber's charismatic leader could be a robber chief or a prophet or religious leader. (He specifically speaks of Jesus Christ as an example of charismatic leadership, for example, but also of the conquerors, invaders, and usurpers of antiquity.) In any case the leader owes his authority to powers and qualities not to be found in ordinary men, and therefore also on his ability to convince his followers that he possesses these exceptional powers. Ultimately, as Weber saw it, the charismatic leader owes his authority to his ability to deliver "booty" to his followers. The booty is not necessarily financial; it can mean spiritual or political advantage. Whether he is a religious prophet or a robber chief, once the charismatic leader loses his "gift of grace," and specifically once his followers cease to believe in him, he has no traditional, or rational, or legal props to fall back on. His authority is gone.

There is much in Weber's theory that illuminates for me the way the modern presidency has developed. But let us concentrate here on the charismatic leader's followers. Under such a leader, lieutenants and officials, too, Weber said, were chosen on the basis of their own charisma, except that where the leader must convince many followers, the followers must convince only one leader of their ability. They are therefore chosen on the basis of utter devotion to their chief. Their authority depends on how well they perform each task the leader sets them, and the leader is the sole judge of how well they do it. His approval is arbitrarily given, and just as easily withdrawn. Where the essence of bureaucracy is order, law, rationality, predictability, continuity, organized into a code of rules which all can understand and all must follow, the "disciple-officials" of the charismatic chief work without organization, without rules, and their authority is conferred not by law or by discoverable rules but "solely by the judgment of the ruler."

It sounds like a job specification for a White House aide. There has long been a strong charismatic element about presidential authority. Max Weber himself, who visited the United States in 1912 and therefore had an opportunity to watch Teddy Roosevelt's version of the thing, said that it was characteristic of "leader-democracy" that it involved "a highly emotional type of devotion to and trust in the leader." Shortly after his death, his own Germany was to experience an even more extreme form of charismatic leadership. But Weber pointed out that "leader-democracy" tended to favor the type of individual who "is most spectacular, who promises the most, or who enjoys the most effective propaganda measures in the competition for leadership." There were limits to the degree of rationality that could be expected from administrations run by leaders of this type, he warned, and then added dryly: "Even in America it has not *always* come up to expectations."

Franklin Roosevelt's grasp on the government was emphatically charismatic rather than bureaucratic. He detested the orderly, the predictable way of doing things, and he loved to make himself the arbiter of each member of his administration's authority. As his postmaster general, James Farley, wrote in his memoirs: "White House confidence on politics and policies" in the Roosevelt administration "went to a small band of zealots, who mocked at party loyalty and knew no devotion except unswerving obedience to their leader." Kennedy's postmaster general, J. Edward Day (curiously, Kennedy suspected that Day would be his most unsparing memoir-writer), looked down the cabinet table and saw the charismatic chief at work: "His absorption with politics, publicity and foreign policy allowed him little time to be concerned about the domestic departments, unless they had an immediate political aspect."

This is the plight of the modern President. He must deliver booty to his followers in the shape of credible political power which they can use for their own purposes. To do this, he must be concerned with "politics, publicity and foreign policy"—which, as we shall see, is all too often little more than a form of publicity for all the permanent effect it has on the world—since these are the only fields of activity that promise much hope of delivering bankable political booty in the time frame within which he must work. He has "little time to be concerned about the domestic departments." The best he can do is to rely on the hasty, hectic efforts of his "small band of zealots" to ensure that the great, slow machine of the bureaucracy, whose proper function is to administer the delivery of services to the citizens, delivers political booty to the President with which he can reward his followers and retain the loyalty of his "disciple-officials." As a result, the

President is effectively isolated from the very machine that ought to be both his link to the "real country" and his means of acting upon it. So far from being the chief executive, there is a sense in which his role is hardly executive at all. The gigantic machinery of the executive branch, like the chancery of the medieval king, has drifted out of his control and obeys its own rules.

IV The Paradox of Congressional Power

The doctrine of the separation of powers was adopted by the Convention of 1787, not to promote efficiency, but to preclude the exercise of arbitrary power.

—Mr. Justice Louis Brandeis, dissenting, in *Myers* v. *United States* (1926)

Gentlemen, I am very glad indeed to have this opportunity to . . . verify for myself the impression that the President of the United States is a person, not a mere department of government hailing Congress from some isolated island of jealous power . . . that he is a human being trying to cooperate with other human beings in a common service.

—President Woodrow Wilson, address to a joint session of Congress, April 1913

If every man insists on knowing what he's voting for before he votes, we're not going to get a bill reported before Monday.

—Senator Russell B. Long, Democrat of Louisiana, chairing a meeting of the Senate Finance Committee, 1975

IN POLITICS, they say, there are no final victories. Lawrence F. O'Brien, shrewdest and most jovial of politicos, who served both Kennedy and Johnson as head of their liaison operation with the Congress, knew enough to choose the phrase as the title of his memoirs. He had, after all, won with Kennedy in 1960, only to see him assassinated; won with Johnson in 1964, only to see him forced to abdicate; and lost to Nixon as chairman of the Democratic National Committee in 1972, only to see him driven from office. Presidents *can* win victories in their dealings with Congress. They are well advised to make sure that they are not victories *over* Congress. Victories of that sort, as Richard Nixon learned, are likely to be implacably revenged. It is hard enough for Presidents to do what they want to do through the agency of what is ostensibly "their" branch of government. But if they choose to act through Congress, or if the action they want to take can only be taken with the consent of Congress, then the road is rockier still.

Even if a President wants to get a firmer grip on the executive bureaucracy, he must still work through the processes of the Congress, processes that can be frustrating, chancy, and bewildering in their complexity. Jimmy Carter discovered all this and more when he set out to transform his sweeping campaign promises to "do something" about the federal bureaucracy into a specific measure of civil service reform. The episode illustrates a good many aspects of the reality of the relationship between a President and the Congress. It shows the sheer complication of the congressional process itself, the number of committees and subcommittees that get in on the action, the variety of individual interests and egos that have to be accommodated in one way or another. It glosses a saying of Congressman Richard Bolling, one of the pioneers of reform in the House of Representatives and now chairman of the Rules Committee. "Everything that happens on this Hill," Bolling said to me one day, "is a seamless web."

Jimmy Carter discovered that the fate of his civil service reform could come to depend on a congressional primary election in North Philadelphia. It demonstrates the raw power of special interests and veto groups, though it has to be said that the groups involved in this particular saga, the veterans' lobbies and the public service employees' unions—though not without muscle—are frail compared to some of the organized agglomerations of lobbying power a President may have to confront on Capitol Hill. Lastly, it certainly does emphasize that while a President can win his victories, they will not be final victories, and that while he can reasonably hope to persuade Congress to give him some of the things that he wants, what he gets from Congress will be at best a far cry from the original scheme he had in mind.

There was no theme Jimmy Carter stressed more in his campaign for the White House than the need to reform the federal bureaucracy in Washington. Carter had succeeded in carrying through fairly sweeping reforms as governor of Georgia; local opinion is divided about how effective his efforts there were. The theme harmonized with Carter's sense that a Populist, antielitist wind was blowing through the land. The shape of his thinking about administrative reform was influenced, too, by a sophisticated bureaucrat, Jules Sugarman, a former welfare commissioner from New York City who had become Atlanta's chief administrative officer. Between Carter's nomination and the November 1976 election, Sugarman and others began to put in proposals for a sweeping reform of the bureaucracy, concentrating not so much on the pruning of the structure of agencies, something Carter had talked a good deal about, but on improving the personnel and the management of the bureaucracy.

By the time Jimmy Carter was inaugurated President, his instinct that something must be done to cut the fat out of the Washington bureaucracy had become focused. (Several of his closest aides played important roles in this process, including Jack Watson, the Harvard-trained Atlanta lawyer who was in charge of the transition; Stuart Eizenstat, who was emerging as the top policy adviser; and Hamilton Jordan, whose attention was drawn to administrative reform by a paper written by Ed Lyle, a young lawyer on Eizenstat's staff.) The heart of the problem, it seemed to the President's advisers, was how to restore the President's capacity to manage the government. Many lines of thought converged on this central proposition. There was the widespread public perception of abuse: of waste, fraud, and incompetence in the bureaucracy. There was concern about "whistle-blowers": the question was how to protect men and women who were punished by their superiors in the bureaucracy when they stood up for what they saw as the public good. There was a general sense that the quality of the bureaucracy's performance needed to be improved and made more responsive to the President's intentions. And lastly, certain specific ideas for reforming the civil service were percolating through from the public administration professionals: from men like Sugarman and Alan K. ("Scotty") Campbell, a former comptroller of the State of New York and head of the LBJ School of Public Affairs in Austin, Texas. Campbell was brought in to head and drastically reform the Civil Service Commission, a somewhat lethargic institution left over, like a beached whale, from earlier attempts to reform public administration in Washington.

In April 1977, Campbell became chairman of a task force with over a hundred members called the Federal Personnel Management Project. His deputy was one of the key officials in the Office of Management and Budget, Wayne C. Granquist. Campbell beat the drum for a major reform of the civil service. He held public hearings in seventeen cities across the country. His key idea was that the civil service system must be made less rigid so as to develop and retain more high-powered executive talent in the federal service, and so make the government more responsive to presidential leadership.

It was not until December 1977 that the Campbell-Granquist

task force sent its recommendations to the President. It proposed two measures: a reorganization plan, something the President can implement without legislation provided he lays it before the Congress for sixty days before acting on it, and a major civil service reform bill. The details of the legislation were worked out by a working group chaired by Jules Sugarman, now one of the three civil service commissioners, and made up of the assistant secretaries for administration from each of the cabinet departments, so that when the proposals went to the President all the members of his cabinet had already signed off on them. Even so, the President didn't accept them automatically. He held three long review sessions with Charles L. Schultze, his chief economic adviser, and James T. McIntyre, Jr., director of OMB. And at this point the President made a serious political miscalculation.

The professionals knew that there was no hope of passing civil service reform unless it was acceptable to the public employees' unions, and especially to the American Federation of Government Employees (AFGE). They also knew that while there is little interest in Congress in the broad question of bureaucratic reform, those members and subcommittee chairmen who *are* concerned are primarily responsive to the unions. They had therefore carefully included in their package certain things that the unions wanted: most important, legislation to grant government employees' unions bargaining rights. The unions demanded that bargaining rights be guaranteed by legislation. The Carter administration task force proposed to guarantee them only by executive order. In the end, the President and his advisers simply backed off and dropped all mention of federal employees' bargaining rights from the legislation sent to the Hill.

The result was that civil service reform legislation was in bad trouble even before it reached Capitol Hill. The administration proposed to create an entirely new Federal Senior Executive Service for the top nine thousand or so bureaucrats in the government: for these high-flying administrators, civil service rules would be substantially relaxed and salaries would be linked to performance. Ambitious administrators would be tempted to stay in government service for the chance to trade job security for higher financial rewards and greater career flexibility. The Rule of Three, which requires agencies to fill vacancies with one of the three highest-ranking applicants, would be relaxed. Veterans' preference in civil service hiring would be modified. The Civil Service Commission itself was to be split in two: a board to oversee the fairness of the merit system and a new Office of Federal Personnel Policy to act as the President's personnel manager.

The political miscalculation Carter and his advisers made was to underestimate the power of the unions. They were impatient with the issue of union bargaining rights and saw it as extraneous to the real issue: how to make the government more efficient. They thought it would make their plan less controversial to Congress if they left bargaining rights out. They were wrong. The chief union involved, AFGE, announced that it would oppose any reform that didn't by statute grant it bargaining rights on behalf of federal employees. The AFL-CIO, to which AFGE belongs, was even more implacable on the issue.

In the Senate, which reformed its unwieldy committee structure somewhat in 1977, both the legislation and the reorganization plan came under the jurisdiction of the Government Operations Committee, chaired by Senator Abraham A. Ribicoff (Democrat of Connecticut). In the House, the plan had to "lie before" the Government Operations Committee, but the legislation fell under the jurisdiction of the Post Office and Civil Service Committee chaired by Representative Robert N. C. Nix (Democrat of Pennsylvania). At this point the seamless web becomes a labyrinth.

In 1978 Nix claimed to be sixty-eight. Many maintained he was much older. Certainly, whatever his physical age, in style he was a figure out of an earlier generation of big-city politics. He was rewarded for many years' loyal service under former Mayor William J. Green in the Philadelphia Democratic machine by being sent to Congress to represent the devastated North Philadelphia slums as the city's first black congressman. In time, Nix transferred his allegiance to the machine's new master, the harsh law-and-order mayor, Frank Rizzo. But like old-time machine politicians all over the country, and especially old-time black machine politicians, Nix was learning that times were changing. His old boss's son, William J. Green, Jr., after a stint in Congress, was getting ready to challenge Rizzo for mayor. And young Bill Green was backing an attractive candidate with a background in the civil rights movement, the Reverend William H. Gray III, in his challenge for Nix's seat. In 1976, Nix only managed to hold Gray off by 339 votes. The rematch was due in the 1978 Democratic primary on May 16.

Unfortunately for the administration, Gray was an old friend from civil rights days of the President's free-spoken ambassador to the United Nations, Andrew Young. On two occasions, Young had visited Gray in North Philadelphia. To Nix, though he pretended otherwise, it looked like an administration endorsement of his opponent. He was furious. The White House was furious, too. Only a couple of weeks earlier at the Camp David meeting called to review staff ineffectiveness, the President told his staff to pay special attention to members of the congressional committees with power over civil service reform. Here was a cabinet member mortally offending the congressman with most power over the legislation. So the White House worked assiduously to soothe the old man's ruffled feathers. They assured him that Andy Young was a law unto himself. They rushed federal money into the district. Still, Nix openly threatened to hold up the civil service legislation in his committee if he were beaten in the primary and left a lame-duck chairman. "The only adverse effect," he told a reporter with a slow smile, "would be if I were defeated. It would be delayed and certain compromises that will be necessary would be much more difficult to effectuate."

The spring of 1978 was going by, and civil service reform was going nowhere. Chairman Nix spent more and more of his time in the fight for his own political life in North Philadelphia. The legislation was stuck in three subcommittees of the House committee: Gladys Noon Spellman's, on compensation and employee benefits, Patricia Schroeder's, from Colorado, on employee ethics and utilization, and William D. Clay's, on civil service. The House subcommittee system chops the issues pretty fine. It looked as though the unions would be able to kill the bill unless their price were met. Mrs. Spellman, who represents Prince Georges County, Maryland, a dormitory for Washington federal employees, was particularly responsive to their concerns. The veterans' organizations were also making felt their displeasure at the proposal to curtail veteran preference. It looked as though the White House was going to be given an object lesson in how much harder it is to change the system in Washington than to talk about changing it in the campaign.

Nix was thrashed by Gray in the primary. In the meantime, however, the White House had found a way around the impasse. With Nix's consent, leadership on civil service reform passed to the number two Democrat on the House committee, who happened to be none other than the President's unsuccessful rival for the 1976 Democratic presidential nomination, Congressman

Morris K. Udall of Arizona. Udall agreed to do what he could to work out a compromise.

The thing was carefully and professionally done. Fortunately Ed Derwinski of Illinois, the ranking Republican on the committee, was sympathetic to the principle of civil service reform and was generally helpful. (It is remarkable how much help Jimmy Carter has had from Republicans in Congress.) Udall went out of his way to show himself sensitive to labor's concerns. He met with labor people and with those members of the committee, especially Congressman Bill Clay of Missouri and Congressman Bill Ford of Michigan, who were identified with labor. The AFGE's president, Kenneth T. Blaylock, who had already been called in for some gentle arm-twisting by the President, was in a fight for reelection. Udall flew out to Chicago for the union's convention and got himself booed by Blaylock's opponents for making a speech there. Members of Congress from the Washington area, with large numbers of federal employees in their districts, like Mrs. Spellman and Congressman Herbert Harris from northern Virginia, were sensitive to fears that civil service reform would remove job protection and so "politicize" the bureaucracy. Udall took trouble to reassure them as best he could.

Gradually the compromises were worked out. Udall accepted an amendment from the Schroeder subcommittee that softened the blow for the veterans' organizations; the White House didn't like it, but had to accept it. He accepted an amendment from the Spellman subcommittee, limiting the new Senior Executive Service to an experimental two-year period and in only three federal agencies at that. (That was to be changed in the final Senate-House conference.) And even this is only an oversimplified list of the concerns that had to be mollified. Everyone was given a chance to air his or her concerns. If a disagreement could not be resolved in the committee's open markup sessions, then all parties would adjourn to Udall's office, and a compromise would be worked out in private there.

In the meantime there was trouble in the Senate too. Senator Ribicoff also was anxious to protect the unions' position. The ball was carried on critical votes by others, notably Senator Lawton Chiles (Democrat of Florida) and Senator Charles Percy (Republican of Illinois). Senator Charles ("Mac") Mathias (Republican of Maryland), normally the most reasonable of men, went so far as to threaten a filibuster at one point: he, like Mrs. Spellman, had to think of the fears of his voters in Washington's Maryland suburbs. In spite of everything, the bill passed the Senate with only one dissenting vote and with only minor amendment on August 24. And on September 13 the House voted it by 387–10 on final passage. Most of the ten were from the Greater Washington area.

The versions passed by the two houses were different, so there had to be a conference committee, which met in late September. There were still tense negotiations, day-long debates in the conference, and threats of breakdown before the President finally had a civil service reform bill to sign.

It was the damnedest of close-run things. As late as May, few gave the bill any hope of passing. If any one of a dozen turning points had gone otherwise, the President would have been denied. Moreover, the legislation that Carter sent up to the Hill was already very different from the kind of reform he was talking about in the campaign. And the legislation he signed was very different from what he sent up to the Hill. "His" bill was the product of an immensely complex process of lobbying, trade-offs, and pulling and hauling within the executive branch in the first place, and then of an even more complex process of dealing and compromising on the Hill. Perhaps most important of all, the President could only get his legislation through the Congress by in effect giving away control of it. He had to leave Udall, and to a lesser extent other players in the congressional game, the freedom to make compromises the President would rather not have made, and so freedom to pass legislation essentially different from what the President believed the country needed. If the President is, as the textbooks say, the leader of Congress, he must sometimes lead, like the Duke of Plaza-Toro, from behind. The truth is that he shares power with the Congress in a system that has become dangerously fragmented, confused, and unpredictable.

2

For a very long time now, the separation of powers has been anything but absolute. A fiction of absolute separation is maintained in theory, perhaps, but in practice the executive and the legislative mingle and interpenetrate in an infinity of ways. Iron triangles of every size link executive bureaux and legislative committees together on every subject imaginable. People move from jobs on congressional staffs to jobs in the executive bureaucracy, or from Congress to cabinet posts, or vice versa. Ideas floated on Capitol Hill are picked up downtown: the Peace Corps is a celebrated example. Constantly and in an infinitude of different ways, people from the Congress and their staffs and people from the White House and the federal departments and agencies are meeting, talking, making deals, fighting, and working together to hammer out governmental action that can therefore rarely be truthfully ascribed either to the President, or to the Congress, alone.

The strict dichotomy between legislative and executive is of dubious relevance to the realities of the modern relationship between President and Congress. What does remain fresh and vital is that other inheritance from eighteenth-century theory, the doctrine of checks and balances. It is not essential to the health and safety of the American political system that there should be an impenetrable wall of separation between the Congress and the executive branch. Indeed, it would be highly impractical if there were. What is vital is that neither the President nor the Congress should grow overmighty. Each branch must retain enough practical power to check the other if there is a danger of the balance of power between them being dangerously upset, as Congress was able to do, after a tussle, when that danger arose in 1973.

The doctrine of the separation of powers also has had the effect of confusing exactly what is meant by the legislative function. Because Congress is known as the legislative branch, it is natural to describe everything Congress does as legislation. In reality, Congress has several distinct functions, and legislation in the proper sense of the word is only one of them. In its simplest form, the theory is that Congress makes the laws and the President takes care that they be faithfully executed. Even in eighteenth-century theory, a considerable degree of interpenetration between the two functions was recognized. The Constitution itself enjoins the President to recommend to the Congress's consideration "such measures as he shall judge necessary and expedient." For the Founding Fathers, law was essentially common law, interpreted by the judiciary, and very occasionally modified, after suitably reflective debate, by statute. That is the quintessential legislative function.

Congress, though, has always done many other things. It has

the right to investigate, so as to know whether legislation is required. It inherited from the eighteenth-century English House of Commons the "right of supply," the vital whip hand over money, which is intrinsically quite distinct from the power to legislate. One of the main issues at stake in the American Revolution was whether this power should be retained by the House of Commons in London or shifted to the colonists in their assemblies in America. The end result of that ancient struggle is that only Congress can authorize the expenditure and appropriate the money the President needs to run the government. (Money bills, of course, must originate in the House of Representatives.) As an extension of this financial control, Congress has in practice acquired the right to oversee the executive branch. And under the Constitution the Senate must advise and consent to treaties and appointments. In all these ways, no President can govern without a degree of cooperation from Congress.

Finally, the President will also need to persuade Congress to pass legislation that he has recommended. If he is to keep his campaign promises, if he is to respond to the challenges facing the nation, he will need to start new programs that can only be established by statute. If he is to put the stamp of his own personality on the political scene, he must present Congress with a coherent package of measures. Partly because they do not wholly trust the existing departments and agencies to respond sympathetically to their political intentions, partly because they want to be credited with innovation and energy, most recent Presidents have shown a strong preference for responding to new problems not only with new programs, but also with whole new agencies. Indeed this presidential habit is largely responsible for the incoherent proliferation of executive agencies that presidential candidates love to inveigh against in their campaigns.

The net result is that the President needs Congress. He must be able to work with Congress. "There is but one way for a President to deal with Congress," said Lyndon Johnson at the end of his life, "and that is continuously, incessantly, and without interruption." But so, too, must Congress cooperate with the President. Just as the "executive" bureaucracy in practice responds to the "legislative" oversight of congressional committees and their staffs, and indeed also responds to congressional initiatives, though this is not the theory of how things are supposed to work, so, too, there are circumstances, and over the course of the twentieth century, at least until the very last few years, an increasing number of circumstances, when the legislative branch can only be given the leadership it needs from outside; that is, by the President.

The development of the "legislative presidency" has followed very much the same pattern as the growth of the modern presidency generally. Theodore Roosevelt and Woodrow Wilson first took the initiative in asserting presidential leadership in Congress. They developed the techniques of liaison between the White House and Capitol Hill. And they began to present Congress with something like a presidential legislative agenda. After Wilson's defeat in the Senate on the Versailles treaty and his illness and eclipse, the three Republican Presidents took a more hands-off attitude toward Congress until the explosion of Roosevelt's Hundred Days in 1933. Then, and again at times later in his administration, Roosevelt certainly did boldly assume the leadership of Congress. He put forward coherent strategies for attacking the country's difficulties. He brought all the powers and influence of the presidency to bear on the job of building coalitions in Congress to pass the legislation he thought the country needed. Even so, he was not overbearing in his dealings with Congress. A high proportion of the New Deal legislation originated on Capitol Hill, not in the White House. He avoided granting to any one aide the role of representing him in his dealings with Congress. He was careful not to miff congressional sensibilities. It is a curious fact that the institutionalization of liaison between the executive branch and the Congress began not with the New Deal, but with the Second World War. During that conflict the War Department was responsible for liaison between the two branches of government. Over two hundred serving officers were assigned to the department's legislation and liaison division.

The first comprehensive presidential program of legislation was sent up to Congress by President Truman in 1947. When Eisenhower first became President, he disapproved of this innovation, and in 1953 he refused to send up a program. Within a few months, the routine workings of the machinery established in Truman's time had churned up so many demands for legislation that Eisenhower was forced to drop his attachment to textbook theories of the separation of powers. In later years the Eisenhower administration, in this as in other ways, followed the new pattern established by Truman. Eisenhower, on the other hand, made an important new departure in 1953 when he established the first formal office for congressional liaison in the White House. It was staffed by General Wilton B. ("Jerry") Persons and by Bryce Harlow, both of whom had worked for the wartime Office of Legislation and Liaison in the War Department. John Kennedy appointed his campaign manager, Larry O'Brien, to run the congressional liaison operation in the White House, and O'Brien was one of the few Kennedy aides to hit it off so well with Johnson that LBJ trusted him as if he had been one of his own Texan protégés.

Throughout the period of the Eisenhower, Kennedy, and Johnson administrations, there was a reasonably close and cooperative relationship between the White House and the leadership in Congress. During the Eisenhower administration, this bond was surprisingly close, in spite of the fact that (with the exception of the two years 1953–54) a Republican President faced Democratic majorities in both houses of Congress. This concord was due in part to the consensus politics of the period. It was also helped along by the *gemütlich* relationship between the autocratic Texans who led the two houses of Congress and a Texas-born President whose achievements as a national hero commended him to their old-fashioned patriotism. Bryce Harlow has recalled the socializing among Ike, Sam Rayburn, and Lyndon Johnson in phrases that have a period flavor:

> The President was from Texas by birthright and they loved to sit together. I'd get them together about once a month at least. They'd "strike a blow for liberty" a time or two or three and everything would liquidize a little bit. They'd just have a ball, enjoy each other enormously, and be totally candid.

By the time one of Eisenhower's drinking companions had moved into the White House himself, something like presidential domination over the formal party leadership in Congress had been established, and—as one academic expert has put it—the line between the congressional leadership and the White House was virtually erased. There were several reasons for that. The men who succeeded to the mantles of Rayburn and Johnson were weaker and less self-assertive. Then again, Mike Mansfield, John McCormack, and Carl Albert were basically in sympathy with what Kennedy and more especially Johnson were trying to do. They were by and large laboring in the same cause. They came to depend more and more on the President's men for the information about Congress they needed to maintain their position: after all, the White House and the executive departments, most of which had by this time their own large congressional liaison bureaux, could deploy a far stronger force of nose-counters and arm-twisters, and a far more persuasive barrowload of sticks and carrots. The congressional leadership at this period met regularly with the President's men whenever legislation had reached a critical corner in its journey through the congressional labyrinth.

It would be wrong to conclude from this increasing domination of the congressional leadership by the White House that the White House dominated Congress as a whole. To make that assumption would mean ignoring the conservative coalition. The most formidable obstacle to presidentially sponsored legislation in the Kennedy and Johnson administrations was not the official Republican opposition nor the official Democratic leadership. It was the unofficial but very real coalition between conservative Republicans from the Middle West and West with conservative Democrats from the South: about twenty of the latter in the Senate and almost a hundred in the House. One political scientist has worked out that between 1961 and 1968 the coalition made its appearance on 277 votes. On almost one-half of those occasions, the President prudently abstained from challenging the coalition's position: in most of those cases, therefore, the coalition won a victory just as surely as if the President had chosen to fight and then lost. There were 159 contests between the President and the coalition. On only 98 occasions did the President win. And in reality the presidency's success in making headway against the conservative coalition was even less impressive than those figures suggest. In 1964, when he tackled the Southerners head-on on civil rights, Johnson won seven out of ten contests with the coalition. And in the Eighty-ninth Congress (1965–66) the conservative coalition was temporarily eclipsed, and Lyndon Johnson wrote the dazzling record of his Great Society legislation.

After 1965–66 the coalition reappeared. Johnson's prestige was tarnished; his magic had left him. People were increasingly disenchanted with the Great Society. In his later years in the White House, Johnson suffered even more from obstruction by the conservative coalition than Kennedy. He was opposed by it more often, and it beat him a higher proportion of the time. Henry Hall Wilson, who was in charge of relations with the House of Representatives for both Kennedy and Johnson, calculates that—except during the Eighty-ninth Congress—the arithmetic was hopelessly stacked against both Presidents. In the House, even if the President got the support of every single Northern, Western, and Border State Democrat, Wilson reckons, he still needed to win more than half the votes of the Southern Democrats. Most of the time, on most votes, that just wasn't on. At the height of the imperial presidency, the President was routinely beaten on a wide variety of issues by conservative Southern Democrats and conservative Republicans working together to block presidential policies.

It is hard to calculate accurately what proportion of the programs Presidents support are enacted into law, or the proportion of votes on which Congress supports the President, if only because Presidents, to make friends and to make themselves look good, have a habit of saying they are in favor of things that are going to pass anyway. But for what they are worth, such computations show a steady downward trend in presidential influence with Congress from the early years of the Eisenhower administration to the present time, interrupted only by the brief heyday of Lyndon Johnson's success between 1964 and 1966. Democratic Presidents naturally do better when both houses of Congress are controlled by their own party than Republican Presidents do when Congress is controlled by the opposition, but not much better. In all there were only four years between 1961 and 1977 when more than half of the President's program was passed into law. And the programs the President sends up to Capitol Hill are not by any means the programs he would like to send up. As the example of civil service reform shows, and as the lamentable history of successive Carter energy plans shows even more clearly, the process of conciliation and compromise begins long before a line of draft legislation reaches the Hill. All in all, it is rare for a President to win passage of a bill he really wants in the form in which he wants it. So much for the prowess of the President as legislative leader. So much for the effectiveness of the congressional connection as a transmission system for presidential power.

3

The accepted view is that since Franklin Roosevelt's time the presidency got stronger and stronger in comparison with Congress until the 1970s, but that then, as a result of Vietnam and Watergate, Congress began to reassert itself, so that the pendulum has swung back, and Congress has now recaptured much of the power and prestige that had been lost to the imperial presidency.

That version of what happened is too simple. It is true that Congress has gradually reasserted itself, first in foreign policy and then over a wide spread of disputed territory. It is probably true, as a consequence, that Congress is now substantially "stronger" compared to the President than, say, fifteen years ago. But the story is more complicated than that, and less comforting.

For one thing, the contest between the two branches of the government is not a zero-sum game. The President's loss is not automatically Congress's gain. No automatic laws of nature like the swing of a pendulum are involved, but rather the infinitely complex outcomes of a sophisticated process of trading, negotiating, pressure, and bluff, with all players fully entitled to claim credit for whatever they please in the result, and no one quite sure what truly deserves to be claimed as a credit. If Congress is weakly led, or lethargic, or deeply split, that makes it no easier for a President to lead. To the extent that all Presidents depend on Congress for help, and they all must, a weak Congress means a weak President. Nor does a weak President strengthen Congress. Congress may get more favorable publicity if the President is seen as bumbling or bungling. But if the President cannot or will not come up with ideas for meeting the nation's difficulties, and cannot put together the political support for pushing those ideas through, there is no alternative way of supplying national leadership from inside Congress. The Speaker of the House cannot do it, nor the majority leaders of the two houses, nor the whip or the chairmen of the Rules and Ways and Means committees. Perhaps one day the caucus will once again evolve into a source of political authority, as it was in the nineteenth century. Perhaps it should. But that has not yet happened.

To portray an imperial presidency first scoring power off a somnolent Congress, then losing it again as Congress reawoke, falsifies history. It was more that, during the twenty years after Roosevelt's death, President and Congress shared power in an imperial Washington. In foreign and national security policy, the presidency was indeed imperial in its style and its ambitions in those years. In domestic and economic matters, it was on the whole meek by comparison and left decisions on many routine domestic matters to Congress.

Architecture is not a bad guide to the self-image of those who commission it. During the years when Congress is supposed to have been allowing its power to be filched by the White House, the Senate commissioned and completed a second office building, subsequently called the Dirksen Building, at a cost of $24 million. In 1972, the Senate appropriated a further $85 million to extend the building in the same overwhelming style. But the Senate's architectural achievements pale by comparison with the House's Rayburn Building. Altogether the House appropriated $135 million for the new office building and for renovation of the two existing buildings. Nine stories high, 240 yards long, with 50 acres of office space, only 15 percent of which, however, is actually used for congressmen's offices, the building was described by *The New York Times*'s then architectural critic, Ada Louise Huxtable, as "a national disaster" when it opened in 1965. "It is quite possible," she wrote carefully, "that this is the worst building for the most money in the history of the construction art." More wittily, another critic said it could be defended "only militarily." Leaving aside refined aesthetic judgments, this immense pile of the most expensive available bronze, marble, and granite, with its cavernous wasted spaces, its late-Roman baths and gymnasia, and even its "slumber rooms," betrays a collective self-esteem that need not fear comparison with any executive conceit. Neither Nelson Rockefeller in his Albany mall nor Lyndon Johnson in any of the works of the Great Society is as pompously commemorated as that quiet seeker of consensus, Mr. Sam Rayburn.

It has become customary to point to the growth in the numbers of the White House staff as a tangible measure of the growth of presidential ambitions. Yet in the very years when the White House staff was growing so fast, congressional staffs were growing even faster. As late as 1914, senators and congressmen worked in an Early American simplicity. In that year, for example, there were fewer Senate employees than senators, and as late as 1935 there were no more than two employees for each member of the House: many congressmen thriftily put a son or a wife on the staff to keep the income in the family. By 1975, there were more than 6000 personal employees, and it seems a safe bet that they included more mistresses than wives. In 1965 the Executive Office of the President employed more than 1500 in permanent staff jobs; the Senate and House committees between them had about 1000, more or less equally split. Ten years later, the Executive Office employed 2000, the Senate and House committees between them, 2072. Altogether by the middle of the 1970s there were more than 11,000 staff working for senators, congressmen, and their committees, and a total of more than 30,000 employees of the legislative branch as a whole, including the Library of Congress, the world's greatest research library; the Congressional Research Service; the Congressional Budget Office; the General Accounting Office; and the Office of Technology Assessment.

Capitol Hill has a folksier style and perhaps a genuinely more democratic spirit than the executive world downtown. (Here again it is dangerous to generalize: the atmosphere in the office of, say, some members of the New York or California delegation is very different from that in the offices of some of the older Southern senators.) Perhaps the knowledge that they are answerable to the voters every two years keeps congressmen humble. Even a six-year Senate term seems to leave most senators with a more modest demeanor than service at the pleasure of the elected prince downtown. But you should not be taken in. Friendly they may be. Relaxed many of them are. Most congressmen allow themselves, for example, more horseplay than, say, most assistant secretaries of state. But neither senators nor congressmen, as the expressive French vulgarism has it, mistake themselves for the backside of a pear. They do not underestimate either their power or their dignity in comparison with those of the executive branch or anyone else. In the very days when legend has it that Congress was being trampled underfoot by executive arrogance, its halls were full of those imperious and headstrong men whom Lyndon Johnson used to call the "whales."

In the Senate in those days you could find men like Richard B. Russell of Georgia, acknowledged life president of the Inner Club; Robert S. Kerr of Oklahoma, "uncrowned king" of the Senate because his hands rested on the strings of so much public money and private power in public works, aerospace, and oil; Everett McKinley Dirksen of Illinois, with his voice like that of a Victorian actor-manager giving a recitation and his horse-trader's cunning; Harry F. Byrd of Virginia, living on his apple orchards in the Blue Ridge in a feudal style like that of his colonial ancestors; J. William Fulbright of the Foreign Relations Committee; Lyndon Johnson himself. And in the House, wily, stubborn men like Rayburn; Judge Howard Smith of Virginia, chairman of the Rules Committee for donkey's years; Carl Vinson of Armed Services, the old "swamp fox" from Georgia; Wilbur Mills of Arkansas and Ways and Means, who never reported out a bill until he had the votes to win on the floor; and many others like them, appropriations subcommittee chairmen, for example, controlling tens of billions in public money every year, much of it virtually unnoticed by press and public, except in their own districts.

These men were not indifferent to power. They had power, the kind of power that was real to them, over the kinds of government actions and the kinds of government expenditures that rewarded their friends, punished their enemies, and those—whom they did not always distinguish from enemies—who resisted their power. They made sure of their return to Capitol Hill, year after year, decade after decade. They could afford to leave to Presidents the splendors and miseries of foreign policy. They had seen Presidents come and go, after all. When one of their junior brethren from the Senate moved to the other end of Pennsylvania Avenue in 1961, for example, Richard Russell had been in Congress since the Hundred Days, Judge Smith for thirty years, and Vinson since 1914—three years before the new President was born.

To speak of the power of Congress is a double abstraction. Those who wield power there are not prone to deal in abstractions. They are interested not in the power of Congress as a whole, but in their own power; not in power in the abstract, but in the power to do certain things and to prevent other things being done. To try to quantify the power of Congress as a whole and to compare that aggregate with the power of the presidency is meaningless. Apart from anything else, as men like Rayburn, Johnson, Russell, or Mills were well aware, without a certain minimum of cooperation from Congress even the ablest and most popular President has very little power. What is more to the point is to look at where power lies within the Congress. And as soon as one begins to look at that, it becomes plain that power by no means lies where it did.

To some extent, if one compares the present situation with that in the 1950s, power has departed from the official, party leadership in Congress. It is not a point that should be pushed too far. It is true that Speaker Thomas P. ("Tip") O'Neill cannot guarantee to the President, or to anyone else, that he has the votes to deliver a bill in advance, as Speaker Rayburn really could. O'Neill may well have more power in that regard than the two intervening speakers, John W. McCormack and Carl Albert. It is possible that the Speaker's power is greater now than it has been for almost twenty years. But that is partly a function of personalities and only partly the result of the need to offset the fragmentation of power in Congress.

There is a much clearer trend: since the 1960s power has been dispersed from a small oligarchy of committee chairmen to a far larger number of subcommittee chairmen. There were in the Ninety-fourth Congress 174 subcommittees for one hundred senators; the most sweeping reform in many years still could not cut the number of subcommittees down below the number of senators. In the House, almost a third of the members chair a subcommittee of their own.

Recently House Democratic whip John Brademas (of Indiana) reminisced in an interview with the author about the changes he had seen since he arrived in Congress in 1959. Congressmen are younger, better-educated, feistier, and more independent than they used to be, he said. They can no longer be led by an elite, or by the Speaker, or by the White House. But the greatest single change, he thought, was the reform of the committee system, which had broken the power of the committee chairmen. "When I came here," Brademas said, "the committee chairman was the great feudal baron. We now have a hundred and forty-four subcommittee chairmen." Often enough, the subcommittee chairman holds subcommittee meetings alone with his staff or perhaps with a single Republican present, then goes to the full committee with a unanimous report. That means that the subcommittee chairman often writes the law. Committee chairmen, who were once literally a law unto themselves, must now win the approval of majorities on their committees. They can therefore no longer flatly defy Speaker and President as they used to do, and bottle up legislation in "their" committees. (Instead, subcommittee chairmen now sometimes exercise the same prerogative.) In practice the task of leadership, whether it is to be exercised by the Speaker and the majority leader or by the White House, has become enormously more burdensome because there are so many more independent-minded individuals to be shepherded along. In the 1940s, if the President asked half a dozen members what Congress would do, he would be given the same answer, and as likely as not it would be accurate. Now, no one knows what Congress will do until it is done.

In the House, members used to display less independence than senators. Party discipline was stronger there too. But over the years the House has become more like the Senate. House members have bigger staffs. They are less interested than they were in favors from the White House and in the approval of the leadership. Party means very little to them. Patronage means less than it used to. And the administration has less patronage to offer, now that many political jobs have been brought under civil service. In the city of Chicago, for example, there are some 80,000 federal employees in regional offices. One of President Carter's aides complained that the White House had only five jobs to give there. "That's not even one appointment for each Democratic House member from the city, much less the rest of the state, or the Democratic senator from Illinois." Instead, House members increasingly look in fear or for favor to the special interests, and especially to the single-issue groups who, they believe, can defeat them back in their district. The result, if not chaos, is something like the traditional picture of the eighteenth-century Polish Diet, where hundreds of independent members, bound by no ties of party and each as proud as a sovereign, jealously guarded the power to block anything the king might attempt, without ever organizing any means of putting forward alternative policies of their own.

The power of the committee chairmen was broken by a process of reform that had its origins, before Vietnam and Watergate, in a third great event of recent American history: the transformation of the South by the civil rights movement. The power of the committee chairmen was rooted in the seniority system, by which the longest serving member of a committee inexorably became its chairman. Obviously in such a contest in longevity, senators and congressmen from one-party states and districts had a decisive advantage. In practice, when there were Democratic majorities in the two houses of Congress, as there have been for all but four years since 1931, that meant that the advantage went to senators and congressmen from the South, and to a much lesser extent to Northern liberals, like Emanuel Celler or Adam Clayton Powell, with equally lopsided majorities in certain big-city districts. Above all, the seniority system guaranteed an outrageously disproportionate preponderance for the ideologically unreconstructed South.

The sharp hearing of some Southern backwoodsmen detected the first clunk of the ax laid to the roots of their supremacy in 1962 when the Supreme Court held, in *Baker* v. *Carr*, that the courts could rule on the apportionment of legislative districts. The next five years saw something like a social and political revolution in the South. Massive black nonviolent action for civil rights and voting rights, confrontation with the federal government, sporadic violence, rapid industrialization and the opening up of new job opportunities for both blacks and rural whites, massive migration into Southern cities and suburbs: all these things combined to bring about the downfall of the Southern congressional oligarchy. At the beginning of the sixties, in all but a few urban enclaves in the South, conservative Democrats were certain to be elected. By the end of the decade, nothing was certain. Some Southern whites had been converted to the more moderate policies of a new generation of Southern Democrats, including men like Governor Reubin Askew of Florida and Governor Jimmy Carter of Georgia. Millions of blacks were voting, most of them swelling this moderate Democratic vote. In 1973 Barbara Jordan of Texas and Andrew Young of Georgia took their places as the first blacks representing Southern states in Congress since 1901. On the other hand, for the first time a substantial proportion of Southern whites, tempted by Richard Nixon's "Southern strategy," had begun to vote Republican. The era of the one-party Solid South, which had endured since the Compromise of 1877, was over at last.

Of all the many bastions commanded by the Southern conservatives in their long rearguard action against change from the 1930s onward, one of the most strategically sited was the Rules Committee of the House of Representatives. Originally, with eight Democrats and four Republicans on the committee, Judge Smith, the chairman, only needed to win the votes of two fellow Southerners to add to those of the four Republicans, and he could safely delay liberal legislation forever, if necessary. Smith's absolute rule was temporarily curtailed when Speaker Rayburn succeeded in negotiating an enlargement of the committee in 1961. The committee remained a rock-girt fortress in the path of progressive legislation. In 1966 Judge Smith was at last defeated in the primary in his Virginia district. But he was succeeded by

Congressman William Colmer, Democrat of Mississippi, a conservative, if possible, deeper dyed even than Smith. Early in 1967, however, Colmer lost control of his committee, which adopted a set of rules for its own procedure for the first time. One of these required a majority vote on the committee before a bill could be tabled. The autocracy of that particular committee table was over.

By the 1970s the survivors of the Southern feudal baronage which had ruled Congress for so long were fewer, older, and ever more drastically out of touch with the sentiment of most other Democratic members. Each successive election—1968, 1970, 1972, 1974—returned fewer of the Old Guard of Southern paladins. The rising national tumult over the Vietnam War further discredited the Southerners' grip on the two houses of Congress. The Armed Services committees (not to mention key subcommittees on appropriations) had been firmly in the hands of Russell of Georgia and his ally John Stennis of Mississippi in the Senate, and Vinson of Georgia, L. Mendel Rivers of South Carolina, and F. Edward Hébert of Louisiana in the House. Once upon a time, the power of these patriarchs had been enhanced by the toga of patriotism they loved to draw around themselves. By 1971 even a Republican (admittedly a maverick one) like Donald Riegle of Michigan confessed to his diary an overpowering urge to "smash Hébert in the face" because of his feelings about the war. Even a charter member of the Southern committee chairmen's club like Wilbur Mills of Arkansas, either because he was a realist or because he cherished presidential ambitions, was constrained to put distance between himself and colleagues like Hébert. Nixon's election in 1968, too, meant that there was no longer any motive for discontented liberal Democrats to rally round the President out of residual party loyalty, as many of them felt obliged to do so as long as Lyndon Johnson sat in the Oval Office.

At the height of Johnson's popularity in the middle 1960s, about 180 such Democrats, unhappy about conservative Southern control of their party in the House, belonged to the Democratic Study Group, founded in the 1950s by liberal House members like Eugene McCarthy of Minnesota, Lee Metcalf of Montana, and Richard Bolling of Missouri. In 1967 to 1969, with Congressman James G. O'Hara of Michigan as its chairman, the DSG persuaded the House leadership to revive the caucus, which had fallen into disuse since the early years of the century. The DSG was not to reap the rewards of its long struggle in opposition, however. O'Hara led it at a time when the membership was deeply divided over the war. Membership had fallen to 120 by 1969. It was not until 1970, with Donald Fraser of Minnesota as its chairman, that the DSG began to keep its members together enough to turn the caucus not only into a forum for pressing attacks on conservative leadership on the war, but also into what it was to become: the key instrument for carrying out structural reform in the House.

A reform bill drafted by a joint committee chaired by Senator Mike Monroney of Oklahoma and Congressman Ray Madden of Indiana died in the Rules Committee in 1968. But the caucus succeeded in reviving the bill, in more modest form, in 1970 as the Legislative Reorganization Act. Among other things, it prescribed that committees must have written rules and must make their roll-call votes public. In 1970 the caucus also set up a committee under Congresswoman Julia Butler Hansen of Washington. In January 1971 the caucus accepted the Hansen committee's reform proposals. There were two key reforms. First, there should be a separate vote on who was to be chairman of each committee, and it was explicitly stated that recommendations for chairman need not follow seniority. Second, members of committees must have no more than one subcommittee chairmanship each. But the Hansen committee did not disband after seeing these proposals accepted.

In January 1973 the Democratic Study Group liberals pushed two further reforms through the Hansen committee and won acceptance for them from the caucus. Each carried the attack on the committee chairmen a stage further. Now there must be an automatic vote on committee chairmen, with a secret ballot if 20 percent of the caucus wanted it. And now there was to be a "bill of rights" for subcommittees. They must have fixed jurisdictions, the right to hold hearings and hire their own staff, and independent budgets of their own. No longer could a committee chairman manipulate the fate of a piece of legislation by sending it to a temporary subcommittee, headed by a crony and meeting heaven knew when or whether.

In the same spirit the caucus abolished the "closed rule." This was a device whereby a committee chairman could report out a bill, and amendment on the floor of the whole House would be out of order. Now the caucus insisted that a closed rule could be ignored if fifty Democrats voted to open it. The closed rule had been one of the main techniques used by Wilbur Mills as chairman of Ways and Means to keep great power in his own hands. It not only enabled him to make the House vote on important tax measures, for example, as a whole, which meant it was not likely they would be voted down. It also gave him powerful leverage for bargaining within his committee. Mills tried to defend the closed rule, and such was the feeling in the majority in the House by 1964 that he would probably have suffered for his stubbornness had his career not been cut short as a result of his undignified escapade with an Argentinian stripper who called herself Fanne Foxe. The fall of the titans on Capitol Hill was surreally accelerated by the peccadilloes of Mills, Wayne Hays, whose adventures with Elizabeth Ray gave great pleasure to all who had suffered under the lash of Hays's tongue, and Speaker Carl Albert, who contrived, after striking several blows for liberty, to drive his car through the front window of a Georgetown hostess's town house. It was strange, but somehow reassuring, that such pillars of public rectitude had such traditional tastes in private relaxation, somewhat as if a number of bishops had been in the habit of attending blue movies at a frat-house stag night. Even these self-inflicted wounds did not bring the fall of the oligarchy, however. The coup de grace, ironically enough, was administered by Richard Nixon.

It was the "Watergate class" of seventy-five new Democratic freshmen who finally convinced the waverers and tipped the balance against the committee chairmen. When the Ninety-fourth Congress organized in December 1974, the caucus voted to make appropriations subcommittee chairmen on all fours with committee chairmen as far as voting went, and then the steering and policy committee, the caucus's engine in the whole reform process, voted to replace two of the chairmen: Wayne Hays and Wright Patman, the veteran Texan of Banking, Currency and Housing, were to be replaced by Frank ("Tommy") Thompson of New Jersey and Henry Reuss of Wisconsin. But the full caucus demurred, accepting Reuss and rejecting Thompson, not for personal reasons, but because members wanted to keep power in their hands as a caucus and not conjure up a new tyranny in the shape of a steering committee to replace the one they had just overthrown.

In certain respects, it is true, power had begun to seep back from the committee chairmen, not to the members as a whole, but to the Democratic leadership in the House. The caucus took the power of assigning members to committees—and there are few powers that mean more to members—from the chairman of Ways and Means to the steering and policy committee, of which the Speaker is the chairman. It gave the Speaker power to nominate the members of the Rules Committee. Speaker O'Neill took another important step when he created an ad hoc committee to coordinate the many committees claiming jurisdiction over the President's energy legislation in 1977. Congressman Richard Bolling, veteran leader of the liberals' siege of the citadels of the conservative coalition, and now symbolically the new chairman of the Rules Committee, claims no more than that "we have accreted to the leadership significant power."

It was in the Democratic majority in the House of Representatives that the battle for reform was bitterest, and the results most clear-cut. But the same mood produced similar if less dramatic changes both in the Senate and on the Republican side. In the Senate the Republicans actually modified the seniority system in 1973, the Democrats not until 1975. In 1975 the Senate at last adopted a change in its rules to make it easier to apply the cloture to a filibuster, though the change is not expected to make much difference in practice. Over the years a number of liberal senators in both parties tried with little success to reform the Senate's cumbersome committee structure.

In July 1976, Senator Adlai E. Stevenson III of Illinois, a Democrat, and Senator William Brock of Tennessee, a Republican, circulated a letter to their colleagues complaining of "too many assignments, unequal workloads, jurisdictional overlap, underused committees, a poorly organized system and wasteful scheduling," for a start. Somewhat to everyone's surprise, this effort succeeded where earlier ones had failed. Succeeded, that is, relatively speaking. After a determined lobbying campaign by veterans' groups, Native Americans, small business, and public employees' unions, all of whom foresaw the destruction of "their" committees, the reformers, who had set out to reduce the number of the Senate's committees from 31 to 15, ended up with 24 committees. In the end, only one senator, the unfortunate Quentin Burdick of North Dakota, who had seen his Post Office and Civil Service Committee shot from under him, voted against the reform resolution. So in spite of the stolid resistance of special interests, few senators saw themselves or their interests as threatened by reform.

A detailed study of this Senate reform battle concludes with a perceptive comment: a mixed coalition of senators voted for reform of the committee system, wrote Judith H. Parris of the Congressional Research Service, "for a variety of reasons: modernization, efficiency, rationalization, benefits to junior senators, benefits to the minority, responsiveness, more limited government, a better public image, and making their own work more convenient and productive." There is a highly significant omission from that list. Few, if any, senators were motivated to vote for reform out of any desire to make the Senate better equipped to match its strength against that of the presidency. Still less was that motive present in the House. Senators and congressmen wanted to make their own political lives more bearable, more productive and satisfying. Above all, they wanted to prolong them.

Incumbents, especially in the House of Representatives, have a tremendous advantage. Between 1968 and 1978, in a period of unremitting turmoil, during which three Presidents were in effect defeated and thrust from office and a fourth seemed at times to be hanging on by his eyelids, 94 percent of House members who sought reelection were successful. Senators, surprisingly, were less armored against fate. Only 73 percent of them, over the decade, won reelection, and in 1976 the proportion fell to below two-thirds. The reason is simple. A Senate seat is sufficiently conspicuous that challengers find it possible to raise the huge sums now required for a successful campaign. In the House, except in rare cases where a challenger is possessed of very substantial personal wealth or is generously staked by business or other interests, the advantages of incumbency are almost always enough to see you home. A large staff, including one or more offices in the district, facilities for free mailing, radio and television appeals bombarding the voters, prominence and a recognizable name, not to mention the help and contributions of all those whom the congressman has helped or who count on him to help in the future: what challenger can match these assets, unless the incumbent has unforgivably offended powerful interests or utterly wasted his time in Washington? "There is no excuse for an incumbent losing his job," says conservative Republican Guy Vander Jagt from Michigan. "His voting record usually doesn't matter if the challenger does not have substantial resources." From the opposite end of the ideological spectrum, retired Massachusetts Democratic Congressman Mike Harrington put the matter even more bluntly before he left Congress of his own wish in 1978: "We've got a lot of guys in Congress now who have mastered the technique that will keep them in office. But how many can offer you a coherent sense of the whole? How many would even try?"

Reform did not come about in Congress because its members deliberately sought to equip it to compete more effectively with the President. That was not their conscious purpose. Yet over the past ten years Congress has been engaged in a struggle with successive Presidents on many fronts. And as a result of that struggle, Congress is now asserting powers and prerogatives it did not claim before.

4

Many Americans assume that foreign policy is the exclusive province of the President. To the extent that they are aware that Congress does from time to time intervene in the making of foreign policy, they tend to see this as meddling or even usurpation.

The mistake is understandable. It is the President, together with his secretary of state or his national security assistant, whom we see conducting the foreign relations of the United States. It is they who climb into aircraft and depart for foreign capitals on the evening television news. It is they who announce dramatic events: an opening toward Peking, a Camp David negotiation, a tense moment in relations with the Soviet Union. It is to the State Department, not to the Senate Foreign Relations Committee, that U.S. embassies abroad report, and it is officials of the State Department who conduct U.S. diplomacy. An important and growing role, certainly, is played by other institutions: the National Security Council and its staff, the Pentagon, and the Central Intelligence Agency and other arms of the "intelligence community." But all these, too, report to the President in the first instance and only secondarily to Congress.

Yet it is still wrong to identify the responsibility for foreign policy as lying wholly with the executive branch. Not only is this wrong in constitutional law, it is also an oversimple reading of actual practice.

The framers of the Constitution deliberately divided responsibility, giving some to the President, some to the Congress. To Congress went the power to declare war; to the President, the duty of waging it. The President could make treaties—but only "provided two-thirds of the senators present concur." Over the past two centuries, time and the way the world works have given more and more practical power to conduct foreign policy to the President. Yet Congress always retained the ultimate sanction of the purse.

Deliberately or otherwise, the Founding Fathers also left a substantial area of doubt as to where the President's powers over foreign policy end and those of Congress begin. As early as 1793 Alexander Hamilton and James Madison, writing as "Pacificus" and "Helvidius" respectively, joined in a classic controversy as to whether the President possessed powers in foreign policy that were implied but not spelled out in the Constitution. Hamilton said that he did. Madison said that he did not. Whoever is regarded as the winner of the argument, there is no doubt that Hamilton has been proved right by history. The President *has* taken powers in foreign affairs, whether they are called inherent, implied, emergency, or anything else, that are not specified in the Constitution. But not all those powers together have succeeded in stripping Congress of a coequal role. The question is, how Congress can perform it.

Until comparatively recently, the whole thrust of American history seemed to be in the direction of strengthening and legitimizing those "implied" powers of the President in foreign policy. Relying on their constitutional authority as Commander in Chief and on their duty to protect American lives and property, Presidents between 1789 and 1970 ordered the use of armed force abroad on at least 165 occasions. On only 5 of those occasions was there a declaration of war by the Congress. Over the same period, Presidents concluded over 1100 treaties; only one in a hundred of them failed to be ratified. Moreover, Presidents increasingly conducted foreign relations, not by means of treaties, over which the Senate had a theoretical veto, but by executive agreements which—it was then widely accepted—did not need to be ratified by Congress at all. In the thirty years from 1940 to 1970, Presidents concluded no fewer than 5653 executive agreements and sent only 310 treaties to the Senate for its advise and consent. Some of the most important agreements in the mid-twentieth century were not presented to the Senate, including the wartime agreements at Teheran, Cairo, Yalta, and Potsdam.

In 1934 the Congress even surrendered to the executive branch one of its most important prerogatives in foreign affairs: the negotiating of the tariff.

In 1937 the Supreme Court, in the person of Justice George Sutherland (a former member of the Senate Foreign Relations Committee), came close to consecrating in constitutional theory the paramountcy which the President had established in practice. In the Curtiss-Wright case (which arose out of the aircraft manufacturer flouting a presidentially imposed embargo on the sale of armaments to the belligerents in the Chaco war in South America), Sutherland made a novel claim on behalf of the presidential prerogative in foreign affairs. Whereas at home the President was strictly circumscribed by the Constitution, Sutherland believed, abroad he had inherited the powers of sovereignty from the British Crown. "The President alone," Sutherland wrote in the Court's majority opinion, "has the power to speak or listen as the representative of the nation."

It is notable that this opinion was given, with only one justice dissenting, by the very Court that was locked in constitutional conflict with the President over domestic affairs. And it was given in 1937: that is, *before* the opening of the international crisis that was so vastly to increase the President's powers and prerogatives. Before World War II, before the collapse of the European democracies and the emergence of the Soviet threat, before nuclear warheads or intercontinental ballistic missiles, before containment and globalism: the Supreme Court already believed that foreign affairs were the peculiar province of the President.

President Truman, former senator though he was, took an even higher view of presidential prerogatives than President Roosevelt. In the years after World War II, Congress for the most part accepted a secondary role that was made more palatable by being presented as "bipartisanship." Politics, members of Congress said, stopped at the water's edge. Only twice in the late 1940s and the 1950s did the conservatives in Congress rebel against the predominance of executive authority, committed as it was to the once-hated doctrine of internationalism. In 1951, in the so-called "Great Debate" opened by Senator Robert Taft, conservatives and former isolationists contended that the President had no authority to send troops to Korea or to Europe without congressional approval. President Truman did not hide his conviction that the decisions were his and his alone to make. In 1953 and 1954, in the debates on the Bricker amendment, the same conservatives failed, though only by the narrowest of margins, to give expression to their opposition to the United Nations and to their resentment at the President's use of executive agreements to circumvent the Senate's right to ratify treaties.

The high water of both practice and prerogative by the executive in foreign affairs was reached in the middle 1960s. In 1964, President Johnson got a blank check from Congress to escalate both ground and air war in Indochina with the Tonkin Gulf Resolution. Only two members of the Senate and no member of the House voted against what later appeared to have been a prescripted exploitation of North Vietnamese retaliation against provocative naval action by U.S. and South Vietnamese forces. The true nature of this action had been deliberately distorted by the administration to deceive Congress. Later a legal memorandum by the State Department on the constitutional justification for presidential actions in Indochina made this remarkable claim: "The Constitution leaves to the President the judgment to determine whether the circumstances of a particular armed attack are so urgent and the potential consequences so threatening that he should act without formally consulting the Congress." The constitutional role of the Congress had thus been reduced to a purely consultative role, to be exercised only when the President decided it would be appropriate for Congress to be consulted: or, in effect, virtually to zero.

If the Tonkin Gulf was the high-water mark, it was also the turning point. Within a couple of years, resentment of the way Congress had been hoodwinked by Lyndon Johnson, reinforced by real, slowly growing concern over both the fortunes and the justification of the Vietnam War, began a long process by which Congress gradually asserted a new claim to be consulted in foreign policy or, more accurately in constitutional terms, reasserted its long-eroded prerogatives. The authority of the presidency was weakened by the war before it was shaken by Watergate.

The mood of Congress changed, too. It became yearly more touchy about its own dignity and less willing to take anything on trust from the President and his men. To some extent this reflected the internal changes in Congress. The net effect, however, was a Congress less willing to accept presidential leadership in foreign as much as in domestic policy. Indeed foreign policy was one of the first causes of the new assertiveness. In the Senate, especially, a group of members who opposed the war began a seven-year campaign to bring the President to heel. It began with the hearings held by Senator Fulbright as chairman of Foreign

Relations into the foreign aid appropriation for South Vietnam in the spring of 1966. It may be said to have reached its climax with the passage of the War Powers Act of 1973.

The congressional armies advanced on four separate tracks in their campaign of resistance to what a growing number of senators and congressmen regarded as presidential usurpation of Congress's powers and responsibilities in the foreign field.

First, there was the campaign to end the war itself. Between 1966 and 1972, Congress in one house or the other voted 94 times in recorded votes on issues related to the war and at least another 455 times in unrecorded votes. The largest number of members ever to vote against the war in the House before 1973 was little more than one-third of the membership: 177 on August 10, 1972. While the series of votes reflected growing disenchantment with the war inside and outside Congress, very few congressmen took this to the length of actually voting against appropriations of money to carry on the war. From 1965 to 1972, on all appropriations bills related to the war, more than 95 percent of all members of the House present voted in favor of the bills in aggregate. It was not until May 1973, two months after the United States finally pulled its last troops out of South Vietnam, that the House indulged in what had become an empty gesture: it voted to cut off all funds for combat in Southeast Asia.

Nevertheless, even if congressmen were reluctant to lay themselves open to the charge of failing to support American fighting men in the field, Congress did slowly but surely assert itself in opposition to a presidential war. In 1969 it voted to restrict U.S. military activity in Thailand and Laos. In 1970 it voted for what started as the Cooper-Church amendment, denying the President funds for waging war in Cambodia. In 1971 it twice voted to set a date by which the President must withdraw U.S. forces from the war altogether. It is true that President Nixon, like President Truman before him, insisted he was not bound by such votes. But they did demonstrate a political climate, a political reality of which the President and his advisers could not help but be aware. There was danger for the President in ignoring such signals of disapproval from the Senate. And once the disapproval had spread to the House, with its control over the spending power, the President would be bound to comply.

Second, the Congress addressed itself to the theoretical and constitutional issue of the war power. As early as 1967 Senator Fulbright reported out of the Foreign Relations Committee a resolution that it was "the sense of the Senate" that the President should not commit the United States without affirmative action by the Congress specifically approving that commitment. The point of principle was made more relevant by the revelation of a whole series of secret commitments undertaken by successive U.S. governments to Thailand, the Philippines, Spain, and other countries. These seemed in some circumstances to bind the United States government to take armed action without the people of the United States knowing that any such commitment had been made, and without Congress being consulted. In June 1970 the national commitments resolution finally passed the Senate. Senate liberals long wanted to assert Congress's control over the circumstances in which the President could start an undeclared war. But it was the House which in November 1970 passed overwhelmingly a joint resolution defining the President's warmaking powers. Two years later, the Senate passed a general bill restricting the President's use of armed forces without congressional approval. The Nixon administration lobbied strongly against the bill, and it was much amended in the House. No serious attempt was made to reconcile the two versions in conference and the bill died.

But in July 1973—again, after the war was long over and with the President already visibly in trouble over Watergate—Congress passed, over Nixon's veto, a strong, though ambiguous War Powers Act. It required the President to disengage troops committed in an undeclared war within sixty days unless Congress specifically authorized him to continue it. Some of the bill's own original sponsors, Senator Thomas Eagleton (Democrat of Missouri), for example, thought it "a historic tragedy," arguing that Congress had in effect given the President a blank check for sixty days of undeclared war, and that after that interval it would either be too late or too unpopular to compel the President to withdraw. The President, however, in spite of his now parlous situation, fought the bill as tenaciously as if he truly believed it would clip the wings of presidential hawks. The general consensus is perhaps that, though the bill does not prevent Presidents from waging wars in the future where they believe that either the national interest or their political interest requires them, still Congress has made such unauthorized warmaking more hazardous and therefore less likely. In any case, the mere passage of the

War Powers Act certainly marked a new high point in congressional assertiveness.

The third way in which Congress strove to make itself more effective in controlling presidential foreign policy in the early 1970s was by trying to win better access to secret information. And in this, too, Congress was in the end rather successful.

The Second World War and the Cold War espionage mania that followed brought an elaborate system of government secrecy, legally founded on nothing more than unchallenged assertion of presidential authority and a general acceptance of the executive's right to withhold information about any matter even distantly related to national security, not only from press and public, but also from Congress. The affairs of the Central Intelligence Agency were scrutinized by two subcommittees, one in the Senate, one in the House, that were trusting to the point of somnolence. Throughout the 1950s and the 1960s and even into the 1970s, many senators and congressmen actually preferred to be free from knowledge that could be of no political advantage and might be politically dangerous.

Still there were some all along in Congress who understood that, deprived of knowledge, Congress was also being deprived of power.

Both the Kennedy and Johnson administrations had covered many military or paramilitary operations in secrecy and had not hesitated to deceive Congress or even if necessary to lie about them. The Bay of Pigs and the naval operations in the Tonkin Gulf are only two of the more notorious examples. The Nixon administration took this, as it took other assertions of the executive's prerogatives, to outrageously greater lengths. In March 1972 it came out with an executive order which, while purporting to liberalize the system for classifying secret documents, actually extended the reach of the secrecy system. A year later it introduced a bill which would have the effect of an American version of the notorious British Official Secrets Act, making it a criminal offense for an official knowingly to disclose classified information to an unauthorized person. It not only concealed the air war in Cambodia, in which more than three thousand raids were flown, it argued that it was justifiable to give *false* information to Congress. At the same time Henry Kissinger's diplomacy, which not only employed secrecy, but essentially depended on it, revived the old suspicion of "European-style" secret diplomacy. A number of episodes, of which the covert interventions against the Allende government in Chile were perhaps the most disturbing, made a suspicious Congress wonder just how much it was being deceived by the executive.

The result was the establishment of two committees, one in the House chaired by Congressman Otis Pike (Democrat of New York), the other in the Senate under Senator Frank Church (Democrat of Idaho). The Pike committee collapsed as a result of internal disagreement, in part caused by intensive lobbying by the White House and the CIA, in part by the fuss over the leaking of documents to a television reporter, Daniel Schorr. (The executive can interfere in the affairs of Congress, just as Congress can interfere in the internal affairs of the executive bureaucracy.) The Church committee, even if it did not get to the bottom of all the administration's secret actions, was more effective. By its hearings—amplified by the media—and its reports, the committee succeeded in 1975 and 1976 in persuading the consensus in Congress that its suspicions were not unfounded, that secrecy had indeed led to many abuses in the conduct of U.S. intelligence agencies, abroad and inside the United States. The result was the establishment of a new system. Intelligence agencies were laid under a statutory obligation to keep a special Senate intelligence committee informed—not merely to respond truthfully to congressional inquiry. Few doubt that the intelligence agencies, under the new system, continue to do things that Congress never learns about. Yet it is clear, too, that Congress has strengthened its position in a vital area.

The same new spirit also led Congress to show greater assertiveness in a range of other specific foreign policy matters. In the antiballistic missile (ABM) debate in 1969, the Congress forced a national debate on a major weapons system. Throughout the late 1960s and the early 1970s Congress began to question more and more aspects of the administration's defense and foreign policy. At first, this challenge came mainly from liberal senators and some congressmen who were opposed to presidential warmaking in Indochina. But that concern began to be matched by increasing skepticism of the Nixon-Kissinger foreign policy from conservatives. While liberals fought to restrain Henry Kissinger from bellicosity in Southeast Asia, conservatives suspected him of conceding too much and gaining too little in his dealings with the Soviet Union. There was growing concern, too, in Congress about the Middle East; overwhelmingly, it was concern that the United States was not doing enough, or might not do enough, to safeguard Israel. These two concerns came together in support for the Jackson amendment in 1974, making trade concessions to Communist countries conditional on liberalization of their emigration policies, which in political terms meant their policies with regard to the emigration of Jews to Israel.

By the middle of the 1970s, the President and his advisers had to reckon with Congress when choosing the line of their foreign policy. The White House did not necessarily have to fear defeat in direct confrontation with Congress. It did have to take account of the fact that in a whole gamut of graduated ways Congress could make its disapproval of presidential foreign policy felt, make it hard for the President to carry out successfully, and help to create opposition in the country that could ultimately touch the President where it would hurt: in the polls and at the polls.

5

The long struggle arising out of the Indochina war left the post-imperial presidency festooned with new chains. New laws oblige future Presidents to inform Congress about executive agreements, national emergencies, the deployment of armed forces abroad, and foreign military sales. By a mere concurrent resolution, Congress can tell the President not to take actions abroad that Presidents earlier in the twentieth century would have taken without feeling called upon even to inform Congress. Nor are these new powers merely theoretical. On the sale of advance electronic warning aircraft to Iran, on the embargo on arms sales to Turkey, and on aircraft sales to Israel, Egypt, and Saudi Arabia, Congress has succeeded in modifying presidential plans in foreign policy without even having to push matters to a showdown.

The modern President is even more effectively constrained at home. The mood of suspicion caused by the war set the stage for this domestic struggle. No doubt some degree of conflict was always in the cards between a Republican President whose domestic policies took on an increasingly conservative tone and liberal Democrats in Congress who had succeeded in freeing themselves —at least for the time being—from the tyranny of the conservative coalition. But it is plain from the sequence of events that what set off the rebellion was Watergate and the high-handed style that Nixon had already begun before Watergate and which indeed led to the Watergate retribution.

After the 1972 election Nixon proposed to put his friend Roy Ash in charge of the Office of Management and Budget, created, as mentioned earlier, on Ash's own recommendation in 1970. But Ash's firm, Litton Industries, had been caught in some horrendous cost overruns on government contracts. And as Ash's deputy at OMB, Nixon proposed to install Fred Malek, a hard-edged loyalist of the classic Watergate stamp who had worked for H. R. Haldeman and whose last job had been at the crepuscular Committee to Re-elect the President itself. Both appointments were simply too much for the Democrats in Congress. Helped by the raging Watergate excitement, they succeeded in passing a bill requiring Ash and Malek to be confirmed by the Senate before taking up their jobs at OMB. President Nixon vetoed the bill, and his veto was sustained in Congress. Then, early in 1974, as Nixon's grip slackened on Capitol Hill, Congress passed a new bill; it accepted Ash and Malek, but made all future directors and deputy directors of OMB subject to Senate confirmation. The bill passed so easily that Nixon did not attempt to veto it. Congress had not only successfully headed off his attempt to put the federal government further out of Congress's reach: it had obtained a veto over appointments to two of the key posts in the President's own political household.

Congress has acquired a veto in a more literal sense in hundreds of other specific areas of domestic policy. Occasionally since as long ago as the 1930s Congress has included in the legislation incorporating an agency, a program or appropriation provisions that empower Congress, after the event, to pass on the legality of what has been done. As early as the 1950s, for example, the Joint Committee on Atomic Energy applied a form of control over the Atomic Energy Commission by requiring AEC to keep it "fully and currently informed" on nuclear reactor development. This "legislative veto," as it has come to be called, became enormously commoner in the early and middle 1970s. The energy bill passed under the Ford administration, to cite another example, authorized the Federal Energy Administration to take various steps to increase the production and improve the conservation of energy. At the same time it required the FEA to report back to Congress and empowered Congress to reverse actions the FEA had already taken. This same technique of giving the executive a length of rope, but keeping the end firmly in Congress's hand so that a sharp tug would bring the President and the bureaucrats back to heel, has been applied to foreign policy as well as at home: for example, in the now common practice of allowing arms sales, but in the same legislation giving Congress the power to cancel the sales if it changes its mind. Both President Ford and President Carter have protested vigorously against the legislative veto. In June 1978 President Carter sent a message to Congress stating that it was his view and that of his attorney general that the legislative veto is unconstitutional. The matter will probably be tested in the Supreme Court before long. But for the time, at least, the legislative veto is irresistible to a Congress that is jealous of its own power and suspicious of the President's use of his.

The most important of all the new techniques Congress has evolved for competing with the President in the shaping and oversight of domestic policy is the new congressional budget process. It is also most directly the consequence of Richard Nixon's highhandedness. The congressional budget was Congress's answer to Nixon's impounding of money appropriated by Congress. Impoundment in itself is not new. It merely means refusal by the President to spend money appropriated by Congress. Jefferson refused to spend money that had been appropriated to build gunboats. But until World War II no President had impounded appropriated funds explicitly on policy grounds: he had done so, ostensibly at least, to save money. During the war Roosevelt refused on occasion to spend money on policy grounds, but the circumstances were exceptional and the sums not large. During the 1950s and 1960s successive Congresses often appropriated, to demonstrate their vigilance and patriotism to their constituents, more money than even the vigilance and patriotism of the Pentagon could think of ways of spending on weapons systems, and several Presidents impounded such monies. Lyndon Johnson ordered deferral of billions of dollars of expenditure for macroeconomic reasons: to prevent overheating of an economy already beginning to suffer from inflation.

What Nixon began to do after his sweeping victory in the 1972 elections was different. It was different in scale. It was blatantly aimed at programs the President disliked for ideological and political reasons. It was an unblushing attempt to unwrite laws that Congress had written. Most delicate of all from Congress's point of view, it looked like a deliberate attempt to challenge Congress's cherished control of the money power.

To be fair to Nixon, he had good reason to try to control government expenditure. It was not just that inflation threatened great harm to the economy with unpleasant political consequences. There was also the problem of the relentless growth of what budget makers call "uncontrollables": payments made to entitled beneficiaries under programs such as Social Security, unemployment insurance, Aid to Dependent Children, veterans' benefits, and the food stamp program. (Ironically enough, the problem was that Congress had *not* imposed a legislative veto on these programs: once enacted, the money flowed out uncontrollably to however many Americans were entitled to it under the terms of the original law.) In the four years between 1971 and 1975, nearly three-quarters of the increase in the federal budget had been swallowed by these uncontrollables. And over the decade from 1967 to 1976 the percentage of the federal budget as a whole that was committed in advance to these uncontrollable expenditures rose from under three-fifths to a whisker under three-quarters.

Nixon had grounds for some action to bring the federal budget back under control. But the course he chose made conflict with the Congress inevitable. And his choice of programs for making savings might just as well have been picked expressly to cause the maximum irritation on Capitol Hill. Even before the 1972 election, he proposed to freeze federal expenditures at the arbitrary figure of $250 billion, a meat cleaver approach which brought the venerable George Mahon of Texas, chairman of the House Appropriations Committee for the best part of a decade, down onto the floor of the House to rumble about "a dangerous transfer of legislative authority to the executive branch."

After the election, with a landslide victory and a supposed "mandate" behind him, Nixon proceeded to impound money on a truly imperial scale. Altogether he impounded $18 billion or more of money appropriated for programs he disliked. Defense spending was spared altogether. Half of the money impounded was destined for water projects, many of them politically dear to congressmen and the fruits of long and tortuous logrolling. Most of the rest was to come out of welfare programs of one sort or another. There may have been justification for saving much of this money. But Nixon had chosen to do it by simultaneously alarming the constitutional traditionalists, outraging the liberals, and threatening the less scrupulous in their supply of pork from the pork barrel. The reaction was predictable.

Dozens of suits were brought in the courts to dispute the results of impoundment actions. Eventually, in February 1975, the Supreme Court handed down its ruling in *Train* v. *City of New York*. The Court found that the federal Environmental Protection Agency had exceeded its authority in impounding funds authorized by Congress in its 1972 amendments to a water control act. Before this litigation could work its way through the courts, Congress had acted. A joint study committee on budgetary control was set up, and in April 1973, with the Nixon White House falling to pieces before everyone's eyes, the committee issued a prompt report recommending the creation of a revolutionary congressional budget process. Congress also considered several bills outlawing impounding, and amended the Anti-deficiency Act to make sure that funds could be left unspent only in certain specified circumstances. Finally, in July 1974, less than a month before his final fall and departure, Richard Nixon was constrained to sign the Congressional Budget Act, incorporating as its tenth title an Impoundment Control Act.

One of the key tools that had enabled the modern presidency to evolve was the control of the budgetary process. The Budget Bureau's move from the Treasury into the President's Executive Office symbolized the presidency's newly institutionalized determination to keep the levers of power in its own hands. Then Nixon had deliberately set out, with the help of Roy Ash, to make the budget more than ever the technique with which the President would rule the whole government. Now for the first time Congress had equipped itself with the machinery it needed to compete with the presidency in a business that lay at the very heart of government: setting macroeconomic targets, setting priorities within government in accordance with that overall strategy, and making sure that Congress's appropriation process did not conflict with either that strategy or that order of priorities. Congress set up, under the Brookings Institution economist Alice Rivkin, a new congressional budget office. It set up two new budget committees, one to each house. Most surprising of all to cynics—and there are plenty of cynics around on the subject of Congress's ability to transcend local interests—it also accepted the discipline of a timetable for reconciling all authorization and appropriation bills in a binding concurrent resolution by a set date every year, and further provided that Congress cannot go home until this exercise has been carried out. The system established itself quickly, and so far it appears to be working satisfactorily.

The congressional budgetary system may not fulfill its sponsors' highest hopes. It certainly does not take the play away from the President and his Office of Management and Budget. But it does represent the most convincing evidence to date of a proposition that Presidents and their advisers will have to take seriously. The political will now exists in Congress to reform Congress's procedures and structures so that it can not only serve the interests of senators and congressmen and their constituencies, but also compete with the presidency in claiming to serve the nation as a whole.

The modern presidency was perceived as the modern element in the federal government. It was seen as the efficient element, the national element, and above all, because the President alone was "President of all the people," as fundamentally the more democratic element. In reforming itself, though that was not always the intention, Congress has lessened its disadvantage in comparison with the presidency in each of these respects.

6

The paradox of congressional power exactly matches the paradox of presidential power. The power of Congress is enormous; it is still not enough to do the things that must be done.

Congress has succeeded in reforming itself to an extent that would surely amaze a Representative Van Winkle who came back to Capitol Hill after twenty years underground. It has woken up. Senators and representatives are better informed, better staffed, more professional, less provincial, less parochial, and more independent than they were. The power of the committee chairmen, the very embodiments of the traditionalist and the fundamentalist, has been broken up and shared around. For better and for worse, Congress is greatly more responsive to outside influences of all kinds than it was. It stands up to the President more than it used to; *even* more than it used to. It has brought under control the presidential power to make agreements with foreign countries, to gather intelligence and conduct secret operations, and to make war. It has forged new tools to supervise the presidential bureaucracy, and it now claims a share in what used to be the presidential monopoly over economic strategy. It has shown itself, in many recent instances but not least over the Strategic

Arms Limitation Treaty, fully capable of repudiating presidential foreign policy, even when the President is deeply committed. And it has taught all Presidents the sharpest of object lessons about congressional power by first calling to account and then (in everything but name) impeaching a strong President who defied its authority. Still, all this adds up to is that Congress has ample power to impede presidential leadership; it has no power whatever to supply leadership in his place.

This stalemate merely compounds the President's difficulties. He has enough trouble in persuading Congress to give him the things he needs more or less as a matter of routine: to approve his budget, to authorize his programs, to confirm his appointments. He cannot now be certain that the House will let him carry out his foreign military sales program, a vital factor in U.S. relations with many countries; nor that the Senate will ratify his treaties, even when he has staked his own prestige and that of the United States to them as deeply as Carter did with SALT. But those are all things he needs Congress's help for merely to operate the machinery of government and respond to events as they happen. If he is to give bold leadership he must be able to innovate.

Take the example of the energy crisis. The President has not done his job if he merely passes an energy bill once in his four-year term. He must respond in many ways over a long period. He must have access to the best thinking on the problem, and he will then want to draft a many-pronged campaign: to reduce dependence on foreign imports, to stimulate domestic production, to develop new sources of supply, and to press ahead with research into and development of alternative sources of energy supply. The White House will have to deal directly with many of the interests involved. But Congress will necessarily be involved in many ways and at many levels. (In fact, Carter's original 1977 energy legislation fell under the jurisdiction of at least five committees in the House and of several more in the Senate.) Of course he and his advisers will have to listen to contradictory cases made in many quarters and to resist pressure from many directions: from "the oil companies," no doubt (though at any given moment it by no means follows that all kinds of oil companies are pressing in the same direction), but also from gas pipeline operators, coal owners, foreign embassies, consumer interests, labor unions, regional lobbies such as the New England heating oil users, and many, many more.

In the nature of things, he will have to modify and probably soften his program, perhaps many times, even before he sends it to the Hill. Then it starts to run the long gauntlet of the same interests' representatives there. He will find, as Richard Bolling put it, that everything that happens on the Hill is indeed a seamless web. He may have to compromise on what he considers vital aspects of his vast, complex, long-term energy plan if he is to win ratification of a treaty which he believes engages the faith and credibility of the United States, or to pass some equally important legislation on something quite different, or simply to win consent to the nomination of a key member of his administration. Or he may choose to preserve the integrity of his energy policy, with all its trade-offs; in which case, he must expect to pay a high price in terms of other parts of his program.

It is not that the President gets no help in Congress. He can always count on getting a good deal just because he is the President. It is less alarming for politicians to find themselves fighting the White House now than it was a few years ago, but it is still something politicians avoid if they can. He will get help from the Democratic leadership if he is a Democrat. The present Speaker, Tip O'Neill, sees it as part of his job to help the President. There will always be senators and congressmen who will help, too, on the merits of the case, because they think the President's program is a good one and they know something has to be done. As Jimmy Carter has learned, a President can count on getting support surprisingly often from the opposite party. But the point is that he must take the support available on every vote, on every issue, and add to it, slowly, laboriously, and always at some political price, enough other votes to give him a majority. He has no other way. There is no automatic mechanism of party to do the job for him by delivering a precast majority most of the time. The second of the vital relationships on which a President must rely is not highway driving. It is a matter of hacking every step forward with the machete. Too often the presidential arm grows weary and the presidential step falters long before the end of the road.

V Every Man for Himself: Politics Without Parties

Political parties are the instruments through which democracy works.
—President Harry S. Truman, March 24, 1946

1

A French traveler in early nineteenth-century India, when there were both British and French colonies there, shrewdly observed that a French administrator, when he was the only European among ten million of his fellow human beings, would boast that he was the first among ten million; the Englishman in the same situation would lament that he was alone. Increasingly, Presidents, once first in war, first in peace, and first in the hearts of their countrymen, now find themselves simply alone.

The end of party has left politics to the independents: to independent congressmen and senators facing independent interest groups without the shock absorber of party to soften the contact. It also has left an independent in the White House to confront this confused and dangerous political war of every man against every man. It is now common for candidates to Congress, particularly Republican candidates, to play down their party allegiance in their campaign publicity, and presidential candidates are beginning to imitate them. In 1972, Nixon minimized his ties to the Republican party by inviting voters to "reelect the President," while George McGovern had to be persuaded by the chairman of the Democratic National Committee, Larry O'Brien, not to caption his TV commercials "McGovern . . . for the people," and to have them say instead, "McGovern . . . Democrat . . . for the people." In 1976 Gerald Ford ran as the incumbent President, rather than as a partisan Republican, while Jimmy Carter kept his campaign headquarters firmly anchored in Atlanta and allowed the Democratic committee no role to speak of in his campaign.

In this respect, as in others, the demands of winning and keeping office have taken precedence over the requisites for effective action in office. Presidents run as independents. It is not surprising, therefore, that they find themselves cut off, in office, from the sources of support that parties were originally organized to provide. Nominally leaders of their party, they have in practice less and less power to reward or punish congressmen, let alone senators, where it counts most, in the senators' or congressmen's prospects for reelection. In short, in the Presidents' relations with their party, as in their relations with the bureaucracy and the Congress, the connections have broken down.

In 1947 the big decision facing President Truman, harder in many ways than the decision to aid Greece and Turkey, was whether or not to veto the Taft-Hartley bill. Congress had passed the bill, which sharply cut back the rights of labor unions, by a comfortable margin. There was a good deal of sentiment for the bill in the country. Yet any Democratic officeholder in those days had to think twice before alienating organized labor. And labor was making Taft-Hartley *the* test of whether a politician deserved its support. The unions saw the bill, not altogether without justification, as a deliberate attempt to cancel out all the gains they had made since the founding of the CIO a decade earlier. While Truman agonized over this decision, the Democratic National Committee, on his instructions, polled the two national committeemen and the state chairman and vice-chairman for each state "for advice on what action the President should take."

A third of a century later, such a step would have been inconceivable. Almost the last direction in which a hard-pressed President would turn for comfort and enlightenment would be to the functionaries of the regular party organization. In July 1979, for example, President Carter came back from the economic summit in Tokyo to find his energy policy in tatters and his personal popularity and indeed credibility at disaster levels. He canceled plans for an energy speech, and it became even more urgent to find something to say to calm the country's fears and restore his position. It was, his domestic adviser Stuart Eizenstat told him, "the worst of times," a crisis comparable to the sharpest in the history of the modern presidency. In a political crisis of the first magnitude, pregnant with ominous implications for his fortunes in 1980, the President retreated from Washington to Camp David to take counsel. Whom did he turn to? Not to his cabinet: one of the main suggestions put before him by his White House staff was that he should ask for the cabinet's resignation, and in the event he fired four cabinet members and a fifth quit within the week.

He summoned all his close advisers from the White House. He invited more than 130 citizens from outside his administration to add their advice. They included senators and congressmen, governors and mayors—not all of them Democrats—businessmen and labor leaders, clergy and professors, former officials and representatives of ethnic groups, not to mention no fewer than eighteen journalists. He did not invite the Democratic national committeemen and committeewomen, nor the state chairpersons and vice chairpersons. It would have been astonishing if he had done so. He did not even ask the chairman of the Democratic National Committee. Nor did he ask all of the Democratic leadership from either the Senate or the House of Representatives.

There could hardly be a more graphic demonstration: in trouble, a President no longer looks to his party either for advice or for help. Richard Nixon did not look to the Republicans, as a party, to save him even when he was in extremis. Jimmy Carter does not look to the Democrats. Presidents nowadays scramble into the White House with a minimum of help from the party, and when they are there they give the party a minimum of thought. To all intents and purposes, as a resource for presidential leadership, party no longer exists.

2

Under the American two-party system of democracy as it operated in its classic form, for much of the time from the 1830s until the 1960s, and for almost all the time from the end of Reconstruction in the 1870s until the coming of the New Deal in the 1930s, the party as an organization determined who was going to be President and in return gave him help in vital ways to do his job.

Under that classic system, the parties chose their candidates. Today the successful candidate for the presidential nomination takes the party by storm or stratagem from the outside. In the past, the parties financed the campaign. Now, candidates, whether for the presidency or for any other office, generally raise most of their campaign funds (apart from what they get in public finance) for themselves. Once, the parties provided the candidates with all but a margin of their vote; most voters stuck to the straight party ticket, and most stuck to a party loyalty they more often than not had inherited from their parents. Now ticket splitting is increasingly common, and a third of the electorate claims no party affiliation and thinks of itself as "independent." One-third of all those registered Democrats who voted crossed party lines to vote for Nixon in 1972. A comparable proportion of Republicans voted for Johnson in 1964.

Once in the White House, the party used to expect the President to carry out the platform it had adopted at its convention. Thirty years ago, the platform was a serious statement of common principle, and elected officials were expected to stand by it. At his last press conference as President, in 1953, Harry Truman admitted that he did not expect 100 percent support from all those elected to Congress on the same platform with him. But he did believe, he said, that once the platform had been adopted by the convention, those who ran on it "should generally abide by its detailed construction by the national candidate," meaning by the President. Few committee chairmen followed the party platform more than half the time, the outgoing President grumbled, but that was an aberration, it was "very bad."

In theory, as late as the 1950s the President was supposed to stick to the party platform. In return, his fellow party members in Congress could be expected to vote for most of the legislation he recommended. In practice, it did not work quite like that. The conservative coalition between Southern Democrats and Republicans made its appearance in Franklin Roosevelt's time, and when Roosevelt tried to purge the Democrats who persistently opposed his program, he was only partially successful. By the 1960s, the platform committee's deliberations at the convention had become something of a farce that reflected the growing separation between the presidential candidate and the party as a whole, or between presidential and congressional parties. Presidential candidates and their staffs secretly laughed at the elaborate, artificial compromises arrived at by the platform committees. By the 1960s, only a very naive political reporter would suppose that the victorious candidate's party platform offered any practical guide to his probable legislative program. But really candidates and their staff laughed at their own peril. Once in the White House, they would find that they still had to resolve those same conflicts for which the platform committee once acted as a lightning rod; only now the fierce competing interests zapped right in on the President himself.

Beginning with John Kennedy in 1960, if not indeed with Eisenhower and his backers when they rolled over the Taft regulars in 1952, candidates and their people thought they had superseded the cumbersome, old-fashioned rigmaroles of party. You simply didn't need to go through all that anymore. Television would enable you to reach the voters directly over the heads of the party. Professional advisers—pollsters, media men and women, consultants of every kind—could do everything for the candidate that the party organization had once been able to do, and all they wanted in return was money. John Kennedy and his lieutenants were always elaborately polite to the old-line party leaders, to Richard Daley of Chicago, David Lawrence of Pittsburgh, Bill Green of Philadelphia, and John Bailey of Connecticut. It was always "the mayor," and "Mister Green," "Mister Bailey." But in their hearts they regarded them as obsolescent if not obsolete. They were only half right. It was true that you could win the nomination and the election, too, with next to no help from the party. They proved that—though Kennedy did get some pretty old-fashioned help from Mayor Daley. What they failed to understand was that in the process they were depriving themselves of resources they would need to govern when they got to the White House.

Parties have traditionally performed certain essential functions to make the American political system work, just as they have performed and continue to perform those same functions in essentially similar ways in all other democratic systems. They chose candidates, making sure in the process that no candidate would be nominated for the presidency unless he was at least adequately experienced and commanded the support of a consensus in the party. They pooled money and so to some extent acted as a buffer so that no candidate was too directly beholden to specific sources of campaign finance. (Though admittedly there were parts of the country where for many decades that role was never more than feebly performed. Few Republicans ran for office in California in the second quarter of the twentieth century without the blessing of the Southern Pacific Railroad, for example, and few Democrats in Georgia without the blessing of Georgia Power & Light and of the Atlanta banks.) More broadly, the parties mediated conflicts between the interest groups.

Once they had nominated and elected a candidate, the parties made the system work *for the President.* They acted as two-way channels of communication, letting the President know what was on the voters' minds and allowing him to educate and lead them in return. They weighed and accommodated the conflicting interests and ambitions of different groups. By mediating these conflicts and by helping to establish priorities, they left the President, as party leader, with only the most important decisions to make—those that could not be brokered or compromised at some lower level. That enabled the President to resolve most issues in the name of the party's collective authority, and so spared him the necessity to dicker with his own stock of political credit for every political asset he needs, as Presidents must now do in an age without parties. They provided the ready-made coalitions that could deliver the votes in Congress for most of the agreed-upon planks of the party's platform and for carrying on the routine business of the government. This, too, spared the President the need for him to put together a separate coalition in Congress, at some political cost to himself, on every vote.

The modern President must recruit his army anew for every engagement in the war. The old parties created coalitions of interest and opinion throughout the country. They provided an ideology and a strategy within which Presidents and other party leaders could work together. So in the 1860s the young Republican party, taking advantage of the coincidence of interest between abolitionist idealists and capitalist expansionists, forged them into an effective coalition. And so in the 1930s the Democratic party saw that there was an unlikely harmony of interests between city workers in the Northeast and Southern farmers, and made them in turn the heart of a conquering coalition.

It would be foolish to idealize the old parties. They were not run by sentimentalists. The word does not describe either Marcus Hanna or James A. Farley. Deep cynicism was often involved in the accommodations the parties reached, and there were always victims. Someone had to pay the price of the compromises the parties made, whether it was the Southern whites in the 1860s, the Southern blacks in the 1870s and the 1930s, or the middle-class people who were largely bypassed by the Great Society programs of the 1960s. Still, parties did make it possible to resolve the titanic conflicts of America for a hundred years. They were rough-and-ready ways of discovering consensus, but in a rough-and-ready way they did work. Specifically, they bound together the President and Congress, separated powers in constitutional theory, just enough to allow the President to emerge as the effective leader of the government and to respond, in the persons of the two Roosevelts, Wilson, and Truman, to the great new challenges of the first half of the twentieth century.

3

It started—like so many things that appear to be a good idea at first—in California. The people who swarmed there throughout the 1930s and the 1940s came from everywhere: from the South, the dust bowl, and the Middle West, as well as from the East and from Europe. They brought very different experiences of life with them and widely different political prejudices and attitudes. But on the whole they left their partisan political affiliations behind. Even if they didn't, they were moving into a society that was politically plastic. California was growing so fast that in many communities there was no existing party organization and certainly no machine. In the San Francisco Bay Area, labor was powerfully entrenched. In Southern California powerful economic interests—banking, real estate, the railroads among them —were fiercely defended by an oligarchy whose voice was the *Los Angeles Times*. But in the state as a whole, party organization was minimal. Since the reforms in the early part of the century, California had had crossover primaries. And so there grew up in the California of the great mid-century boom a new form of politics that was centered around the candidate, not around the party. It was a model that was to spread across the country.

The candidate might be his own man, as Earl Warren was, recruiting his own financial support. Or he might be the creature of a business oligarchy, like Richard Nixon in the early phases of his career. Sometimes the politician succeeded in balancing different sources of support, like the successful 1950s governor of California, Goodwin Knight, a Republican, who managed to be backed both by labor and by the Chandler family of the *Los Angeles Times* and their conservative friends in the Southern California business community. But in any case the candidate needed money. California was already a big and populous state, and the new California-style campaign depended on media. There were no party organizations at block or ward level, few ethnic clubs and—outside the Bay area—few labor unions. Candidates, and more especially statewide candidates, had to use the media to reach the voter directly: advertising on billboards, in newspapers, on radio, and later on television, and shrewd use of the news media to project the right image. It was all to become familiar nationally. But in California in the late 1940s and the early 1950s it was new, and the politicians needed experts to advise them on how to reach the voters and how to put across the right image when they did reach them.

And so California saw the birth of one more new industry: the professional political consultancy business. Some of them started as lawyers, like the legendary Murray Chotiner, who managed brilliant campaigns in the new style for Earl Warren, for Senator William Knowland, and for Nixon before he blotted his escutcheon in a number of dubious political affairs outside California. Some of them came from the advertising industry and the almost equally new world of public relations, like the Southern California firm of Spencer-Roberts, pioneers of the new profession of political consultancy. Before the end of the 1950s, all the essential elements of the new politics were commonplace in California. All were present in such statewide campaigns as those of the Republicans Warren, Knight, Nixon, Knowland, and Clair Engle and the Democrat Edmund G. ("Pat") Brown. The elements were: a candidate-centered campaign that stressed the candidate's personality rather than his party's platform and consciously aimed at independents and ticket splitters; a heavy reliance on the media to reach the voters directly, short-circuiting such party organizations as there were; massive fundraising and expenditure; and campaigns controlled by mercenary professionals, not by party regulars.

There are certain similarities between this new kind of campaign and that waged by the liberal Republicans who successfully ran General Eisenhower against the Taft people who dominated the regular Republican organizations in most states in 1952. And on the Democratic side, Senator Estes Kefauver was the forerunner of a new kind of insurgent: the patrician as radical, using the media, and in particular the new high-tension transmission lines provided by television, to cut the knots of party politics. Kefauver was the first in the line of rebels from the left wing of the Democratic party—Gene McCarthy, Robert Kennedy—who finally triumphed with George McGovern in 1972; triumphed and failed, just as Barry Goldwater failed when the Republican Right finally succeeded in nominating him in revenge for what had been done to Taft. But if Kefauver was a man aware of the possibilities of the new politics, he was never nominated for President. And the man the Democrats did twice nominate, Adlai Stevenson, was deeply out of sympathy with the new politics of manipulation and technique: he was, in particular, neither attuned to nor in sympathy with television. Television did not create the new politics, but it was television that was to accomplish the political revolution more than any other single force.

Later a great confusion spread about the notion of "new politics." People mixed up the new politics of technique, developed originally in California and mainly by Republicans, with the other new politics of protest and rebellion that arose in response to the Vietnam War. Ideologically, the two had nothing in common. The new political techniques, if anything, were more likely to suit conservative candidates than liberal ones, if only because the reliance on "media"—meaning in this context essentially paid advertising—and the use of professional consultants in place of party regulars were bound to be expensive. Coincidentally, some wealthy liberal candidates did take up the new political techniques—Robert Kennedy in 1968, for example. But in general, insurgents were less likely to be able to afford lavish media campaigns than incumbents, and liberals less likely to be able to afford them than conservatives. And the exponents of the "new politics" of protest could rarely afford the "new politics" of media technique at all.

As it happened, though, the first successful candidate for the White House to campaign in the new way was a Democrat, and a liberal Democrat at that. The Kennedys were always more aware of what was happening in California than most Easterners, perhaps partly because of Joseph P. Kennedy's long business association with Hollywood. In 1960 Fred Dutton, an able California political operator who had worked for Pat Brown and knew the new style of politics inside out, worked on the Kennedy campaign. But Kennedy didn't need to copy the new politics from the Californians. He was a new style of candidate anyway and tailor-made for a new style of campaign. His was bound to be a candidate-centered campaign in the first place, because he started as an outsider. His Senate service and his run for Vice President in 1956 had given him some visibility in the Democratic party: they had nowhere near established him as a leading figure. Then he was bound to run a candidate-centered campaign for another reason: he was such a superb candidate. First, people would vote for Kennedy not because they felt comfortable with his policies but because they found him exciting. Second, he was made for television. His style was television style: cool, wry, relaxed, relying on the overall impact of his personality, not on the force of the words or the intensity of the feeling. The biggest single edge he had over his two strongest rivals, Johnson and Humphrey, lay precisely in his superiority as a user of television; and in the run-in with Nixon, it was television again that gave Kennedy the decisive margin. At every critical stage of the campaign and on every potentially lethal issue—when he had to deal with the issue of his youth at the convention, for example, and when he had to confront the religious issue in West Virginia and again at the famous meeting with the Protestant clergy in Houston—Kennedy turned to television. It served his purpose perfectly.

Kennedy was also the first major politician to use polls in a new way. Louis Harris first worked for Kennedy in 1958. (He also worked for Pat Brown and Fred Dutton in that same year.) He did a survey that showed Kennedy he had nothing to fear from a potential rival for his Senate seat in Massachusetts, Foster Furcolo. In 1960 Harris did something more important for Kennedy. He used polling techniques to identify the themes Kennedy ought to be sounding—and those he would do well to avoid. In a sense, he was more than a pollster. He was a professional political adviser in the new style. Harris and pollsters like him were professionals not just in the sense that they earned their living by doing what in the past amateurs had done for fun or out of public spirit. They were professionals in the sense that a doctor or a lawyer is a professional. They implicitly—and sometimes explicitly—made the claim that their advice was based on a body of specialized knowledge, that it was scientific. They were not saying, "*I feel* you should be talking about this issue and not talking about that," they were saying, "*I can demonstrate* that these are the issues you should be talking about." Lastly the Kennedy campaign was in the new politics tradition in that it was very expensive: and not only that, the money was raised privately and not from party sources, or even from the whole of the usual spectrum of Democratic givers.

In all those ways, the Kennedy campaign in 1960 was the first appearance on the national stage of a new kind of politics. Yet the point should not be pressed too far. Kennedy may have done things that weakened the influence of party. The whole impact of his style both as candidate and President may have reinforced that effect. But Kennedy did not consciously seek to weaken the party. On the contrary, he devoted a good deal of time and effort to trying to strengthen it. He thought of himself as a good party man. In the very first speech of his campaign, he repeated Truman's point about parties being an essential part of the democratic process. Legislative leadership, he said, "is not possible without party leadership.

> No president . . . can escape politics. He has not only been chosen by the nation—he has been chosen by his party. And if he insists that he is 'President of all the people' and should therefore offend none of them—if he blurs the issues and differences between the two parties—if he neglects the party machinery and avoids his party's leadership—then he has not only weakened the political party as an instrument of the democratic process—he has dealt a blow to the democratic process itself.

The difficulty, as Kennedy saw, is intrinsic to the dual role of the American presidency. The President is "President of all the people." He is the symbolic and ceremonial head of the nation. But he is also the head of the executive government. As such he needs the support of a majority in the legislature for his budget and his programs and his policies. Party is the best mechanism for assuring him of a reliable majority, rather than one he must cobble together afresh on every occasion. And so the President must square the circle. He must be President of all the people and at the same time President of some of the people more than he is the President of others.

Kennedy recognized the dilemma and acted accordingly. He took care to distinguish between the ceremonial functions of the office, in which he acted to emphasize national unity, and the political functions, where he acted in an unashamedly partisan way. More specifically, Kennedy recognized that part of the President's problem was not partisanship as such, but the imperfect partisanship of the conservative coalition. What made it hard for a Democratic President to get what he wanted out of Congress was not the fact that the majority were partisan Democrats, but the fact that a substantial fraction of the majority were not really loyal Democrats, or at least not loyal to the modern, national Democratic party. Like Roosevelt, Kennedy did his best to change that. He went out of his way to support national Democrats in the South, speaking for them and helping them in other ways. If he had been President for eight years, it is possible that this political effort, superimposed on the changes that were taking place spontaneously in the map of Southern politics in response to the civil rights revolution and to economic change, might have been successful. In that case, Kennedy might have handed on a far more unified party to his successor in 1969.

There is no means of knowing. What we do know is that Kennedy's actual successor, Lyndon Johnson, in the end proved no more successful as a party leader than Kennedy. In the end: because for a time Johnson seemed destined to be remembered as the man who had revived the Roosevelt coalition. His victory in 1964 demanded comparison with Roosevelt's in 1936, and in one sense it was a party victory. Johnson swept thirty-eight new Democrats with him into the House of Representatives. As a Texan with solid ties to the Inner Club of Southern conservatives in the Senate, who was at the same time an old New Dealer who had led the fight for civil rights legislation during the Eisenhower administration, who was further out than Kennedy himself on the civil rights issue, Johnson was uniquely fitted for the task of trying to reconcile the Southern Democrats to the mainstream of the party. He had a strong sense of the party as "one big tent"—a phrase he often used of the coalition he had put together. As ringmaster in the Senate he earned the respect (even if it was sometimes the grudging respect) of Southern segregationists and Northern liberals alike. At times he worked the White House switchboard like a virtuoso, personally calling up friends and political allies all over the country to generate support for his programs. On such occasions he took special care to maintain good relations with powerful Democrats outside Congress, such as Mayor Daley of Chicago, the lawyer-politicians Eugene Wyman in Los Angeles and Edwin L. Weisl in New York.

Yet after Johnson had been in the White House for almost five years, the 1968 campaign left the Democrats in greater disarray than ever. For a while the shock seemed fatal. Not one but three desperate insurgencies—under George Wallace, Eugene McCarthy, and Robert Kennedy—ripped away great hunks of the party's living flesh. And when Johnson turned to the party regulars in an effort to restore unity and discipline, he only made a bad situation worse.

The conventional view is that the party was torn to pieces over the single issue of the Vietnam War. It is true that the party utterly failed to accommodate the passionately felt dissent on the war or a more diffuse unease about it which by early 1968, according to poll data, had spread to a majority of the American people. But the war was not some peripheral or coincidental thing. It was the direct consequence of the Democrats' foreign policy, stubbornly pursued for twenty years. The "loss" of China had cost the Democrats the White House. There must be no more Chinas. The war was the inevitable result of that resolve. Nothing could have been more firmly rooted in domestic electoral politics. For more than a decade, as David Halberstam succinctly put it, "a series of American Presidents tried to hold Saigon so that they would not lose Washington."

Still, the war was only one cause of the divisions that the party system failed to handle. The country was deeply divided over the black rebellion and over the Johnson administration's bold decision to discriminate positively in favor of blacks in the effort to endow them with "not just equality as a right and a theory but equality as a fact and equality as a result." The country was divided over the turmoil and violence in the cities that seemed the first fruits of that policy. And so was the Democratic party. On the war, on civil rights and the whole scope of what were known as "urban problems," on the liberal program and the liberal ideology as a whole, the division ran right through the middle of the Democratic party. Politicians at every level found that their constituency was torn apart by the war. Many felt threatened by the war on poverty with its provisions for "maximum feasible participation." Many were swept along by the rebellion against the war; others were swept away by it. After 1965, the consensus that had guided the Democrats since the New Deal, and originally supported Lyndon Johnson's program, fell apart with alarming speed. This was true at the level of theory. It was also true at the level of practical politics.

One by one, each of the main components of the Roosevelt coalition began to flake away. The intellectuals were not important to that coalition in terms of numbers; they were vital to it because their ideas were the cement that held it together. In the late 1960s, some came to the conclusion that liberal policies had failed, and wanted to proceed more cautiously. Some thought they had never been fairly tried, and wanted to go faster. Both groups were impatient with the steady plod along the *via media* of traditional Democratic policy. Many who had once been firm liberals were deeply troubled or outright shocked by the war. Many more lost the robust optimism that had powered the old liberal creed and adopted more or less radical critiques of society. Blacks remained one of the most reliable groups of Democratic voters; even so, many were attracted by more radical styles of political leadership, while others were disillusioned with politics altogether. The time was past when Democratic candidates could safely count on winning the black vote without working hard to earn it. Once, the Democratic candidate could count on a massive share of the ethnic vote. Catholics, Jews, immigrants, and the children of immigrants voted overwhelmingly Democratic in the 1930s and 1940s. Not anymore. Catholics, in particular, seemed strongly attracted by the new conservatism, and by Nixon. And at the same time the South was no longer unquestioning in its ancient Democratic loyalty.

In 1968, battered and driven from office by the insurgents, Lyndon Johnson formed the Old Guard of Democratic politics into a hollow square and succeeded in beating off the raiders. He got the nomination for his candidate, Hubert Humphrey. Once he had dissociated himself from Johnson, and with crucial help from organized labor, Humphrey ran creditably well. At the end, he was coming up so fast that in another week he would have overhauled Nixon. In the process he cut the Wallace rebellion down to size. But the naked muscle with which Humphrey had been imposed on the party; the bitterness left by the treatment of the Kennedy and McCarthy Democrats; and the cold fact of defeat in November, and defeat at the hands of the old enemy, Richard Nixon, at that: all of this made it inevitable that there would be a powerful impulse to reform the party. The reform movement culminated in the McGovern-Fraser commission and the decision to adopt, in the shape of the notorious guidelines A-1 and A-2, what amounted to, even if they were not intended to be, quotas for women, for young people, and for minorities in the selection of campaign delegates. The McGovern commission led to the McGovern nomination and to the party's collapse in the 1972 contest with Richard Nixon and his "new American majority."

A new wave of activists had already been brought into Democratic politics by the McCarthy and Kennedy campaigns and by the peace movement or rather—because in truth it was not only concerned with the war—by the Movement. These new recruits to politics were unsympathetically described by Harvard sociologist James Q. Wilson as the "amateur democrats." The term was not meant to be flattering, but the new Democrats did in fact have some of the more attractive characteristics of amateurs, one of them a remarkable degree of disinterestedness. They were, as Jeane Kirkpatrick noted:

> college educated, geographically and socially mobile, [they] had relatively high incomes, [they were] young, heavily Jewish . . . [they] brought to politics distrust for party organization, disdain for the organization regulars and the paid professionals . . . distaste for a politics based on party loyalty, and a high regard for . . . politics based on ideology rather than on economic interests.

They also proved themselves in both 1968 and 1972 clearly superior to the surviving professional organizations at their own game: the amateurs thrashed the professionals again and again when it came to organizing crash campaigns at high speed to win a primary. In 1972 they captured the Democratic nomination for George McGovern. One of the most dazzling virtuoso performances of political management ever put on at an American party convention was turned in by a twenty-four-year-old graduate student, Rick Stearns, McGovern's floor manager there, who effortlessly achieved the supremely difficult feat of shedding support between votes for tactical reasons and then bringing the votes together again when he needed them.

The insurgents did not just capture the nomination, they captured the convention as well. The established leaders of the party were left to watch the convention on television. The most piquant symbolic defeat was that of Mayor Richard Daley, who had ruled the 1968 convention as a tyrant. Even more truly significant was the failure of dozens of elected Democratic officials—senators, governors, congressmen, and state legislators—who had attended every convention for a generation, to win selection as delegates. Many of the front-rank leaders of organized labor were omitted from their state delegations, as I. W. Abel of the Steelworkers, for example, was passed over by Pennsylvania. Only nineteen of the thirty Democratic governors attended the convention as delegates.

The resentment of the defeated regulars was deep and bitter. At the best of times, they did not like to lose. Still less did they relish losing to young men and women who dressed like graduate students and scarcely bothered to hide their feeling that the regulars were corrupt, unprincipled sellouts. The regulars were also genuinely shocked by the insurgents' positions on "moral" issues such as abortion and drugs, and most of all by the candidate's position on amnesty. Their own honor was being challenged and by people whose ideas of ethics and patriotism seemed to them utterly haywire. So many of the party regulars simply went fishing. Labor gave McGovern none of the full-hearted, last-minute help that almost saved Hubert Humphrey in 1968. It would be wrong to say that the defection of the party regulars cost McGovern the election. Nothing could have won it for him. But after the catastrophe, after Nixon had carried every state except Massachusetts and the District of Columbia, there was nothing left of the national Democratic party except a bundle of debts, a bundle of lawsuits, and a party label that might be worth fighting over again at some time in the future.

All the three insurgencies in the Democratic party in 1968 were new politics campaigns in a sense. They were necessarily centered on the candidate. The Robert Kennedy and McCarthy campaigns were also to a very great extent single-issue campaigns; other concerns and motivations were subordinated to the crusade against the war. For a brief time in 1972, the insurgency actually became the Democratic party. But again it is important to distinguish the two kinds of new politics. The volunteers who worked for Robert Kennedy, McCarthy, and McGovern were practicing, not the new politics of technique, but a new new politics in which commitment and belief replaced both the traditional brokering of interests and the single-minded ambition of the pure candidate-based campaign. The style of 1960 was that of corporate management. The style of 1972 was that of the graduate school. People supported George McGovern, after all, not because of what they could get out of it, and certainly not because they were overwhelmed by his charisma, but because they shared his convictions on the war. In these ideological crusades, just as much as in the Kennedy adventure in 1960, the traditional role of the party was all but irrelevant. The party was no longer choosing the candidate. The candidate was doing his best to kidnap the party.

What was happening to the Democratic party between 1967 and 1972 was so dramatic and bizarre that few people noticed that something not altogether dissimilar was happening to the Republicans. The Republicans, too, were bitterly divided. The true believers on the Right of the party had never forgotten nor forgiven the way their hero, Robert Taft, had been passed over for the sake of Eisenhower and victory in 1952. In 1964 they had had their revenge. They nominated Barry Goldwater. The satisfaction was short-lived. But they refused to draw the lesson that a candidate of the Right could not win. They hankered after a candidate of their own, and they found him in Ronald Reagan. Then there were the liberal Republicans, their base in the cities and the plusher suburbs of the Northeast. Their candidate was Nelson Rockefeller. As long as they could look to his money, and his high-powered political staff, and his base in Albany, and his continual capacity to project himself to the media, they could continue to hope, though as the decade wore on and the conventions went by, 1964, then 1968, Rockefeller looked less and less plausible as a candidate. The Republicans were hardening. They were setting their face against compromise and consensus. They wanted to win, but perhaps they would not need to give up their true beliefs as the price of victory.

Through the middle came Richard Nixon, the conservative with a chance of winning. After the debacle of his campaign for governor of California in 1962 and the tragicomedy of the "last press conference," Nixon worked his way back from political exile by what looked a little like a conventional party strategy but was not. He traveled incessantly. He spoke at fundraisers the length and breadth of the land, punishing himself to squirrel away a rich bank account of political credit. He cultivated party figures of every kind: congressmen, state chairman, county leaders, big givers. But he was not doing all this to help the Republican party. He was doing it for Richard Nixon.

The little band who stayed loyal to Nixon throughout the years of his long march—Pat Buchanan, John Mitchell, John Sears, and Len Garment in the law office in New York, Haldeman and the rest of the veterans of 1960 and 1962 in California—were not regular Republicans. They were working to nominate and elect Nixon. Like the followers of Max Weber's charismatic leader, they were for Nixon *both* because they believed in his exceptional political gifts *and* in the hope of reward. And this mixture of motives, after all, was not so very different from that of the little band of *condottieri* who were "for Kennedy before West Virginia" in 1960 and were richly rewarded when their adventure prospered. Few of those who worked for Nixon in 1966 and 1967 had much connection with the Republican party as such, except insofar as it was represented by Richard Nixon. And there was an additional reason why a Republican with serious ambitions of winning the White House should play down party even more than a Democrat would. By the late 1960s no more than a fifth of the voters were registered Republicans. A Republican could be chosen only if he could draw the votes of vast numbers of independents and also of registered Democrats. Already in 1968 Nixon ran a personal rather than a partisan or an ideological campaign. In 1972, he deliberately worked almost wholly through the Committee to Re-elect the President, not through the Republican National Committee, and for that same reason. There is even evidence that he ultimately intended to replace the Republican party with his "new American majority."

By the 1970s the political parties had little more than a vestigial function in presidential politics. Almost their only remaining asset was a prescriptive right to nominate one candidate each for the presidency, one of whom was certain to be elected. Reforms intended to make the parties' internal procedures more democratic had had the effect of erecting ever more elaborate assault courses to eliminate all but the richest, the most daring, and the most charismatic *condottiere* who had the most talented and devoted retinue of political soldiers of fortune. The more successful the campaign, it seems, the more it is centered upon the personality of the candidate, projected by way of the media by professional image-makers lavishly supplied with funds, and the less it stresses party loyalty, or substantive issues, or any clearly defined political program. The presidential campaign has largely ceased to be a contest between two alternative political philosophies or even between two broad coalitions of interests. Increasingly the political warfare is conducted by means of daring cavalry raids on the glittering prizes of power, fortune, and reputation. It is an exciting and an intriguing game. Whether it is the best way of choosing a President of the United States is another matter. Even if it is, it does little to equip the winner with a clear mandate understood by President and people alike.

4

As long ago as 1963 the political scientist James MacGregor Burns, in a book called *The Deadlock of Democracy,* put forward the thesis that there were no longer only two major political parties in the United States; there were four. The presidential Democratic party had become so sharply differentiated from the congressional Democrats, Burns argued, and the presidential Republicans from the congressional Republicans, that they had become to all intents and purposes four distinct parties, with different programs, different leaders, and different goals—though of course dependent on the same voters. In effect, Burns had spotted the arrival on the presidential scene of the new politics of direct media contact with the voter, and had rightly contrasted it with the more traditional style of the congressional parties. What he did not foresee was that the new politics would gradually spread to Congress as well. By now, most statewide races in the bigger states are organized and conducted like miniature presidential campaigns, with the same emphasis on the candidate's personality and the same reliance on media; similar tactics are now spreading to House races in many parts of the country and at comparable cost. It is not unknown for candidates to the House of Representatives to spend half a million or even a million dollars to be elected in states such as New York and California.

There has been an even more profound change in Congress. That is the rise of the special interests and in particular of the single-issue interest groups. You can see the power of the interests in the most graphic way on Capitol Hill any day when Congress is in session. The members hurry over from their offices for a vote. Overwhelmed by all their other work—speeches to be written, constituents to be greeted, subcommittee and committee meetings to be attended—the congressmen often have only the sketchiest idea of what a vote is about and of what underlying issues are involved. So the lobbyists cluster around the door to the House chamber, literally to tell the members how to vote. Sometimes they find time for a whispered word. Sometimes the decision is communicated with the brutal simplicity of the Roman circus: thumbs up or thumbs down.

There have always been lobbyists on Capitol Hill, of course, In the raffish years after the Civil War, Samuel Ward, brother of the writer of "The Battle Hymn of the Republic," was known as the King of the Lobby. It was Ward who coined the happy phrase that "the way to a man's aye is through his stomach"; he kept an appropriately lavish table in consequence. What is new is the intensity of the pressure for particular issues—some of them business interests, some passionately held moral beliefs like those of the pro- and antiabortion lobbies. What is new, too, is the vulnerability members feel to these pressures and the sheer volume of money that is now flooding the Hill.

"What you are watching," said Congressman John Brademas in an interview, "is the interests learning how to work with the post-Watergate scene."

Among them are new interests that used not to try to influence Congress, learning to use their elbows alongside the traditional economic lobbies of business and labor. Recent changes in campaign finance law have intensified these trends. With the coming of public financing for presidential campaigns and with the growth in the publicly perceived power of Congress, money that used to go to presidential candidates is now available for congressional candidates—if their position on the issue is right. The 1974 campaign finance reform act (technically a set of amendments to a 1971 act) allowed both corporations and unions to contribute up to $5000 to as many "political action committees" (PACs) as they wish. Almost two thousand PACs, formed by corporate employees, trade associations, and stockholders in particular corporations, as well as by unions and environmental and other "public interest" lobbying groups, contributed a total of more than $64 million to congressional candidates in the 1978 midterm elections. "Congress is increasingly responding not to ideological pressures," Congressman Bob Eckhardt (Democrat of Texas) told me, "but to special interest pressures. For one thing, this is happening because of increasingly expensive elections. Most noticeable is the enormous pressure of the oil and gas interests now that energy is such a leading issue. This is no longer true just of Texas, Oklahoma, Louisiana, and California. Oil is almost everywhere now, because there are refining and distribution interests everywhere as well as production interests."

The most evident change in Congress in his time there (since 1965), says Senator John Culver (Democrat of Iowa), is this emergence of single-issue politics. Historically, Culver argues, parties in America have been broad coalitions that welcomed diversity. Now the influence of the party, which had to reflect the interests of farmers *and* consumers, factory workers *and* small businessmen, the unemployed *and* the middle class, is being replaced by the more sharply focused pressure of "often strident and self-righteous" groups. He mentions the well-organized lobbies on abortion, the Panama Canal treaty, labor law reform, gun control, and homosexuality. Each measures the worth of every member of Congress by a single "litmus test": how he or she stands on that one issue. The pressure is increasingly brash, and not surprisingly, because congressmen and senators feel increasingly vulnerable to it. "We may not be able to make your boss see the light," a lobbyist told one of Culver's legislative assistants, "but we can sure make him feel the heat." And they can.

The power of parties to deliver votes in congressional elections has declined. The power of patronage is much diminished. The cost of elections has gone up. Voters are increasingly independent, not to say indifferent. In many congressional districts margins are closer than they used to be. Yet the incumbent congressman is generally safe—unless a well-financed interest group decides to go after him. If the congressman won by a margin of 2 percent of the vote in the last election—and many won by smaller margins than that—and if the right-to-life people, or the environmentalists, or the opponents of the Panama treaty can deliver 3 percent of the vote in his district, then unless the congressman is a man of quite heroic resolution, he is going to vote the "right" way on abortion, or the environment, or Panama. Increasingly, writes political scientist Thomas E. Mann, congressmen are "responsible for their own margins of victory or defeat, and the electoral constraints they face are defined in their own districts." The constraints may be felt in the district. But all too often they are defined in Washington by the representatives of single-issue interest groups of one sort or another.

So in congressional politics, as well as in presidential politics, candidates are campaigning in new ways. They have learned to reach the voters directly in their own behalf, not as foot soldiers in the army of a party. At the same time new pressures brought to bear by the single-issue interest groups are replacing party ties or loyalty to ideology in Congress. But these are not two isolated trends. They are intimately connected. They are two stages in the dissolution of the party system. First, politicians learned to bypass the party and to win office for themselves with the media techniques of the new politics. Then the citizens learned to use those same techniques to make the government do what they wanted. The first to learn this lesson did so out of passionate conviction about what they considered to be moral issues of transcendent importance: the war, equal rights for blacks, for Native Americans, for women, for homosexuals, for fetuses. The same strategy—ignore the party and use your strength directly on the windpipe of the individual congressmen—was swiftly adopted by groups of every other kind in the effort to build majorities for a bewildering variety of propositions. The result, as David Broder put it in the *Washington Post* in 1979, is that "independent, autonomous office-holders are confronting independent, autonomous interest groups in a kind of unmediated power struggle that leaves the national interest in shreds." The political scientist Walter Dean Burnham puts the same point differently. American electoral politics are undergoing a long-term shift into routines designed only to fill offices; at the same time the process is evaporating all intermediaries between the people and their rulers. Burnham called his article "The End of American Party Politics." The rivalry between President and Congress today, says Congressman Wyche Fowler of Georgia, is between people who got to the White House and Capitol Hill in the same way, by being proudly independent and anti-Establishment and in effect campaigning against Washington. Presidents, like congressmen, arrive there to find that they have exchanged the encumbering and sometimes embarrassing alliances of party for the loneliness of the traveler who must defend himself against the marauding interest groups.

VI The Electronic Mephistopheles

"Well, when you come down to it, I don't see that a reporter could do that much to a President, do you?"

—President Dwight D. Eisenhower, at his first press conference, 1953

"You guys . . . All you guys in the media. All of politics has changed because of you. . . ."

—Former President Lyndon B. Johnson, 1971

1

AT FIRST glance, the President's relationship with the news media—unlike his relations with the bureaucracy, with Congress, or with his party—might seem to be an upbeat one. The rise of the modern presidency has been closely linked with the rise of the modern media, so closely that it would be a defensible thesis to argue that the modern media created the modern presidency. Theodore Roosevelt and Woodrow Wilson, the forerunners of the modern presidency, were also the first two Presidents to understand what the new, mass-circulation newspapers and magazines that had sprung up since the Civil War could do for them. FDR knew how to make use of the writing press to neutralize the hostility of the publishers; he also learned how to use radio to free himself from dependence on publishers and politicians altogether. John Kennedy, Lyndon Johnson, and Richard Nixon learned to use television as Roosevelt had used radio. They turned the modern presidency into the television presidency.

"Since 1960," Joseph Califano has written, "the name of the deadly serious game of attaining and exercising national leadership has been television." He does not exaggerate. Television is vital to the candidate and no less vital to the incumbent. And Presidents know it. "We wouldn't have had a prayer without that gadget," said John F. Kennedy of his 1960 campaign; and in office, "We couldn't survive without TV." Nowadays a candidate emerges even before the elongated series of primaries because the opinion polls show that he has a following: it is television that gets him into the opinion polls in the first place, and television that gives him first recognition and then popularity. The print media play their part, too. It was *Time* magazine's profile of Jimmy Carter in 1975 that first brought him national attention as a leading contender for the nomination. But if the national media as a whole pay no attention to a candidate, he has no chance of becoming President. The contest for the two parties' presidential nominations is therefore carried out through the mass media, and more and more via television.

In office, television is a President's best way of reaching the American people, and reaching them, moreover, directly, without intermediaries. President Ford used television skillfully in his dogged and almost successful bid to hold off candidate Carter in the closing stages of the 1976 campaign. President Carter has reached for television in every one of a series of tight corners as his one hope of persuading the voters that, even if his policies evidently were not working, no other policies would have been more effective. In the future, candidates will be even more intent on using television to project themselves, and Presidents even more driven to use television to defend themselves. Television has become more than one of the techniques of American politics: it has become the main forum in which American politics (and also, increasingly, the politics of other democracies) are conducted.

Still, if television is the most important medium for politicians, it is not the only one. The most educated and consequently most influential section of the electorate gets its more detailed information almost as much from print as from electronic journalism, and that group includes the men and women who produce and write television shows. So newspapers, newsmagazines, wire services, and publications of every kind, from *Aviation Weekly* to *The Village Voice*, play an essential role in setting the agenda for television, and so for politics.

As their rivals and opponents are never slow to point out, the news media give Presidents great advantages. No one can dominate the news like the President of the United States. Only he can make news by going for a walk in his Rose Garden. The nation's eyes are always on him. They are kept focused there by the busy machinery of Washington journalism—by the bureaux, the columnists, the two thousand accredited White House correspondents, not to mention the White House press secretary's office, with its staff of fifty and its seven-figure budget.

The President is literally always front page news. Twenty years ago the political scientist Elmer Cornwell painstakingly counted stories on the front page of *The New York Times* and of his local paper, the *Providence Journal,* from 1885 to 1957, and was able to show how the coverage of the President has steadily grown over that period, upstaging coverage of Congress and of state and local governments. More surprisingly, perhaps, a recent study has shown that the same trend has gone on even while Congress struggled to regain some of the ground lost to the presidency. The President's share of all news-column inches on the front page of *The New York Times* has continued to expand, from 62 percent in 1958 to 73 percent over the whole period 1970 to 1974.

The advantage the President has in getting his story across in the print media is nothing compared to the advantage he has on television. Metal plates set into the front lawn of the White House cover the sockets into which electronic cameras can be plugged at any moment, so that the three networks' White House correspondents can report with marginally different pictures of the White House facade behind their heads: the picture is electronically bounced off a tall building to the east of Lafayette Square to the networks' headquarters in northwest Washington. At any moment the President can ask to preempt network television to speak to the nation: unless he grossly abuses this prerogative, his request will be almost automatically acceded to. Even more effectively, he can always do something, go somewhere, say something that the networks dare not leave uncovered. He can go to the country, to Camp David, to China.

None of the President's political or institutional competitors can hope to match his power to use television—not even a Senator Edward Kennedy. There is no leader of the opposition to demand equal time after a presidential speech. Stung by President Kennedy's success in using TV to get his message across in his first year in office, the Republican leaders in Congress at the time, Senator Everett McKinley Dirksen of Illinois and Congressman Charles Halleck of Indiana, neither of them, admittedly, natural star material for television, insisted on putting on what was soon dubbed the "Ev and Charlie Show." It bombed. As Russell Baker reported in *The New York Times* in March 1962:

> President Kennedy's news conference yesterday was attended by 391 persons. For this morning's "Ev and Charlie Show," the authorities of the Capitol press gallery had set up facilities for seventy-five reporters. Seventeen showed up.

All projection is valuable for politicians. Free projection over network television of the kind the President can count on virtually every day of the year if he wants it is more valuable than much fine gold. But the truly revolutionary importance of television for Presidents—as with radio before it—is that it enables them to communicate directly with the people, without their words and appeals being filtered through any mediating or editing process. And this, too, Presidents understand.

"Time after time," wrote FDR, "in meeting legislative opposition . . . I have taken an issue directly to the voter by radio, and invariably I have met a most heartening response." "I'm going to put it right to the housewife," he once said in a radio broadcast; "maybe she can hold the boys in line better than I can." FDR saw, too, even before he became the first President to appear on television, which he did briefly at the New York World's Fair in 1939, that the new medium would emancipate Presidents from the constraints of hostile publishers and competing politicians even more than radio had done. "Sometimes," he wrote to a friend as early as 1938, "I wish the advent of television could be hastened."

On November 14, 1959, *TV Guide*, the biggest circulation magazine in the United States, carried an article titled: "A Force That Changed the Political Scene." The author was Senator John F. Kennedy and the force was television. Kennedy's thesis was that TV would emphasize the candidate's image above all. He was right. Both Kennedy and Nixon subsequently came to believe that it was Kennedy's more attractive image (not to mention lighter makeup) in their first and most celebrated TV debate in Chicago that decisively swung the course of the campaign, though Kennedy used television with subtlety and effectiveness throughout the campaign. "It was," says David Halberstam justly, "the day that changed politics." But it should not be forgotten that Nixon, too, was a politician of the television generation and had used television to brilliant effect before.

Television was not widely in use in the United States during the 1948 campaign, but by 1952 there had been an extraordinary boom. There were estimated to be 19 million sets in the country that year. Two years before, President Truman had gone on television to talk to the nation about the outbreak of the Korean War. It was a portent: the first of many such solemn occasions. "History was personalized last night," wrote Jack Gould in *The New York Times* the next day. But the first important political event that was purely a television happening had Richard M. Nixon for its hero. It was the Checkers speech in September 1952. With his deft appeal to patriotism and sentiment, Nixon used the NBC-TV network (and the CBS and Mutual radio networks) to deflect the hue and cry over his alleged slush fund; overnight, he saved his place on the ticket and transformed himself from a liability into an asset for Eisenhower.

Both Eisenhower and Stevenson used television effectively in the closing stages of the 1952 campaign, Eisenhower more effectively than Stevenson, who retained to the end of his life a certain old-fashioned disdain for television. In the White House, Eisenhower's press secretary Jim Hagerty knew how to manipulate TV as part of his armory for protecting and projecting his boss. Still, it fell to Kennedy to be the first television President. The networks carried nineteen Kennedy speeches live, many of them given added impact by the fact that they came at moments of crisis, like his dramatic speeches on the Cuban missile crisis on October 22, 1962, and on the rioting caused by the admission of James Meredith to the University of Mississippi in the previous month. The conversation with television correspondents was a creative innovation, an extremely effective way of explaining administration policies without serious risk of sharp questioning or criticism. Even more daring was the decision to allow cameras to cover the President and his brother, the attorney general, as they looked for ways of responding to Governor George Wallace's "stand in the schoolhouse door" in June 1963: the issue was the integration of black students into the University of Alabama. He encouraged his wife to do "the Jackie Kennedy Show," a one-hour CBS special. Forty-six million people watched the First Lady stroll from room to room in the mansion, explaining the beautiful things there—those that had always been there, and those that had been added as a result of her enthusiasm.

Kennedy understood the added advantage he drew from his family's glamour, but he was not taken in by the glamour of the media in return. He knew exactly what television could do for him, and why it was so valuable. So did his press secretary, Pierre Salinger, a man with a certain star quality of his own, in spite of his weight and his lamentable stogies. "The publishers of seven out of ten dailies had come out for Nixon," Salinger wrote later. ". . . FDR, when he was under strongest attack, took his case directly to the people . . . I felt JFK would have to do the same eventually—and live TV was the way to do it." Kennedy put the same thought more brutally to his friend Ben Bradlee, then with *Newsweek*. "Well," he said to Bradlee after the successful "conversation" with three network correspondents in 1962, "I always said that when we don't have to go through you bastards, we can really get our story over to the American people."

Kennedy was aware of what television could do for him; he was also aware of what it could do to him. He understood the danger of overexposure. He did not want to become "the national bore," he said, and he asked Salinger to look up how many fireside chats Roosevelt had made every year and take that as a guide to the right number of his own appearances. (Though in the end he appeared on TV far more often than Roosevelt had spoken over the radio.)

Lyndon Johnson had fewer inhibitions about becoming the national bore; he had fewer inhibitions altogether. In his first year in office he went on television more often than Kennedy had done in three years; in his first two years, more often than Eisenhower had done in eight. He developed a new technique: rushing to a network studio at fifty miles an hour at the last moment to appear on the nightly news and make an announcement in person. He even encouraged the networks to install a permanent studio in the White House itself, with cameras ready and warmed up at all times: an experiment that did not endure. Johnson was far less skillful at using television than Kennedy. As a result, he did suffer from overexposure, and he did become something of a national bore. More seriously, his attempts to manipulate the media (print as well as TV) were so crass and transparent that they backfired, leaving the White House with a serious "credibility gap." In the end, people simply didn't believe a word the White House said about the progress of the war in Indochina. *The New Yorker* put it elegantly:

> Our leaders have often told us they can see the light at the end of the tunnel. They have been wrong about the light, of course, but they have been right about the tunnel.

Even before the major escalation of the war in Southeast Asia, Johnson was already overplaying his hand badly. In April 1965, after a rebellion in the Dominican Republic, Johnson went on television to announce that he was sending in 400 Marines to protect American lives. Within days, more than 24,000 U.S. troops had invaded the small Caribbean country; the President spent hours personally attempting to convince newsmen that this was justified because "fifteen hundred innocent people were murdered and shot and their heads cut off," which turned out later to be pure myth. During the same crisis Johnson more than once personally interrupted the network evening news. Such heavy-handed efforts to dominate and manipulate the news predictably had the effect of the little boy who cried wolf. Johnson's credibility gap was terminal, and it was self-induced.

Lyndon Johnson's experience, however, did not prevent Richard Nixon from picking up the television weapon, although Nixon, too, had long been aware of the danger of overexposure. As long ago as the second Eisenhower administration, Nixon was quoted as saying that there was "a very early point of diminishing returns in using television," and that people "probably got tired of seeing their favorite programs thrown off" in favor of presidential or political speeches. In office, he continued to be aware of the danger; at one point he held a press conference for print journalists alone, explaining that "television has probably had as much of the President as it wants at this point." Yet when he first arrived in the White House, Nixon unleashed a positive blitzkrieg of presidential speeches on television and to devastatingly successful purpose.

The high point of opposition to the Vietnam War (as opposed to sentiment against the war, which grew even stronger later) came with the October 1969 "moratorium" demonstration in Washington, which drew an estimated half million protesters to the capital. Nixon and his circle were appalled. They thought the Republic was in danger. Nixon took to television. On November 3, 1969, to an audience of 72 million, he made his "silent majority" speech, contrasting the protesters with his own supporters. "North Vietnam cannot defeat or humiliate the United States," he said. "Only Americans can do that." The Cambodia crisis in May 1970 later undid much of what Nixon had achieved by that speech and by his efforts to display himself as the harbinger of peace. But the silent majority speech was, as David Broder of the *Washington Post* (no uncritical admirer of Nixon, certainly) put it, "a devastating use of television." Nixon's own speechwriter, Ray Price, went further. "Judging by results," Price wrote in *Broadcast* magazine, "it was the most effective use of TV that's ever been done. You had the massively accelerating peace movement. But after the speech, the balloon just fizzled."

The key to Nixon's use of television was the idea of control. Nixon had been burned by television. It had, he thought, lost him an election. He had also been saved by it. So he had learned how to turn the medium to his advantage. And he was surrounded by aides and advisers who had either worked as television executives or worked with television as advertising men. He did his best, therefore, to exclude from his use of television the faintest possibility of the unpredictable happening. He calculated the effect of television, and at first brilliantly. During his first three years and three months in office, the CBS network has computed, he made thirty-one special appearances in prime time, compared with twenty-four such appearances by President Johnson in five years and ten by President Kennedy in three years. By going on TV in prime time (between 7:00 P.M. and 11:00 P.M.), Nixon roughly doubled the size of his audience. By moving his press conferences to the evening, he gave them far greater exposure than Kennedy's intrinsically more exciting conferences had received.

During and after the 1972 campaign, Nixon changed his tactics sharply. Where before he had sought every opportunity of going on television, now he avoided it. He even switched to radio, a medium on which he felt he came over to better advantage. The reason was simple: he knew he was ahead and saw no reason to risk his lead.

All Presidents since Kennedy have found television an indispensable resource. They have used it to put their case across and to defend themselves when in trouble. They have learned to make the most of the special position they enjoy because in the United States the same man is both the ceremonial and the political leader. They can therefore not only count on deciding when and how to appear on television, they can count on being treated with deference when they do. Even Gerald Ford, perhaps the least telegenic of recent Presidents, learned to confine his appearances during the 1976 campaign to bland ceremonies in the White House Rose Garden, while Jimmy Carter appeared on the news every night under siege from one opponent or another. Ford's State of the Union message in 1975—hardly the most compelling viewing—was seen by 75 million people; when Democratic congressional leaders demanded equal time, three broadcasts they made on three different evenings were seen by a total of only 47 million.

There is evidence that presidential use of television to project a favorable image has worked. A study by Louis Harris, introduced as evidence before a 1970 congressional subcommittee, found that support for President Johnson's Vietnam policy rose by 30 percent after he had expounded it on television, and that support for Nixon's Vietnam policy similarly rose, though only by 18 percent. Again and again, when a President has gone on TV and spoken out in presidential terms about some danger threatening the Republic and set forth the actions he proposed to take to forestall it, his popularity as measured by the opinion polls has risen sharply—more sharply than he could make them rise by taking any other kind of action. The boost he received by taking a decisive posture was certainly enhanced by the fact that he could be seen doing so in tens of millions of living rooms.

Thus President Truman's rating rose by twelve points after he announced the Truman Doctrine and aid for Greece and Turkey, as did President Roosevelt's after he declared war on Japan. President Kennedy's stock rose by the same twelve-point margin after the Cuban missile crisis in 1962 and President Nixon's by 16 percent after he announced the Vietnam peace agreement in January 1973. President Ford's popularity rose from 40 percent to 51 percent after the *Mayagüez* incident in 1975, and President Carter's rating rose by the highest sudden jump ever recorded, seventeen percentage points from 39 percent to 56 percent, after his summit meeting with President Sadat of Egypt and Prime Minister Begin of Israel in September 1978. Television, more than any other single force, has nominated and elected modern Presidents (all except Gerald Ford), established their authority, and kept them in power.

2

Are Presidents grateful to television for the incomparable facilities it puts at their disposal? Do they turn with relief from the frustration of dealing with the bureaucracy and the Congress to their dealings with the media? Do Presidents love the media?

They do not.

Roosevelt got on well enough with reporters, though he could get angry with them. He pinned the Iron Cross of Prussia on John O'Donnell of the *New York Daily News* and told another reporter to wear a dunce's cap. But he believed to his dying day that the newspaper publishers as a group were out to get him. And he was not altogether wrong about that.

Harry Truman used to get furious with the newspapers and never felt at ease with radio or television.

Eisenhower never forgave the reporters for not treating him in the White House as they had treated him when he was Allied supreme commander and a national hero, and one protected by press officers with all the authority of military discipline to back them up. In private, he used military language about the press.

John Kennedy liked reporters. He found them good company, and newsmen like Charles Bartlett and Ben Bradlee were among his genuine intimates. He had even been a reporter himself briefly as a young man.

But none of that meant that Kennedy trusted the press or television. He assumed that publishers were hostile. He not infrequently called up individual reporters and bawled them out if he didn't like their stories. He canceled the White House's subscription to the *New York Herald Tribune*. At a New York dinner of the American Newspaper Publishers Association he harshly indicted the press for publishing information that the nation's enemies would "otherwise hire agents to acquire through theft, bribery or espionage." In return, the Kennedy administration was angrily criticized by publishers, working reporters, network executives, and television news professionals alike for practicing "news management." *The New York Times*'s Arthur Krock charged this was "enforced more cynically and boldly than by any previous administration in a period when the United States was not at war."

Assuredly, relations between the Kennedy administration and the media were not always sunny. But they were an idyll compared to relations between Lyndon Johnson and the media. And under Nixon, relations deteriorated dramatically.

Lyndon Johnson's experience of the media before he succeeded to the presidency was limited. In the Senate, he had manipulated a small group of specialist correspondents with great skill. But his television manner was as labored as Kennedy's was effortless. His appearance was unmistakably old-fashioned, his accent a stumbling block to many Northerners, and that included most network television executives and most of the elite of the Washington press corps. There were many influential people in the media who were frankly prejudiced against Lyndon Johnson. They thought him uncouth and felt he fell short of the standards of grace and elegance that John Kennedy had set for a new generation, their generation, and for an America come to maturity as a power and as a civilization. Lyndon Johnson sensed this. He suspected prejudice in the media, and so he exaggerated it. "I don't know whether we are far enough away from Appomattox," he told one columnist, "that a Southern President can really unite the people of this country, particularly against this big, Eastern intellectual press. They're trying to cut me up."

There was an element of paranoia in Johnson's attitude toward the media. But in the end, of course, the media did turn against him. And it is true that it was the "big, Eastern, intellectual press," *The New York Times* and the *Washington Post*, which became most critical of his policies. But the media's enthusiasm for Johnson's Democratic challengers might have been restrained had it been clear, as the opposition to Johnson and his policies surged in 1967 and 1968, that the eventual alternative would turn out to be Richard Nixon.

There is no getting away from the fact that, to large sections of the media, both in print and in television, Nixon had been a *bête noire* for years. The older Washington reporters, many of them sympathetic to the New Deal, had not liked the role he had played in the Hiss affair, and the fact that in the end it looked as though Nixon had been right on the substance of the case did not make them love Nixon any the more. Many of the younger Washington bureau chiefs, correspondents, and columnists were actively committed to Kennedy, and saw Nixon as the defeated rival of 1960 returned from the grave. At the best of times, Nixon lacked charm in his dealings with the press. He was not good at the background chat packed with calculated indiscretion, at the quotable quote or the relaxed wisecrack. He never felt at ease with reporters, and in his famous outburst after his defeat in California in 1962, he let his fear and his dislike of them show.

Still, neither network television executives in New York nor Washington correspondents got where they are by being quixotic or sentimental. Their job was to get on with those who had access to stories, which meant with those who had power. They were good at that. Moreover, while it is likely that a majority of the more influential people in the media in the late 1960s and the early 1970s thought of themselves as liberals, and disapproved of Nixon, in practice many of them had become quite conservative. Many had been upset by black protest and shocked by student demonstrations. Many were not unsympathetic to the Nixon administration's policies, even if it stuck in many of their throats to admit that they approved of Nixon. (This helps to explain the prodigious popularity of Henry Kissinger with the Washington media people. Kissinger did what Nixon wanted done, but he contrived to suggest that he disapproved of Nixon for wanting it. That went down well with those who hated Nixon, but who had no more sympathy than Nixon for a policy of withdrawal in Vietnam.) In short, Nixon could have had sympathetic treatment from the media, even from the "Eastern Establishment media" he feared and hated so much. The price would only have been a little tact, a little openness. It was too high a price for Richard Nixon to pay.

Nixon's resentments went too deep. He suspected even the *Los Angeles Times* of being hopelessly prejudiced against him, even though that newspaper had done more than almost any other single institution to make him a national figure since his early days in California. He surrounded himself with men like Patrick Buchanan and James Keogh, who believed in the reality of liberal conspiracy, and with men like H. R. Haldeman and John Mitchell, who saw the media as at best a resource to be manipulated in the President's interest.

There was a clash of genuine principle, too, best illustrated in the pivotal case of the Pentagon papers. It was the leak of the papers, after all, that led to the setting up of the plumbers unit, and so, rather directly, to catastrophe. In publishing the papers, *The New York Times*, and later other newspapers, exposed not the shortcomings of the Nixon administration but the follies and deceptions of their Democratic predecessors. Within the White House, one school of thought argued for leaving well enough alone. What harm could it do if the papers exposed the wickedness of the Democrats? Nixon swept such arguments away. Old-fashioned patriotism required that the government protect its own secrecy, whichever party was in office. (So, too, of course, did the interests of the Nixon administration, whose Vietnam policy fundamentally rested on doing one thing and saying another.)

Conversely, Nixon and most of those around him simply had no conception of the ethical imperative behind the media's perverse habit of raising awkward questions, its stubborn refusal to join the parade. The administration and the media were simply talking past one another, and increasingly each side came to suspect the other's motives. At what was supposed to be a friendly meeting with the Radio and Television News Directors Association, Vice President Spiro Agnew made a polite reference to Walter Cronkite's "well-known patriotism." Cronkite quickly put in that neither he nor anyone else in the room thought patriotism had anything to do with reporting the news. Agnew appeared not to understand what he meant, still less why it was so important to Cronkite to make the disclaimer.

Here, in fact, was a clash of two cultures. Ray Price, a moderate if there was one in the Nixon circle, put his feelings about the media into a long passage in his book, *With Nixon*. He related the cultural differences between the White House and the media to the split between the two hemispheres of the brain: the right half, which according to some physiologists and psychiatrists specializes in sensory and emotional perceptions and reactions, and the left side, which is said to be logical and analytical. Price makes a dozen charges against the media. They have too much power, and they use it irresponsibly. They pretend to a high-minded pursuit of truth "when they are really maneuvering to keep the facts from getting in the way of a good story." They are biased. They are self-righteous. Competitive pressures lead them to distort the news grossly, and to distort it always in the same direction, by overemphasizing crime and violence, doom and disaster. They are insular, and they all view the world through the same set of lenses. Paranoiac about criticism themselves, they wrongly see it as their duty to challenge government, when really their job is to challenge all aspects of the power structure, including themselves. They make a fetish of fashion, and they refuse to correct their own mistakes. But all these shortcomings are traceable to the fundamental temperamental, indeed physiological difference: the instincts of the media are those of the right hemisphere of the brain: emotional, artistic, romantic, not coldly logical like those of the men in business and government.

It would not be hard to challenge this thesis. The television networks, for example, are run by men in whom the artistic and romantic instincts are not always uppermost. There is a smattering of truth, at least, in several of Price's charges. The journalistic temperament, however, if there is such a thing, and the professional deformations that make journalists the way they are, are not likely to change any more than the characteristics of politicians and their speechwriters. What is to the point is that if one of the mildest and most tolerant of Nixon's intimates, and one who had himself been a professional newspaperman all his life, felt this way, then it takes little imagination to divine the caldron of fear, resentment, and even hatred that boiled underneath Nixon's own efforts to be civil and dignified with the media. The result was predictable. The volcano erupted. Nixon unleashed Agnew. As the President's surrogate, the Vice President (who felt about the same about the media anyway) made his repeated assaults on the "small group of men" who wielded "a concentration of power over American public opinion unknown to history."

Now it was the turn of the men and women who controlled the media to feel resentment—and fear. Their reaction was not a simple one. On the one hand, those few voices that acknowledged that there might be something in what the Vice President said about concentration and elitism were overwhelmed by the cries of protest and outrage, and by indignant invocations of the First Amendment and the dangers of censorship. More surreptitiously, however, there was a certain accommodation to the angry views expressed by Agnew and apparently shared by large numbers of citizens "out there." There was also a realistic appreciation of the federal government's power, especially over television, an appreciation deepened by one or two broad hints from the administration, as when Dean Burch, conservative Republican chairman of the Federal Communications Commission (FCC), pointedly demanded transcripts of network commentators' "instant analysis," as the White House called it, of a Nixon speech.

Faced with the evidence of the administration's hostility, reminded of its power, and uneasy about how many viewers and advertisers might share its anger, network executives and newspaper editors took added care to make sure that conservative viewpoints did not pass unrepresented. At the same time, the more radical attitudes thrown up by the late 1960s began to fade, like their champions, from the screen. Those who controlled policy at the networks, in the newsmagazines, even at *The New York Times*, in spite of what Nixon's people thought, were neither unredeemably prejudiced nor deeply radical. But after the Agnew episode they were deeply angry. And they were also a little afraid.

The stage was set for Watergate. It is important to avoid a whole crowd of mistakes about the meaning of that long-drawn-out and confused drama, It was not, as Nixon's sympathizers still sometimes try to maintain, the vengeance either of the Kennedy people, or of the liberals, or of the media. Nixon and his palace guard brought it on themselves. Nor was it a trial of strength between the President and the media. Only a small minority even of the Washington-based media played any part in bringing the administration's misdeeds to light: essentially, in the crucial early stages, only the *Washington Post,* with intermittent help from the *Los Angeles Times, The New York Times,* CBS, and a handful of individuals. Other components of the system, besides the media, "worked." James McCord, the honest Plumber, refused to be made a scapegoat. Judge Sirica did his duty. So did the prosecutors and the Congress and the higher courts. Perhaps the most crucial of all the functions performed by the media in Nixon's overthrow was the result of no conscious decision by any one person. That was the decision to carry the Ervin committee hearings live on the networks, so that the American people could see Nixon's people for themselves, could judge the quality of their fanatical devotion to their chief, and could hear for themselves that the President had taped all his own conversations in the Oval Office. Once that decision had been taken, there could be only one ending, and that took no conscious animus; once the hearings had started, once McCord had made his initial charge, the networks had no alternative but to cover them.

Still, having made all these qualifications, it is hard to resist the conclusion that if Richard Nixon had not been at daggers drawn with *The New York Times* and the *Washington Post* and the networks; if he had made even a moderate effort to be conciliatory with them; even—if you have to pinpoint a single moment in such a long campaign—if John Mitchell had restrained himself from screaming coarse threats to Mrs. Katharine Graham down the telephone when *Washington Post* reporter Carl Bernstein first called to check out whether the attorney general of the United States was controlling a secret, illegal fund for political dirty tricks; if, in short, Nixon had contrived to moderate the intensity of his administration's conflict with the media, then perhaps he would have got away with it and lasted out his second term.

If Cleopatra's nose had been shorter, said the French philosopher Blaise Pascal, the whole history of the world would have been different. Few modern historians agree. In the case of Watergate, personal factors may have affected the course of events. But the fact that there was conflict between the President and the media was not solely or even mainly due to personal factors. That conflict preceded Nixon, and has survived him, even if his successors conducted the conflict in more muted tones. The new presidency and the new media, which to a superficial view might have been natural allies, drifted inexorably into antagonism. The imperious temperament of Lyndon Johnson and Nixon's dark and brooding suspicions embittered that conflict and left scars on the collective memory of the media and of the American public. "The majesty and the awe have gone out of the presidency," said President Ford's press secretary, Ron Nessen. "This is the damage Nixon did. He made everybody cynical."

It would be hard to overestimate the damage Nixon did, and some part of the difficulty between Presidents and the media now and in the future must be put down to Watergate. But not all of it. All Presidents are likely to be frustrated in their dealings with the media. The aims, the values, the interests, and the duties of the two sides of the relationship are too different. Lacking other means of organizing support, unable to turn to the federal government, or to Congress, or to a strong, disciplined party for help, Presidents have little choice but to rely on the media, and especially on television, more than it is reasonable for them to do. The danger is that they put more weight on the bridge than it was meant to carry. There is a certain rough justice in their plight, however. It was the politicians who discovered what television could do for them. Now diminishing returns have set in. An increasingly bored and cynical electorate is no longer so easily activated by appeals from the corner of the living room. The power of the magic is wearing off.

3

The key idea that made possible the rise of the modern presidency was the proposition that the President, alone among all elected officeholders, is "President of all the people." Well, now he has competition. Television is the medium of all the people. One of the few things all Americans share together, from the north woods of Maine to San Diego, is television. Virtually 100 percent of the population has access to a television set. The average set is in use for more than seven hours a day, so Americans "watch" TV about as much as they sleep or work. The average American male, it is said, watches it for about nine full years of his life. It is *the* prime source not only of news, but of impressions, prejudices, information, attitudes, fashions, and values generally. Its influence has outstripped that of all competitors. Only perhaps that of the family now competes on roughly equal terms where the church, the school, and the political party have been left floundering far behind, and increasingly what American families do together is watch television.

Television is not completely uniform, of course. Even if we are thinking specifically about news and current affairs, people watch local programs as well as those on the network, and they do have access to a considerable variety of different points of view about local issues and local and state politics. Nevertheless, if we are talking about national and international events and issues, and those are the events and issues that concern the presidency, the great majority of Americans get their information about them from network programming. The differences between the content and emphasis of the three networks are not great. So, for all the infinite variety defenders of television programming can point to, where the presidency is concerned, most Americans get their news from a very narrow band of sources. One of the few things most Americans have in common is a standard set of ideas, images, and pieces of information, accurate in the main, as far as they go, but derived from a remarkably limited number of network news and current affairs shows.

This potent machine, like a cyclotron, directs a stream of highly charged particles into the brain of every man, woman, and child in America. It is ostensibly morally and politically neutral. (Some would say neuter.) It can be used to communicate the sublimest ideas and the most banal. The one constraint those who control it never forget is that they must never stray too far from the middle ground. If they do, ratings will fall, and advertising will move to the competition. A self-correcting gyroscopic mechanism built into every network executive's head will soon bring programming back on course.

Such a machine, able to project personality and policy alike instantaneously into every living room in the country, is every politician's heart's desire. And with this electronic Mephistopheles, Presidents have made a Faustian deal.

Mephistopheles really did give Dr. Faustus the powers he sought. And television has really armed Presidents with magic powers. The snag to the Faustian bargain lay in the dimension of time. The snag about presidential television is that both Presidents and viewers are in danger of becoming addicts. President Kennedy once graphically described the problem of addiction in a conversation with his friend, the historian Arthur Schlesinger. The President was talking about those who were urging him to send U.S. troops to Vietnam. The trouble was, he said, that the troops would march in, and the bands would play, and the crowds would cheer. But in about four days, everyone would have forgotten, and then he would be told he had to send in more troops. "It's like taking a drink," Kennedy added. "The effect wears off, and you have to take another."

There is a good deal of evidence that the effect of presidential television is wearing off. That is true whether the impact measured is that of Presidents as a whole, or that of an individual President, or merely that of a single appearance.

Any individual President must beware of overexposure. Television is a powerful magnifying glass. It shows a President to the people in bold relief. It also shows up every nick and pimple on his face, and ever tic and flaw of his character. Both Lyndon Johnson and Richard Nixon started out by achieving great successes on television. Johnson's first address to the joint session of Congress, five days after the Kennedy assassination, with its closing invocation of America the beautiful, from sea to shining sea, was powerfully moving for many who saw it. Nixon's silent majority speech perfectly caught a mood and tilted the balance of power in politics for a time. But both men were pitilessly exposed by television before they were through.

Emmet John Hughes, who worked for President Eisenhower in the White House, relates a conversation he had on this subject with news analyst Eric Sevareid. Hughes assumed that television was a deadly weapon in the White House's arsenal, but Sevareid questioned this. He suggested that television "not only exposes what a man wants to say, but it also exposes a man. It would seem," he concluded, "that there were some things about Lyndon Johnson and Richard Nixon that television made all too clear—and not to their advantage."

There is perhaps only one thing to be queried in that, and that is the implication that overexposure on television is only damaging where there is some exceptional character defect. Television concentrates the viewer's attention on a face so intimately that it always reveals the personality behind the face as it could never be exposed by still photographs, or the distant sight of a speaker on a platform, or a voice on the radio, or by even the most penetrating newspaper interview. Overexposure to television damaged Gerald Ford and Jimmy Carter, both seen by the American public as "good" men, just as much as it damaged two "tough" Presidents like Johnson and Nixon. Of course, different supposed weaknesses are exposed in different people. The more Richard Nixon tried to appear sincere, the more people suspected that he was merely being more cunningly tricky than ever. (They were not necessarily wrong.) The more Jimmy Carter, coached by his television advisers, attempted to project himself as tough and decisive, the more people wondered whether he was strong enough to be an effective President: only after his spontaneous outrage at the taking of U.S. hostages in Iran did he come across as strong without affectation.

There is another trap for Presidents. To appear strong and "presidential" they must go on television and describe some problem or crisis and then outline what they propose to do about it. To the viewers such appearances are ambiguous. They want strong leadership from the President. But they are also perfectly well aware—and citizens are more cynical about Presidents than they used to be—that the President hopes to improve his political position and his standing in the polls by his performance. So the President is bound to appear in a faintly hypocritical light. On the one hand he is apparently wringing his hands over the shortage of energy, or the capture of an American ship by an unfriendly power, or the presence of Soviet troops in Cuba, or whatever it may be. On the other hand the viewer knows that the President hopes to make political capital, if not out of the bad news, certainly out of his reaction to it. Such television appearances have yielded reliable dividends in the past. They are likely to yield diminishing returns in the future. Presidents have been going on television more and more frequently, eating up the most valuable political asset they have at an accelerated rate.

The impact of any individual television broadcast, too, wears off with time. "Four decades of Gallup Poll measurements of presidential popularity," writes George Gallup, summing up the shot-in-the-arm effect of presidential television speeches, "show that these sudden gains are rarely sustained over a long period of time." There is no shortage of examples to prove Gallup's point. Take Nixon: after the announcement of the Vietnam peace agreement in January 1973, his standing in the Gallup poll rose steeply, from 51 percent to 67 percent in a few days; but within three months, *before* presidential counsel John Dean broke with the White House and started singing, and *before* the televised Ervin committee hearings had put all the President's men on display, it had fallen to 54 percent. Take Gerald Ford: his rating rose from 40 percent approval in Gallup to 51 percent after the *Mayagüez* incident in 1975, but in three months it was down again to 45 percent. Take Jimmy Carter: in July 1978 his popularity languished at 39 percent. After Camp David, two months later, it had climbed to the relative security of 56 percent. Within weeks, as the snags in the agreement with Israel and Egypt began to appear, it drifted back to 50 percent, and there it rested for four months. By July 1979 it was as if Camp David had never been. The President's approval ratings stood in the middle 20s—a disaster level comparable only with those of Harry Truman in the doldrums of the Korean War and the Joseph McCarthy panic, and with that of Richard Nixon immediately before he resigned.

The dismal truth about presidential television is that Presidents have been doing it more and more, and the viewers have been enjoying it less. It is more than a decade since a President has been able to turn public opinion around on a significant domestic issue, the way Kennedy arguably did on racial desegregation, and Nixon certainly did when he gave tongue on behalf of the silent majority. The President, it seems, is an addict who needs a stronger and stronger fix at more and more frequent intervals to offset the havoc wrought on his popularity by the viewers' boredom, familiarity, natural erosion, and the frustration of trying to do something about increasingly intransigent political logjams. The viewers are not exactly addicted to presidential speeches preempting their favorite programs. But they, too, certainly need a stronger and stronger dose of political magic before they feel a buzz.

The appeal of presidential television as a whole is wearing off, along with its novelty. In the early 1960s, journalism was exciting. Americans were fascinated by the unfolding epic of their society. With John Kennedy in the White House, much of that excitement was focused on Washington, the Kennedy family, the New Frontier, and the presidency.

There was an increase in straight news coverage. The reasons why the networks went to a half hour, instead of a quarter of an hour, for their nightly news programs, have more to do with the networks' desire to capture advertising spots from their affiliate stations than with any passion for news. But once the change was made—CBS just pipped NBC to the post in September 1963—the longer news focused more attention on just those national and international issues that are the concern of the presidency. For a rather brief period, too, there was an upsurge in documentary coverage both of the presidency and of those same "presidential" issues: war and peace, nuclear weapons, the gathering storm in Southeast Asia, the civil rights revolution in the South, and the intensifying rhythm of conflict and protest of every kind in American cities. Later, people were to say that TV helped create the mood of crisis of the late 1960s, and in a sense that was true. What is beyond argument is that television, whether it was routinely reporting the news, or putting on spectaculars like the increasingly elaborate coverage of the party conventions, or making graphic the problems only the President could cope with, always concentrated national attention on the man in the White House.

After Nixon, there was less enthusiasm for the presidency as a national spectator sport and perhaps less faith in the presidency as a symbolic representation of the nation and its best aspirations. That remains to be seen. Certainly Americans sat with their eyes glued to the screen while the great Watergate whodunit unwound. That was a kind of catharsis. Afterward, people did not seem to be able to summon up the old innocent fascination.

It is exceptionally hard to distinguish between trends in public opinion and decisions by television networks—most often made in obscure private memos or at meetings by anonymous executives. But there are signs that, quite apart from a slackening of public interest in politics generally and the presidency in particular, there is a new fashion in the Manhattan towers where television policy is decided. Where the presidency is concerned, it seems, eyes in the executive suite are beginning to glaze over. For a long time, network programming executives have been increasingly annoyed by presidential requests to preempt prime time. The more the cost of a spot on network prime time rises, the more painful it is for the networks to pull out a show and put the President on instead. The same goes for political programming generally, except in the rare instance—like the Ervin hearings—where politics become compelling drama, and the networks would make themselves unpopular by not letting the action run. There was one straw in the wind during the 1976 campaign. CBS and NBC covered the Democratic Convention in New York and the Republican Convention in Kansas City gavel to gavel in the usual way. ABC, then in the process of overtaking the other two networks to emerge as number one in the ratings, deliberately cut back political coverage in favor of the Montreal Olympics. In television terms, the decision was right.

Television does not exist to report the news. It does so, on the whole, as well—if not better—than it is reported anywhere else. But that is not the function of the television industry. Its function, and those who control it are very, very well aware of it, is to make profits—if possible, more profits this year than last year, and more next year than this. In order to maximize profits, those responsible for the programming policy of television—at the affiliate level as much or more than in the networks—must maximize advertising revenue. That in turn means that they must maximize their audience. That is their main motivation. *Incidentally,* they also report the news. The power television has acquired over the way Americans perceive their President remains quite incidental to the primary purposes and preoccupations of those who control television.

A distinction must be drawn between two policies. One seeks to make an adequate profit to reward the stockholders for their initial investment and to provide for modernization of plant and equipment, a policy that would allow a television organization to aim at a good audience, but less than the biggest possible audience, all of the time. The other aims at *maximizing* profit. That implies that every element in the programming must be aimed consciously at all times at the largest possible slice of the market, and therefore—television executives' perceptions of the tastes of their audience being what they are—at the lowest end of the market. Sometime in the late 1950s, the networks became too profit-oriented, too big, too corporate, for it to be conceivable for them to aim at anything less than maximum ratings. Once that was so, it was only a matter of time before that goal came into conflict with the ideal of the fullest and fairest possible coverage of news. And once corporate goals and journalistic ideals did come into conflict, it was a foregone conclusion which would win.

Historians of U.S. television agree that the conflict was decided, once and for all, in the middle of the 1950s. The decisive episode came in 1955, to be precise, when William Paley, the founder and despot of CBS, with the help of his sidekick Frank Stanton, "the Statesman of Broadcasting," decided to throw Edward R. Murrow overboard. Until then it was possible to believe that the great tradition of reporting, which had after all just come through one of its epic periods in World War II, and not least, to be fair, at CBS, would be allowed to remain the flagship of broadcasting, with all the various forms of entertainment following in its wake. By the middle 1950s, squeezed between the temptations of profit and the fear of political repercussions, Paley, Stanton, and their opposite numbers at NBC decided otherwise. Corporate profit and corporate expansion must come first. News remained vital, not least because of the federal government's residual regulatory power. News would convince the FCC that CBS and NBC and ABC deserved their monopoly. But it would not be the primary function of the broadcasting industry.

If that decision of twenty-five years ago was historically final, it has to be said straightaway that its effects were concealed for a very long time by a whole chain of circumstances. The first of them was ironic. Ed Murrow's classic current affairs show, *See It Now*, was doomed by the prodigious success of quiz shows. Only a year after the decision to downgrade Murrow (he lingered on until John Kennedy made him director of the United States Information Agency), the great quiz show scandal broke out. There was panic in the boardrooms of the networks. For a while it looked as though the Eisenhower administration might clip the networks' wings. The industry panicked and went into one of its periodic fits of morality. It cleaned up the quiz shows, of course. But the main thrust of its purity drive was a sudden decision to enhance news departments. Television responded to the excitement of the New Frontier and a new, glamorous First Family. But the reason why television was poised to discover the entertainment value of politics was that the need to bury the unfortunate aroma of the quiz show scandal dictated a new emphasis on news.

Throughout the 1960s, news generated its own momentum. The upbeat rhythm of the Kennedy years and of Lyndon Johnson's early triumphs gave way to the equally compelling beat of the Big Muddy blues. (That was what the GIs called Vietnam: the Big Muddy.) Until well into the Nixon years, because of national preoccupation with the war and with various different forms of domestic protest, presidential politics retained some of their show business appeal. (Faced with a President who just did not have that certain something, the media elevated his national security assistant in his stead as one of the most unlikely superstars of all time.) From 1968 on, public interest in the national political drama was beginning to wane. By the middle of the 1970s, it was fading as fast as a tropical sunset. People were yearly more and more interested in social, as opposed to political, questions, and in personal and private, as opposed to public and political, solutions. After Watergate, confidence in politicians generally slumped to a level that wiped out all that had been achieved by the imperial presidency and the imperial Congress in the forty years since the New Deal. Publishers and newspaper editors and television executives could see what was happening. Indeed, they experienced the same disillusionment in themselves. So they gave the public, as they must always do, more of what it wanted. A slow, relentless declining spiral set in. Diminished media coverage led to lower public interest, and lower public interest to still more unenthusiastic coverage.

It is always dangerous to extrapolate from long cycles. The danger is that you draw a tangent to the curve and project a trend to infinity just as it is about to be reversed. Perhaps public interest and media interest in politics are about to revive. Perhaps a hard-fought, close-run campaign in 1980 will wake up the audience. Perhaps a new President will bring back the magic of Camelot. I think not. My own hunch is that the presidency will never again be at the center of the national consciousness in quite the way it was between 1933 and 1973.

There is, in any case, a shorter cycle at work. The presidential biorhythm is intimately connected with a cycle in the White House's relations with the media. George Reedy, since he served Lyndon Johnson as press secretary and so knows whereof he speaks, points out that since the purposes and interests of the media are ultimately different from those of the President, the President cannot in the long run win them over to do his work for him. Inevitably, therefore, the media have come to be seen by the President as the enemy. He vents his spleen on the press, and on television, says Reedy, "never realizing that what he is really doing is venting his spleen against the whole intractable environment that surrounds him."

Two political scientists, Michael Baruch Grossman and Martha Joynt Kumar, have developed this insight into a whole theory of the relations between the media and the President. No President, they argue, is so successful that he can do without the media; influencing the media is a high priority in everything the White House does. On the other hand, no major news organization can cover the presidency without at least a minimum of cooperation from the President and his White House staff.

When a new President arrives in the White House, the interests of his incoming administration and those of the news media accidentally coincide. The media want to portray him and his family and staff to the country. Personality is good copy for newspapers, and it is the very life of television. So in the first phase the administration and the media are allied. But after a few months, the media are in need of new stories. News must be new. Reporters go hunting for conflict, either between the President and his opponents, in Congress and elsewhere, or among the President's own advisers. In self-defense the administration begins to manage the news. It tries to influence reporters by going over their heads to publishers and executives, to reward some reporters and punish others. It begins to draw up "enemies lists." Eventually, it castigates the media as a whole. The news media and the White House, in this second phase, are in competition.

Yet the two parties to the quarrel still need one another. The President still needs the media to put his case across to the wider public and even to transmit signals within the government in Washington. The media cannot ignore the President and the federal government altogether. So the level of conflict that might be caused by the tactics both sides use is never quite reached. The media lose interest in the President and cover him more and more perfunctorily. The President, despairing of justice at their hands, delegates his relations with the press more and more. He tries to see and be seen by the media only in carefully structured situations. A phase of detachment follows the phase of competition.

This is what happened with Lyndon Johnson. It would have happened with Richard Nixon, had not a fourth phase, the hunt to the death, supervened. There are signs that a similar cycle has been followed, in muted tones, in the relations between Jimmy Carter and the media. "The Washington press corps and the Carter White House," reported Dom Bonafede in his weekly column on the presidency in the *National Journal* in early August 1979, "appear to have settled upon a tenuous armistice. This is not unusual for a President two-thirds into his first term, low in the polls, and about to ask for a renewal of his lease at the White House with hat in hand."

Is the Faustian bargain nearing the dramatic moment when the electronic Mephistopheles will materialize in a puff of smoke and demand the President's soul? Things will not happen so suddenly. But Presidents, having allowed the party organizations to rust away, now find it harder and harder to use the media as a substitute. Presidents are in the predicament of the little boy who cried wolf. They have devalued the language of emergency and crisis, invocation and appeal. The signs are that fewer and fewer people are listening.

Presidents still attract the fascinated attention of an influential section of the printed press, and it is very likely that some future Presidents will do so more than Ford and Carter have been able to. They still enjoy a preferential access to the television screen and the power to command the media's attention. Dramatic events like those in Iran and Afghanistan can put the President back in the spotlight for a time. But the media's interest in the presidency seems increasingly tinged with cynicism. The public seems increasingly skeptical and indifferent. A cycle of diminishing returns seems under way, perhaps irreversibly so. The President's isolation is noticeably greater, his voice fainter. The modern presidency has come to depend too heavily on the media. It is not clear that the media can save it.

VII President and People

The truth is that in the presidential office . . . American democracy has revived the oldest political institution of the race, the elective kingship.

—Henry Jones Ford, *The Rise and Growth of American Politics*, 1898

What a party wants is not a good president but a good candidate. The party managers have therefore to look out for the person likely to gain most support and at the same time excite least opposition.

—James Bryce, *The American Commonwealth*, 1888

1

ONCE THEY are in the White House, Presidents have become more and more isolated from the people at the same time as they have been plunged deeper and more intimately into contact with the people on the way there. Government, Congress, party, media: each of these institutions which once connected the President to the people, and provided him with the effective power he needed to respond to the people's wants, either has been weakened or has passed beyond the President's power to control it. Only one element of the system has brought Presidents literally into closer contact with the people over the past twenty years: the nominating and electoral process. In the White House, the President looks more and more like a prisoner. Only in his past, when he was a candidate for election, and in the future, when he will be a candidate for reelection, does he look like the people's hero and the people's choice.

It is sometimes said that what has been happening is that the United States has been moving in the direction of what is called a "plebiscitary democracy." Arthur Schlesinger, for example, has written that "Nixon was moving toward . . . a plebiscitary presidency. His model lay . . . in the France of Louis Napoleon and Charles de Gaulle." In reality, it seems to me, the presidency has been evolving in a more complex way. On the one hand, as cabinet, Congress, and party have atrophied as the intermediary institutions that kept the presidency in democratic contact with the people, the President has come to be linked with the people to an increasing extent by electoral politics alone. But to speak of a plebiscitary presidency suggests that the President is an autocrat for four years whose power is checked only when election time comes around again and he is forced to renew his mandate.

It is not like that at all. For one thing, the President's power is constantly checked, by Congress, by the "iron triangles" within his own government, by the media, and by special-interest groups of all kinds; in extreme cases, like those of Watergate or Truman's seizure of the steel mills in 1952, it is also checked by the courts. Whatever he may be abroad, at home the President of the United States is no autocrat. And his mandate is not only granted by an election every four years. The presidential election now lasts virtually for four years. It is always election year in Washington, and the President has become a perpetual candidate. His power is not now ratified or legitimized by institutional support. It is measured by his political credibility. That in turn is a function of how he is thought to be doing at any given moment in this perpetual campaign.

It was not for nothing that Lyndon Johnson used to carry the latest poll result in his back pocket, ready to cite it, selectively and tendentiously if necessary, to every visitor. The public opinion poll has become more than a mere measuring rod for judging how well a President is doing. In a sense, it has become the key device of the late modern presidency, the gadget that makes it possible for the political system of an unimaginably complex nation of 220 million inhabitants to operate as if it were the "direct democracy" of an ancient Hellenic city-state.

A sort of perpetual election is conducted through the polls. In this way, popular acclaim is offered or withheld as if by the tumultuous assembly of the citizens in the marketplace. The President's effective power is very much a function of his standing in the polls. How characteristic of contemporary American arrangements, too, that such a vital part of the political process should be, in effect, subcontracted to an oligopoly of entrepreneurs, Gallup, Harris, Field, and the rest.

For all the immense power the polls have acquired, and it is only fair to say that one reason why they have acquired it is because they have on the whole proved so reliable, they are only one of the outward and visible signs of an inner, more fundamental reality. The President's effective power is derived not from the mandate of the last election but from the political resources he has been able to accumulate by trading in the Washington market. The currency is his all-important standing, as measured by his fellow traders and the media whose job it is to keep track of it. The perpetual election campaign is, more and more, the reality of the presidency.

The distinction between being a President and being a presidential candidate has been progressively rubbed away. The presidential election campaign is no longer simply the way a President is chosen. It has come to influence the kind of man who is chosen, the men and women he surrounds himself with in the White House, their priorities as they look out at the world from there, and their whole style of operating.

The presidential election itself, in the narrow sense of the final contest between the Democratic and Republican candidates, has changed relatively little in fifty years. Candidates travel by air now, instead of whistle-stopping by train, and so they and the reporters who travel with them are even more cut off from the reality of the country than they were. They rely even more than they did on the media and have perhaps become more skilled at manipulating them. Among the media, television—both in its reporting function and as a medium for paid advertising—has become dominant. That in turn made presidential campaigns prohibitively more expensive, with the result that sweeping legislation to reform campaign finance was passed in the 1970s. Parties as such count for far less than they did, and the modern presidential candidate is less the nominee of a party with continuing existence than he is a political adventurer who has picked up the flag of a party rather as an ambitious soldier of fortune in fourteenth-century Lombardy might have dressed his soldiers in the colors of Guelf or Ghibelline. There have been changes. But in substance the contest between Gerald Ford and Jimmy Carter between Labor Day and Election Day in 1976 was waged in a recognizably similar way to the way Herbert Hoover and Al Smith campaigned in 1928, or even to the way William McKinley and William Jennings Bryan campaigned in 1900. What has changed beyond recognition is the process whereby a man becomes the party's candidate. The key changes in the nominating system have happened in the last twenty years.

Two changes have been especially important. Between them they have had an effect on the presidency as an institution that is still little appreciated. Each was originally the product of indignation at what was seen as the anachronistic and undemocratic influence over the presidential succession wielded by those who were variously denounced as "power brokers," "bosses," and "old pols."

This rebellion against established party leadership has a long history and interesting precedents. Americans have always been suspicious of party politics and inclined to be contemptuous of party politicians. It is an attitude that was justly criticized by the late Philip L. Graham, publisher of the *Washington Post:* it was fantastic, Graham said, to "treat our politicians as unsavory characters while we charge them with preserving our civilization." Historically, moral fastidiousness about party politics has often been mixed up with class disdain toward party politicians, as it was with late-nineteenth-century civil service reformers and early-twentieth-century Progressives.

A new wave of reform, in which educated upper-middle-class heirs to this tradition played a prominent part, was touched off by what many saw as the scandalous process of manipulation by which Hubert Humphrey won the Democratic nomination in 1968. Neoconservatives now interpret the reform movement almost entirely in class terms, which in my opinion undervalues the genuine moral indignation of the reformers, about the war and other issues. Be that as it may, the excesses of the 1968 Chicago Democratic Convention under the auspices of Mayor Richard Daley led directly to the reform of the Democratic party's rules and so to the eclipse of the party's traditional leadership, symbolized with a certain historical justice by the unseating of his honor the mayor at Miami Beach in 1972.

For broadly analogous reasons of their own, and in their characteristically quieter fashion, the Republicans adopted similar reforms. The new ideological conservatives in the Republican ranks were just as suspicious of the compromising instincts of professional politicians as the Democratic Left, just as intent on breaking their power. Rebellion against party politics was in the air. Whatever their origins or the intentions of those who pushed them through, the effects of these changes in the rules for the nominating conventions on the whole electoral process have been far-reaching. Some of their champions believed they were strengthening, by purifying, the party structure. Most observers think that would be a desirable direction for the political system to move. But the actual effect has been the opposite. So far from making the party more "responsible," the rules changes have strengthened the candidate and his personal following at the expense of all other elements in the party. They have made the campaign more candidate-oriented, and less oriented to party loyalty, ideology, or substantive issues. The power of the party leaders has been all but broken. The congressional party has been all but excluded from the nominating process. The party no longer recruits the candidate. The candidate recruits, or perhaps it would be even more accurate to say captures, the party.

The other great change is in the part played by the primaries. Primary elections were an innovation of the Progressive movement in the early years of the twentieth century, and by the 1950s they were passing into disfavor. Harvard professor V. O. Key wrote in 1952 that their principal effect was to kill off candidates, and Adlai Stevenson II, the Democratic candidate in 1952 and 1956, thought they were "more likely to destroy good candidates than to make them." The plain truth, Stevenson said, was that a primary campaign was not "a suitable testing ground for presidential candidates." Harry Truman simply dismissed them as "eyewash."

There may have been a good deal in what these great men said. But John F. Kennedy did not agree. The rise of the primary to its modern dominance dates from Kennedy's decision to take "the primary route" in 1960. It is often forgotten, though, that Kennedy entered only seven of the eighteen primaries of that year, and in only two of them, in Wisconsin and West Virginia, did he have serious competition. The media, however, found the primaries an exciting and glamorous story to cover, even when, as in New Hampshire, Kennedy had a virtual walkover. It was the intense media coverage of the far more exciting primary contests of 1968 that set off the recent increase in the number of states that hold primaries. There were eighteen primaries in 1960, nineteen in 1964, only seventeen in 1968. Then the number began to grow: twenty-three in 1972, thirty in 1976.

The result is that primaries are now decisive in choosing the candidate. In 1960, only some 40 percent of the delegates who nominated John Kennedy were chosen in primaries. In 1968, it was possible for Hubert Humphrey, who actually ran eighth in the number of votes he won in primaries, with only 2.2 percent of votes cast, to sew up the nomination nonetheless. But by 1976 more than three-quarters of the delegates at the Democratic Convention, and more than two-thirds of those at the Republican

Convention, were chosen in primaries; Jimmy Carter owed his nomination by the Democrats almost entirely to his success in the primaries.

The primaries have become decisive in another way, too. Between 1936 and 1968, it has been computed, the primaries never once eliminated a candidate who before them was likely to win, nor did they ever lead to the nomination of a candidate who was not likely to win. That all changed in 1972. In that year the primaries eliminated Senator Edmund Muskie, the front-runner before the primary season began, and led to the nomination of Senator George McGovern, an outsider when the first primary was held.

The basic reason for the proliferation of primaries was a general perception that it was more "democratic" to choose a candidate in that way. This perception is in itself a product of the decay of party in the United States. It does indeed sound more democratic for "the people" to vote for their candidate, rather than for the decision to be taken by "a handful of party leaders." Put like that, there is no argument. But there are other ways of putting the alternatives. What if the decision were taken in a regular and constitutional fashion by party members? If parties were alive and well in the United States, it might now be argued, as it is vigorously being argued in the early 1980s in the British Labour party, for example, that the privilege of choosing the party leader ought not to be handed to the lukewarm masses who take no interest in politics between elections, but should belong to the party faithful who have proven their dedication to the party's principles and program by long years of work. European political parties, of the Left and of the Right, take the duties of membership more seriously than U.S. parties do. It is revealing that members of French and Italian parties, for example, are called "militants." No European party allows the population at large a voice in the choice of the leader. Each, on the contrary, takes that decision in a highly structured way, according to rules carefully laid down, and certainly not in a smoke-filled room. But the argument that choosing the party leader belongs to the party's members is not likely to succeed in the United States, which has neither membership parties nor parties of ideology, and where consequently there are neither party faithful, in the European sense and in the sense in which such paragons once existed in the United States, nor any but the vaguest party principles for them to be loyal to.

The spread of the primary has shifted the point of decision further back: to the process that decides who is likely to emerge from the primaries as the winner. The people, after all, cannot vote for a candidate who is not running. Nor are they likely to vote for a candidate they have never heard of. The first decision is largely taken by the polls, and therefore in the last analysis by the media, for it is from the media that Dr. Gallup and his competitors get lists of candidates to ask their samples about. It is the media, again, that decide which candidates will do well in the polls. In short, the primary process is almost as prone to manipulation as the caucus system: but it can be manipulated by different forces and on behalf of different types of candidates. These may or may not be more desirable on balance than the old system, which numbered both Abraham Lincoln and Warren Gamaliel Harding among its products, but they will be different.

The qualities that make a man a successful candidate over the obstacle course of the primaries are not the same as those that make a successful President. One glaring example results from the American people's curious prejudice against their own government. Jimmy Carter is not the first presidential candidate to try to get to Washington largely by campaigning against Washington. George Wallace and Ronald Reagan have both brought this perverse practice to a fine art, and both Richard Nixon and Robert Kennedy used the technique in 1968. Nixon, who was so intent on monopolizing power in the White House, which is after all located in Washington, that he was actually forced to resign as a result, nevertheless used to fulminate against "the trend to sweep more and more authority to Washington." What was unprecedented about Carter was his lack of knowledge and experience of Washington and of the national and international affairs that are dealt with there. But Carter may have set a new precedent for others. In the last fifty years, most presidential candidates—General Eisenhower and Wall Streeter Wendell Willkie are obvious exceptions—have been either Vice Presidents, governors, usually of major states, or senators. In the future, the primary route may produce candidates with few legislative skills, little experience of government, and nothing but contempt for the way the system has worked in the past. They may be excellent candidates. They are not likely to be effective Presidents.

The primaries give a notable advantage to relatively young men. The brutal months of curtailed sleep, indigestible food, and general dizzying whirl tend to eliminate older men who might be capable of formidable stamina if they could reach the more ordered world of the White House. Even since the introduction of public finance, the primaries favor, in the crucial early stages, men who are either personally wealthy or financed by wealthy groups of backers. They put a premium on charm of a kind that is of little help in steering a bill through Congress or negotiating with the Soviet Union.

In general, the primary system tends to favor consensual candidates with centrist positions. There is a mathematical reason for this. Mathematicians call it "the paradox of voting." It was known to the Marquis de Condorcet in eighteenth-century France, in spite of there being few opportunities for studying voting behavior under the *ancien régime*. It was also pointed out by Lewis Carroll, whose real name was Charles Dodgson, and who was a professional mathematician when he wasn't taking photographs of little girls or writing *Alice's Adventures in Wonderland*. He stumbled across it when trying to reform the voting procedures for university committees in Victorian Oxford. In recent years it has been restated by the Harvard economist Kenneth Arrow:

> Let A, B and C be the three alternatives, and 1, 2, and 3 the three individuals. Suppose individual 1 prefers A to B and B to C (and therefore A to C), individual 2 prefers B to C and C to A (and therefore B to A), and individual 3 prefers C to A and A to B (and therefore C to B). Then a majority prefer A to B, and a majority prefer B to C. We may therefore say that the community prefers A to B and B to C. . . . We are forced to say that A is preferred to C. But in fact a majority of the community prefer C to A.

In other words, as a matter of mathematical fact, there is no absolutely clear and infallible way of making a democratic choice between more than two candidates. In the final stage of a presidential election, there are only two candidates. In the primaries there are always more. In any individual primary there may be anywhere from three to six or more candidates. If the number of potential candidates who polled more than 1 percent support on the Gallup poll is taken as a convenient outer limit of the available candidates, the number rose in 1972 as high as seventeen in the Democratic race and often has been as high as a dozen. Before any candidate can win a victory in a primary, the voters must have made sophisticated choices that may involve voting for a candidate not because he is their first choice but because he is seen as the most likely winner or as the lesser of two evils as compared with some other candidate. The same realities underlie the process at the convention, where the winner's majority is necessarily made up of votes from delegates for whom the "next President of the United States" was the first choice and of others from delegates who in their heart of hearts would have preferred someone else.

The nominating process is therefore an inherently ambiguous way of choosing among the number of candidates normally on offer. It tends to favor candidates who arouse no strong antipathies. There have been real exceptions to this rule, though not as many as might at first appear. Several of the far-from-bland modern Presidents, such as Theodore Roosevelt, Harry Truman, and Lyndon Johnson, succeeded from the vice presidency and might well never have become President by the route of election in their own right. There have been apparent exceptions like Barry Goldwater and George McGovern, ideological "extremists" thrown up by the mechanism of the nominating campaign, which means obtaining not a majority of the electorate but a majority of a rough half of the electorate. Even the strongest of modern Presidents, Franklin Roosevelt, may have been only an apparent exception to the system's tendency to favor the bland. For one thing, he was perceived as far more centrist in the campaign than he was to prove in the White House. And the situation was so exceptional that voters may have been a little less willing to settle for the safe compromise than in calmer times.

The genius of the system makes the mathematical paradox irrelevant by saving the voters from the necessity of making choices between clear-cut alternatives. The politicians, says columnist Garry Wills, "labor long and well, and successfully . . . to sound much the same as each other." The dynamics of elections drive the politicians to concentrate on the center and to tell the biggest groups of voters what they already believe to be true.

The way the nominating system has developed in the last few years may have accentuated the temptation for candidates to try to be as smooth and unexceptionable as possible. Television flatters the cool personality, with no strong passions and at most a quiet charm, with perhaps a dash of wry self-deprecation. Sophisticated issue-polling, instantly analyzed by computers, enables today's candidates to tell the voters what they want to hear with improved precision.

The process requires skills of a high order, in the candidate and in his followers (or handlers). They are not necessarily, however, the skills that are most valuable in government. Nor does the modern campaign call for any exceptional endowment in the candidate of those qualities that are most essential to leadership in the White House: intellectual honesty, administrative decisiveness, and political courage.

So long as the convention holds that presidential candidates are recruited from Vice Presidents, senators, governors, and senior congressmen, the candidate himself will always have some experience of the national government, or some experience as an executive, though rarely both. But the workings of the system offer no guarantee that his key staff will have any experience of any kind that is relevant to running the government. "Typically," David Broder has written, "these are young people with few obligations and limited experience who will gamble for a chance on a ticket to the White House. . . .

> Most candidates will do as Carter did [Broder went on] and take his campaign staff to the White House with them. And they will find . . . that those aides are people who are more adept at, and more interested in, running the campaigns than they are in running a government.

Some of them, indeed, convey a distinct impression that they regard government as a tedious distraction from the real man's work of the campaign. Jimmy Carter's former speechwriter, James Fallows, tells a relevant anecdote: "Flying back on Air Force One shortly before I left, I heard one of the Georgians say to several others, 'You know, there really ought to be a place for people like us between elections, where we could rest up and get ready for the next one.' " There is. It is called the White House.

The problem goes deeper. It is not just that the President's men are chosen for their services in the campaign and show little relish for the dull business of governing. Because the key jobs go to the heroes of the campaign, the White House remains a campaign headquarters for four more years. "The presidential party at the center," wrote James MacGregor Burns fifteen years ago, "is a highly centralized and disciplined political organization. Political decisions are made on the basis of one criterion: what is best for the political standing, prestige, reputation and re-electibility of the *President.*" Power in such a system comes from proximity to the President; the most powerful man commonly has the office physically next door to the President's. Usefulness is measured in terms of personal service to the President. Everything is seen in terms of whether or not it helps the President in his unending campaign, as if he were still on his way into Concord, New Hampshire, on a wing and a poll. "It really does prove to be damned difficult to do anything about energy, for example, or the reform of the government," one of Carter's more thoughtful aides said to me. "You can only talk in terms of solutions that can have an effect within two years."

An absurd example comes from the Nixon White House. The President read the crime statistics over a weekend at Camp David. On the Monday, he told John Ehrlichman that "this must stop." Ehrlichman told one of his staff, Norm McCullough, that something had to happen or the President was going to want a pretty good explanation: "the full resources of the federal government were going to be made available." Poor McCullough! Even with "the full resources of the federal government" to strengthen his arm, he failed to stop crime.

For most Presidents, the campaign that took them into the White House was the most exciting experience of their life. Not unnaturally, they want to make it last. On the night of his nomination in New York in July 1976, Jimmy Carter went down to talk to his own Georgia delegates and told them how he felt about the campaign that had just ended. "The strength of our political effort," he said,

> has been the closeness between me personally and voters around the country. Women in the shoe factories and textile mills. And men driving trucks and making electronic equipment and working on farms and cutting hair and waitresses in restaurants. To a substantial degree they felt they could have confidence in me and that I was close to them. And there wasn't any powerful political figure that stood between them and possibly the next President. And I'll never shake that intensely personal relationship, because I want to be damn sure that when I am in the White House the American people feel: that's my President.

That speech reads a little sadly now. In the White House, Jimmy Carter has tried to keep the "intensely personal relationship" that he felt he enjoyed with the voters during the campaign. Sometimes he has laid aside the text that his speechwriters had carefully written for him and reverted to the speech he gave more than two thousand times in the campaign. At some of the tensest moments of his presidency—for example, just before his energy speech on July 15, 1979, he has dropped in on "just folks" to try to recapture the magic communication of the campaign. It has not worked. The magic, if magic there ever was, rather than curiosity and the yearning for change, has gone. More and more, it seems, the distinction between presidential candidate and President is being washed away. More and more, Presidents are likely to come on like candidates. But it is not clear that this is what the people want.

In the most literal sense, it is true that Presidents are candidates for reelection for an increasing proportion of their time in the White House. In the thirty-five years since Franklin Roosevelt died, the White House has been occupied by a second-term President, free from worries about reelection, for a little more than five and a half years. For the first four of those, Eisenhower's health was so precarious that the possibility of a succession crisis was never far from anyone's mind in Washington. And for most of his remaining eighteen months, Richard Nixon was troubled by equally severe anxieties of a different kind. Typically, the President is in his first term and would like to be elected for a second. Typically, the President *is* a candidate.

And the campaign has been starting earlier and earlier. On July 31, 1979, the *Washington Post* announced that "President Carter has begun to campaign for reelection." That was after thirty months in the White House. The press had routinely treated the President as a campaigner long before that. In March 1979 the *Atlantic Monthly*, an august Boston journal no one could accuse of belonging to the incestuous world of Washington journalism, introduced an article on "Jimmy Carter's strategy for 1980" with the words: "He's running already, of course, for renomination and reelection." On January 31, 1979, the *Washington Post*'s David Broder pronounced that the budget Carter had just sent to the Hill was "aimed at winning the 1980 election." "Although it is still unofficial, undeclared and even unacknowledged," wrote the *New York Times* White House correspondent, Terence Smith, less than a month later, "Jimmy Carter's campaign for a second term got underway last week." Strategy for the campaign, Smith reported, had been laid out in a confidential memorandum by Hamilton Jordan; and Smith even added that Robert Strauss, former Democratic national chairman, was one of those who had chided the President for not starting to campaign still earlier. Some of his aides undoubtedly agreed with that opinion. One of them told Elizabeth Drew of *The New Yorker* early in 1978—when the President had almost three years of his term ahead of him—that "the President is going to be running for reelection" in the 1978 congressional elections.

That remark may have reflected the persisting delusion that a President can improve his political position by campaigning so effectively for congenial candidates in the midterm elections that he improves the complexion of Congress and finds it easier to pass his legislation. As we have seen, it never works. More likely the aide Drew quoted was simply recognizing the reality of the contemporary presidency. Lyndon Johnson was being overly sanguine when he told his aide Harry McPherson that "you've got one year." Or rather, Johnson was thinking in terms of a President's chances of passing his legislation through Congress. The truth is that a President nowadays must be campaigning for reelection from the moment he first walks into the Oval Office, looks around, and decides how he wants the furniture arranged: 1980 began in 1977, and 1984 will begin in January 1981.

A modern President is like a man who inherits a house with two mortgages on it. There are payments due because of the commitments he made in order to be elected. And there are payments to be kept up if he is to be reelected.

The payments due from the last election are the lighter. But they are not entirely negligible. Carter may say he owes the special interests nothing, but it is still true that he supported a cargo preference bill because the maritime unions had been big contributors to his campaign. He pushed for and got a separate Department of Education because he pledged to do so in order to win the support of the National Education Association.

All Presidents make campaign promises. Few, if any, keep them all. This may be a good thing, of course. Whether a President thinks it more virtuous to keep a campaign promise than to break it depends essentially on his judgment on the subject of the particular promise. No doubt it would be better if candidates did not make promises. No doubt it would be better if mankind had been born virtuous. Nixon, for example, made a number of commitments to the Southern Republicans in order to detach them from Ronald Reagan. They may well have been decisive in winning the Republican nomination for him in 1968. He made a specific commitment to protect Southern textiles. He made a vaguer but still recognizable commitment at the Marriott Motor Hotel in Atlanta on May 31, 1968, on busing. He also, at about the same time but separately, committed himself to Senator Strom Thurmond to build a comprehensive antiballistic missile (ABM) system. Thurmond's help was deemed crucial at the time against George Wallace.

Some might think it would have been better if Nixon had made none of those promises or if he had broken all three of them. That is not the point. All Presidents incur obligations in order to be nominated and then incur many more in order to be elected. Whether they honor them or not, those obligations are still part of the political baggage a President must drag with him. If he honors a political commitment, he makes enemies. If he decides he cannot or will not honor it, he makes different enemies. In either case, how he has campaigned to get to the White House has affected in a very direct and palpable way how he behaves once he has got there.

Those who have worked for Presidents tend to agree that the mortgage due on the past election is lighter in their minds than that which will fall due for reelection. "The mortgage to the past campaign has a much shorter life," said James Fallows when I suggested the mortgage metaphor to him. Nixon's chief speechwriter, Raymond Price, agreed. He said he was more aware in the White House of the President's need for reelection than he was of the constraint represented by campaign promises. As a major instance, he cited Nixon's abrupt turnaround on wage and price controls in August 1971. It was hard to isolate the many factors that went into that decision. But, Price said, the decisive consideration was probably the feeling that the President would lose in 1972 unless the administration could get inflation under control.

The same fear looms like an unpleasant specter in any President's head whenever he has a major decision to make. The closer the next election, the more sleep he is likely to lose over it. Successive Presidents continued to escalate the U.S. stake in Southeast Asia out of many complex motives, of which patriotism may have been one and misinformation another. But one consideration that was certainly never far from their minds was the conviction that the electorate would punish any President who "lost" Vietnam. Even Nixon, who saw from 1968 on that the war could not be won, was determined that he should not be seen to have lost it.

The demands of reelection do count with Presidents. But one should not oversimplify. They are only part of a larger concern that is never absent from the President's mind or from the minds of those who serve him. The question is not solely: "What does this do to my chances of being reelected?" It is, more fundamentally: "What does this do to my chances of achieving all the other things I want to do?" It is a distinction with less of a difference than might appear. A President's prospects of reelection are the supreme test and the best measure of his general political credibility and credit. Shorn of institutional aids, such as strong party structures, he is driven to earn his way as best he can by trading in the Washington marketplace. His chances of achieving what he wants to do are as good as political credit: no worse, no better.

He has another recourse, however, or another temptation. If he cannot persuade Congress to give him the help he needs in time to be effective, the temptation is to go back to the original source of his power: the mandate of the people. He won that mandate in the first place by his mastery of the arts of manipulating the media and his consequent popularity as measured by the polls. He is surrounded by men and women who are frustrated by the slow and stubborn processes of government, and who are chafing to get back to the thing they know best. The danger is not that the President becomes too political but that everything he does is measured and motivated in terms of the politics of the campaign.

The presidency has always been an intensely political office. It could not be otherwise, and there is no harm in that. But there are two ways in which we use the word "political." In its fuller and richer sense we use it of the whole democratic process by which all the multitude of desires and aspirations and interests in society are accommodated with one another as best they can be. There is another, narrower, and meaner sense in which the word is used. In that second sense, the political process has no higher purpose than to decide who is to fill a particular office. That is campaign politics. If the White House is occupied by men or by women whose conception of politics reaches no further than how best to use the media to influence a President's standing in the polls, that would be a disaster for the United States and a danger to the world. The question is whether the decay of the instruments with whose help a President might hope to carry out his political task in the fuller and more honorable sense of the word has reached the point where Presidents have no option but to spend themselves in the self-defeating search for a new mandate, and to subordinate all their other functions to the demands of a perpetual campaign.

2

In the spring of 1974, after the Arab oil embargo and the sharp increase in the world price of oil, President Nixon ordered the bureaucracy to find out whether the United States could free itself from dependence on imported oil. The exercise was called Project Independence. The report appeard in November, three months after Nixon himself had disappeared from the scene. It concluded optimistically—as it had been intended to conclude—that if the Organization of Petroleum Exporting Countries (OPEC) persisted in keeping the price of oil at the "unheard of" price of $11 a barrel, then U.S. imports, which had been running at the rate of 6.3 million barrels a day in 1973, could be eliminated by 1985.

In April 1977, in the speech in which he made his much-derided remark about energy shortage being "the moral equivalent of war," President Carter unveiled a National Energy Plan, cobbled together at racing speed by James Schlesinger and a small team of collaborators at the Department of Energy. By now imports were running at 7.3 million barrels a day, or 16 percent higher than in 1973, and the OPEC price had risen to $13.50 a barrel. Carter's plan set a more modest goal than Project Independence: to cut oil imports back to "below six million barrels a day." The specific actions outlined in his plan, it was calculated, would, if enacted, achieve an even more modest import saving and would bring imports down only to 7 million barrels a day by 1985, or to roughly the level they stood at in 1976, the year Jimmy Carter was elected President.

Two years and four major energy speeches later, in the aftermath of a crisis that came close to derailing his presidency and which was directly due to the failures of his energy policy and the consequent gas lines across the country, Carter tried again. On July 15, 1979, with the OPEC price now standing at $23.50 for all producing countries except Saudi Arabia, Carter proposed to hold U.S. imports to their 1977 level of 8.6 million barrels a day; to achieve this goal, so much more modest than the Nixon administration had taken for granted it could achieve with no undue effort, he planned to spend $142 billion in new federal tax revenue over ten years and take the U.S. government more deeply into energy than it had ever been involved in any business with the possible exceptions of Western land in the nineteenth century and the defense industry in World War II. Within months it was plain that the taxation element of Carter's new strategy would be cut to ribbons by the Senate Finance Committee in response to some of the heaviest lobbying ever seen on Capitol Hill. If the overall target for import reduction were reached, it would only be because the impact of the energy crisis on the economy generally had reduced overall demand.

I do not cite this depressing tale merely with the intention of mocking President Carter's performance, though in truth it has not been brilliant in this respect. Still less, certainly, do I mean to imply that any other administration, past or future, would necessarily have played the same hand any better. The moral is different and far more serious. It is, surely, that the complexity and the difficulty of the major economic and social problems now facing the United States are such, and at the same time the constraints upon quick and effective presidential action to cope with those problems are such, that Presidents have little chance of making any real progress in the direction of solving them within their first term in office. Moreover, they have virtually no hope of making *visible* progress toward solving them in time to have a positive effect on their own prospects of being reelected.

The domestic presidency, as an agency for responding to new problems and remedying old ones, seems to be winding down. That is bad enough in itself. What is worse is that, as a consequence, Presidents are tempted to spend far too much of their time and effort on recouping their political fortunes by using foreign affairs to make themselves look "presidential."

Energy is the preeminent example of how hard it is for the President to change the course of the society or the economy. It is not the only one. As long ago as 1945 the Wagner-Murray-Dingell bill first proposed to provide health insurance for Americans of all ages, as part of the Social Security system. Twenty years later, Medicare and Medicaid were enacted, making health care universally available without fee-for-service only to two groups, the old and the indigent. Many of those who supported those two reforms in the 1960s saw them consciously as only way stations on the road to a comprehensive health insurance and health care delivery system in the United States. After another fifteen years, though both President Nixon and President Carter have put forward plans for some kind of national health insurance system, such a system is little nearer. Indeed it may be further off than it was in 1965.

In the meantime the Social Security system itself, perhaps the most universally welcomed of the New Deal reforms, is hovering on the verge of bankruptcy.

Twenty years ago it was all too plain that the welfare system was breaking down. Ten years ago the Nixon administration embarked on a comprehensive reform that would have substituted a guaranteed family income, then abandoned it in the face of apathy and opposition in Congress. President Carter came in promising welfare reform. Still nothing has happened. In the meantime an entire generation of dependent children has grown up under a welfare system that is both indefensibly inhumane and extravagantly expensive. The price of the failure to reform welfare has been the growth of an underclass of angry, bitter inner-city dwellers with few skills and little hope.

It was in 1954 that the Supreme Court, in the *Brown* case, first ruled that school segregation was unconstitutional. Twenty-five years later, segregation de jure in the South had long been abolished, but segregation de facto was still the norm in Boston and Chicago. It was in May 1968 that the Court decided the *Green* case, arising from New Kent County, Virginia, in which it ruled out tokenism, emphasized the word "now" in its desegregation order, and in effect prescribed busing where necessary to desegregate school systems. Since President Nixon's disingenuous message to Congress on the subject in March 1972, three successive Presidents have avoided grasping the nettle on busing. As a result, schools in Boston and other Northern cities have seen the same kind of racial brawls when desegregation was attempted that shocked the nation when they happened in Little Rock, Arkansas, in 1957. After twenty-six years, the law, as declared by the Supreme Court in *Brown*, has not yet been enforced.

Serious as their consequences have been, the failures to reform welfare or to complete school desegregation can hardly be compared in importance with the failure to equip the United States with a just and rational tax system. High theoretical rates of taxation, combined with a veritable warren of loopholes for those who can afford professional advice, have achieved something close to the worst of both worlds: taxation that is heavy enough to be painful and yet inadequate to provide the government with the revenue it needs. The U.S. government receives, year in, year out, around 5 percent less of the national product than the government of any comparable country, yet rates are high enough so that tax rebellion is spreading among the middle class, encouraged by the dubious rationalizations of conservatives. Significant tax reform appears to be impossible. Every time new tax law is written on Capitol Hill, new privileges for corporations and other special interests and for wealthy individuals are duly written into it. Even a timely shift in the direction of tax policy for macroeconomic reasons is generally beyond the capacity of these cumbersome congressional procedures. Lyndon Johnson found this to his cost in 1965–68, when he tried to raise tax revenues to pay for the Vietnam War. His inability to do so may have cost him the presidency. Certainly it spelled the end for his Great Society programs and gave a sharp new impetus to the inflation combined with economic stagnation that has troubled the economy ever since.

Economic management has been, perhaps, after energy policy, the area where the ineffectiveness of the presidency has been most conspicuous. Until near the end of the Johnson administration, the Council of Economic Advisers ritually issued a bulletin every month, hailing another month added to the longest period of unbroken economic growth in history. In those days, Presidents and their advisers were true believers in the gospel according to John Maynard Keynes. But faith in economic management did not survive the onset of chronic inflation. The prestige of Milton Friedman, the high priest of monetarism, has come to rival that once enjoyed by Keynes. But the Friedmanites have been less successful than the Keynesians once appeared to be in finding the formula that guarantees economic growth. For a decade, unemployment has been too high in the United States, and inflation has been too high, and economic growth in real terms too fitful. The biggest and potentially the strongest economy in the world has run a chronic deficit in its balance of payments, and the dollar has fallen steadily in terms of stronger currencies in spite of all the efforts of four consecutive Presidents.

And so Presidents have turned increasingly from those tasks where they are seen to fall to other tasks where they can at least seem to succeed. In the 1970s, Presidents—like U.S. banks and manufacturers—found they could earn higher dividends from their foreign operations than they could earn at home. As Nixon put it, people didn't seem to care how many outhouses you built in Peoria. Peace was what they wanted from Presidents. And if peace was unobtainable, the great discovery made by Richard Nixon and Henry Kissinger was that they could be persuaded to settle for "peace."

"Several incentives converge," wrote political scientist Thomas Cronin, "to induce a President to concentrate on foreign policy at the expense of domestic policy. . . . It is vastly more 'presidential' to be concerned with national security and world peace than with domestic policy . . . At home a President may be hamstrung by an opposition-dominated Congress, by a narrow electoral margin, by a hostile press, or by a scandal in his administration but twelve miles offshore a President virtually is the United States, and few people qualify their loyalty under such circumstances."

Richard Nixon's journeys to the Middle East and to the Soviet Union in May and June of 1974 were so clearly motivated by the desire to upstage the torrent of news of scandal and cover-up in Washington and to portray himself in a "presidential" light that it would not be an exaggeration to say that the President actually ran away from Washington to the Middle East and Moscow. Bob Woodward and Carl Bernstein supply a revealing touch in their account of the Moscow journey. At the Kremlin dinner, carried away perhaps by the vodka and champagne that traditionally flow copiously on such state occasions, Secretary Brezhnev attributed the agreements reached to a "personal relationship that was established between the General Secretary and the President." The Soviet official news agency, Tass, however—which never does such things by accident—reported Brezhnev's toast with a small but highly significant change in the wording. The agreement could be credited, Tass said, to "the relations that have grown up between us," an ambiguous phrase, but one that clearly played down the personal role of Richard Nixon. The President, according to Woodward and Bernstein, was extremely put out, and it is easy to understand why. He had desperately wanted his visit to Moscow to underline not the general improvement in U.S.-Soviet relations but his own personal irreplaceability as the bringer of "peace."

Once he turns to foreign affairs, the President seems automatically freed from the difficulties of each of the relationships that have been the theme of this book. He no longer needs to act through the medium of a slow and perhaps unresponsive bureaucracy. The key elements in his foreign policy—those, specifically, that have potential in terms of his reelection—can be closely held in the White House's national security staff. If he wants to make war or sign a treaty, he will need the permission of Congress: but there are many things he can do, or *be seen* to do, without congressional assent. He can make a speech, meet a foreign leader, travel to a foreign capital. And he can act as suddenly, as secretly, and as capriciously as he likes. That adds drama to his role in foreign policy.

In foreign affairs, he will be treated more deferentially by the media. He is dealing with matters that are relatively unknown to Americans, and where many facts are known only to government, so that his statements are less likely to be challenged than when he pronounces on domestic issues.

Above all, in foreign policy he is more often dealing with questions where fewer special interests are vested. Of course there are vested interests in foreign policy: those of various ethnic lobbies, of defense contractors, or of international trade and banking, among many others. But they are fewer and weaker than the interests affected when a President sets out to devise an energy policy, for example, or attempts to reform taxation. The media are more inclined to take his statements and the briefings they are given by White House staff at face value. "The press corps might be congenitally skeptical in assessing the intentions and ambitions of domestic politicians," David Halberstam has written, "but it brought no such toughness of mind to the politics of foreign policy."

Skepticism still ends at the water's edge. Two recent examples, President Ford's response to the *Mayagüez* incident and President Carter's mediation between Egypt and Israel, illustrate how the essentially domestic political motivation of presidential actions in international affairs is admitted with an almost naive frankness by those around a President, and duly passed on by the press as though it were the most natural thing in the world.

It is now plain enough that the version of the *Mayagüez* proclaimed by the White House, applauded by most of Congress, and reported in the media, which portrayed a hero President responding courageously but with restraint to an intolerable affront to the national honor, does not correspond with the facts. The ship was in what the Cambodian government, rightly or wrongly, claimed as territorial waters. If that claim was justified, then the

Cambodians were also justified in stopping and searching a ship in those waters to determine whether it was enjoying the right of innocent passage or was there for some noninnocent reason, such as espionage. (It is not suggested that the *Mayagüez* was engaged in espionage, only that the Cambodians may well have thought it was.) Several other ships had been stopped, searched, and captured in those same waters the previous week. The timing makes it extremely probable that the Cambodians released the crew as a result of diplomatic approaches which the President did not allow to succeed before he ordered a military response, including bombing and airborne landings. It is nearly certain that those landings and bombing raids were unnecessary and therefore unjustified. At least thirty-eight lives were lost in the operations, ostensibly in order to save the thirty-nine members of the *Mayagüez*'s crew, though it is not at all clear that the crew's lives were in danger. Finally, even if President Ford's rather perfunctory informing of Congress, after he had ordered the assault, is held not to breach the War Powers Act, he certainly rode roughshod over the legislation enacted in 1973 prohibiting the use of funds for U.S. combat activities "in or over Cambodia, Laos, North Vietnam and South Vietnam."

Yet at the time none of these reservations were heeded. The Senate Foreign Relations Committee, which had fought for years to bring the Indochina war to an end, unanimously approved a resolution approving Ford's right to use force after a three-hour briefing. There was, the *Washington Post* reported, "an almost pervasive sense that, the United States having been humiliated in Vietnam it must now strike with force to show it would not tolerate what many saw as an arrogant act of international lawbreaking." The President did not try to conceal the eagerness with which he used force, or the relief it seemed to afford him to be able to do so. On May 16 the *Washington Post*, like many other newspapers, published a White House photograph, taken moments after the decision to unleash U.S. air power against Cambodia, which showed the President, Henry Kissinger, and three of their aides. Ford and Kissinger were grinning with guilty pleasure like schoolboys at a fan dance. It was, the *Post* reported, "only a brief sense of jubilation," though why it should have been an occasion for jubilation, however brief, is not clear.

A *Washington Post* reporter, Lou Cannon, reported an interesting detail. Gerald Ford "was always talking about Truman," one presidential intimate told Cannon. "This time he did what Harry would have done."

Jules Witcover, in the same paper the next day, added another touch, gleaned from "one who was present" at the meeting at which the decision to launch the bombers was taken. "He was very calm and deliberate," this witness related. "For some reason he gave me the impression of being a general himself."

Though all participants said domestic politics were never a consideration in the decision, Witcover went on to report, Senator Barry Goldwater of Arizona thought differently.

"This one act of Ford could be the act that elects him," Goldwater said.

Peace has its victories not less glorious than war. If there was political mileage for Gerald Ford in standing tall like Harry Truman and showing that the United States was not going to be shoved around by Cambodia, Jimmy Carter was able to win even greater political credit by his actions as a peacemaker in the Middle East in 1978. That is not to say that Carter's only, or even his principal, motive in offering himself as a mediator between Israel and Egypt was "political" in the narrow, self-interested sense. Still, Carter was well aware of the temptation to use the foreign policy role of the presidency even before he moved into the White House. Asked in a June 1976 interview by the columnist Neal Pierce whether he would allow himself to be diverted by foreign affairs from hard domestic problems, Carter replied that he would try to avoid that. "I would not use foreign affairs or foreign trips as an escape mechanism to avoid responsibility on the domestic scene," he said.

Three years later, Carter's former speechwriter, James Fallows, concluded that this good resolution had not been kept.

"No matter what his original intentions," Fallows wrote,

> foreign problems were sure to preoccupy him deeply. Like every other President who has served since the United States became a world power, he would inevitably be drawn into the whirlpool of foreign affairs. . . . There were also the familiar allurements of foreign affairs: the trips on fabulous Air Force One, the flourishes, the twenty-one-gun salutes and cheering multitudes along the motorcade routes. More important was the freedom to negotiate with world leaders . . . all the excitements and trappings that go with dealing with momentous global matters that can mean life and death for all mankind.

These foreign spectaculars have another advantage for a President. In Washington, he is at the mercy of the media. They control the environment, so to speak. If the President or his press secretary puts a certain construction on events at a press conference or in a briefing, the reporters are fully at liberty to find some other news source, in Congress, or in the bureaucracy, or in one of the interest groups affected by the President's policy. In the context of domestic policy, they will do so as a matter of elementary journalistic technique, so that the President's view is routinely contrasted with the views of others. That kind of exposure of presidential policy to conflicting and critical points of view happens very much less in foreign affairs. Reporters know less about foreign countries. They feel under less obligation to be fair to the Soviet position, or the Palestinian position, or even to the position of a nominal ally like France or India (two countries that are for some reason habitually unpopular with reporters in Washington). At the same time they will feel a certain duty to give the President of the United States the benefit of the doubt. There are practical factors at work, too.

When U.S. military units are involved in combat, as they were in Vietnam, or in what might be termed "pseudocombat," as in Lebanon in 1958, or in the Cuban missile crisis of 1962, or in Santo Domingo in 1965, or in the *Mayagüez* affair, it is not just that reporters are likely to feel an impulse to rally round the flag. The White House and the Pentagon become their only sources of information. They may pick up inconsistencies or implausibilities in the accounts they are given, as some of the best reporters, like the *Washington Post*'s Murray Marder, did when asked to swallow the Johnson administration's version of events in the Tonkin Gulf in 1964, or as Richard Rovere did in *The New Yorker* within forty-eight hours of the *Mayagüez* operation. But they cannot go and check whether what the President is saying is true.

There is a second way in which the President can control the environment in which the media must work. He can devise events (or what the American historian Daniel Boorstin called pseudo-events) so dramatic in themselves that the media have no alternative but to cover them, and which the media can only cover with the White House's cooperation. Any presidential trip is like that. The only way of staying with the President and being sure to see what he does and hear what he says as he crisscrosses the country on a speaking trip is to go along on the White House press plane. The proposition is especially true of television. For all the minicams and the other technological advances of the past decade, reporting on television in the 1980s is still a little like what one wit called it in the early days: writing with a five-ton pencil. When the President goes to Europe or the Middle East, and recent Presidents have strayed farther and farther from the beaten track, as far as Tokyo and Vladivostok, network television news has to be along. That means the networks are going to need a lot of help from the White House and other agencies of the U.S. government, including the military, whether they like it or not.

The classic example is Nixon's 1972 visit to China. Nixon had already worked the news of the trip for a television spectacular. On July 15, 1971, a presidential spokesman at San Clemente told the three networks that the President had an announcement he wanted to make. He did not say what the announcement was about. Nevertheless the networks agreed to clear time and interrupted their scheduled programming, which happened to be, respectively, *The Dean Martin Show,* a rerun of *NYPD,* and a movie called *Counterfeit Killer.* At 10:30 P.M. the President duly appeared in 25 million homes to announce that he had accepted an invitation from Chinese premier Chou En-lai to visit China.

The White House persuaded the Chinese government to allow live television coverage of the President's visit. Three big cargo aircraft carted a twenty-ton portable transmitter and fifty tons of other television equipment to China, along with more than a hundred technicians, producers, and executives. The presidential visit, in February, was timed to coincide with the buildup of the primary campaign in New Hampshire. Normally the lion's share of the media attention in New Hampshire would have gone to the President's Democratic challengers, since the Democratic race was intrinsically far more interesting than a presidential walkover in the Republican primary.

The schedule was carefully planned to make sure that the more dramatic moments of the visit occurred in prime time in the United States. In the case of the President's return to Washington, that meant a nine-hour stopover on the airfield at Anchorage, Alaska. In the event, the networks, having invested $2 to $3 million of their own money in covering the President in China, naturally did their best to recoup by putting on blanket coverage: some forty-one hours of network time devoted to the trip over seven days, watched by an estimated 100 million viewers in the United States alone. Money could not buy that kind of exposure for a presidential candidate. But from their point of view the networks had no alternative. After all there *was* something dramatic, not to say intriguing, about the spectacle of Richard M. Nixon being received in the Great Hall of the Chinese people and picnicking at the Great Wall of China.

Jimmy Carter's contribution to the technique of the presidential spectacular was to appreciate the suspense that could be built up by a presidential disappearing trick. The dramatic impact of his successful mediation between Egyptian President Anwar Sadat and Israeli Prime Minister Menachem Begin at Camp David in September 1978 was greatly enhanced by the prolonged and total news blackout on the negotiations that preceded it. More dramatic, though less successful, was his decision over the lunch hour on Independence Day 1979 to cancel a televised speech to the nation on energy scheduled for the following day. He built up expectation for the speech he eventually delivered on July 15 by inviting a medley of advisers to deliberate with him on the Catoctin mountaintop, and admitted that one of the reasons for canceling his speech had been a conscious intention of building up the drama. When he paid a surprise visit to an "average" family in Pittsburgh, his host criticized him for canceling his July 5 speech. "Would you have watched it then?" asked the President.

The Carter White House has never seriously tried to conceal the domestic political motivation of the President's peacemaking efforts, as Martin Schram's report in the *Washington Post* on the day the peace treaty between Egypt and Israel was signed in March 1979 reveals with almost embarrassing clarity.

How much impact would the treaty have on Carter's fortunes, Schram asked the President's pollster, Patrick Caddell.

"It's not the kind of thing you can translate into hard specifics," Caddell replied. Then the pollster sat down and wrote the President a letter. In it he quoted the words Edmund Burke used of Charles James Fox in 1783: "He may live long. He may do much. But here is the summit. He can never exceed what he does this day."

One of the President's Georgian advisers put the thing in a more down-to-earth fashion. "When Carter deals with the nitty-gritty, like energy and deregulation and all that," said this worldly wiseman, "it doesn't do much to distinguish him from the pack—from, say, a bunch of senators. But this will have a long-lasting benefit for Jimmy Carter. It will make him look presidential."

A few weeks before, Schram explained, "after Iran had fallen and we were in danger of losing our Yemen," Carter was being told by all his advisers "to do something presidential." That was when he demonstrated his originality. "At a time when others might have called out the *Mayagüez* one more time," as Schram put it, "Jimmy Carter summoned Air Force One instead. And he made his most presidential stand in a most unpresidential way. He set out on a bit of shuttle diplomacy. . . ."

That piece is unusual only in its frankness. The fact is that, at least since John Kennedy's time, the reporters who cover the White House, the President's staff, and Presidents themselves have seen the great events in the outside world far more in terms of the tests and the opportunities they represented for presidential politics than in terms of their own intrinsic importance.

The Camp David summit of 1978 was a brilliant success in this respect. In a couple of weeks, Carter's presidency was born again. All the failures and frustrations of his first eighteen months in office, the embarrassment caused by the disgrace of his budget director, Bert Lance, and the "competence factor," were forgotten. As a result there was something of a summit craze in Washington for a while.

A group of Latin American editors came by the White House and asked why the President couldn't take the problems of their continent to Camp David and work his magic on them.

Someone else said: "Why can't we have a summit to deal with inflation?" If the President can end two thousand years of warfare in the Middle East, the argument went, why of course he can knock a few points off the rate of inflation.

Representative John Conyers (Democrat of Michigan) thought there ought to be a summit on black unemployment.

All of which prompted Mary McGrory of the *Washington Star* to ask a highly pertinent question. Why, if the President could bring peace to the Middle East, or to Northern Ireland, or to southern Africa, couldn't he straighten out the postal service or fix it so that the votes got counted on election night in the District of Columbia? The answer is that it is a lot easier for the President to succeed in dealing with the first kind of problem than it is for him to succeed in dealing with the second.

Of course, if success in dealing with world problems meant really bringing peace to Belfast or the West Bank of the Jordan or Afghanistan, that would be a far harder proposition even than reforming the U.S. mail, though that has defeated the efforts of many successive administrations. It is no easier to change things in the real world abroad than it is to change them in the United States. It is a great deal harder. The United States is a society geared to change; it is one of the few countries where things do sometimes change, and with startling rapidity, whereas in Northern Ireland or the Middle East, fears and animosities seethe on unchanged for hundreds of years.

But from the point of view of even the most idealistic President, let alone from that of his pragmatic political advisers, it isn't what happens in the real world abroad that matters. Years after the American President has "ended two thousand years of warfare in the Middle East," the situation of the Palestinian Arabs living in Bethlehem or Nablus will not have changed. What matters is that the summit should be a success, so that the President looks "presidential." That is what is going to distinguish him from the pack of mere senators and presidential candidates. That may sound cynical. But a moment's reflection shows that it must be true. The President cannot be deeply concerned with the future life of the Palestinians of Nablus, or of the inhabitants of "our Yemen." And even if he were concerned, he would have no business making decisions to change their lives. His concern must be, and rightly is, with what happens in the United States. And if he is to improve the postal service or push through a new national energy policy, he must first of all concern himself with his own political strength and credibility. That includes his ability to win reelection. So when the President negotiates "peace" in the Middle East, he is seeking to achieve a triumph in the real political world of Washington, D.C., which is connected with the real world for the inhabitants of Nablus, but is by no means identical with their world.

Once again, the President is trapped by another aspect of the familiar paradox. The power of the United States in the world is so great and that power is so nearly in the absolute control of the President if he wants to use it to move warships and aircraft about the globe, and in the last analysis even to order their use, that the world's leaders have no alternative but to meet with him if he asks them to. They will say they agree with what he wants to achieve. They may even be constrained to do what he asks. But within the American system his power is not so great.

In an earlier and more celebrated memo to Jimmy Carter, in December 1976, Patrick Caddell urged the President-elect to come out for "postcard registration and energy policy." It is an amusing illustration of the tunnel vision that is the occupational disease of those who practice presidential politics. Everything is related to the overriding goal of augmenting the President's political power and credibility: the future of an issue, like energy policy, that embraces nothing less than the whole shape of American society and the American economy, is jumbled up as if it inhabited the same plane of importance as a mere electoral device like postcard registration. And so it is in foreign policy. Because the unspoken standard by which all is measured is the President's political strength, he is constantly tempted to turn from the intractable and frustrating problems of domestic policy, not to the great issues of foreign policy, with which of course Presidents must concern themselves, but to one theatrical appearance on the world stage after another whose underlying purpose is to bolster his political standing.

It is often said that the United States has been distracted from the real issues for fifteen years by the false issues of Vietnam and Watergate. If Vietnam is taken as the test case for the whole strategy of intervention anywhere in the world where a Communist government might make its appearance, and if Watergate is taken as shorthand for a deliberate attempt to shift the balance between the constitutionally separated powers of the presidency and the legislature toward the executive, then the truth was exactly the other way around. It was because the presidency was unable to tackle the real problems that successive Presidents were drawn into irrelevant adventures abroad. Vietnam was one. There were many, many more: Chile, the Congo, Guatemala, Lebanon, Dominican Republic, Laos—it is hard to think of a part of the world so remote from the United States geographically or so marginal to its interests that an American President has not, at some time or another in the past thirty years, been tempted to intervene there in one way or another, either in order to appear "presidential" in the eyes of the electorate, or in deference to the presumption of its unforgiving rage if any of these territories—many of them unknown to all but a handful of the voters until they flashed briefly into the headlines—should be "lost."

There are, mercifully, signs that both the political attractions of intervention and the fear of being held responsible for "losing" parts of the world are less great than they were. Jimmy Carter has rightly boasted that not a single U.S. soldier has been killed anywhere in the world since he was President. He has also resisted considerable pressure in Congress and in the media to react more harshly than he did to the Islamic revolution in Iran. The temptation, for Carter, has been to spend too much of his time making peace, not making war. And that is all to the good. Moreover, there are signs that the political incentive to go in for foreign policy spectaculars of any kind may be diminishing. The signature of the treaty between Israel and Egypt, for what that is worth, brought Carter only a single point in the opinion polls, whereas the negotiation of the "framework of agreement" for the treaty brought him sixteen points. More generally, it is quite likely that diminishing returns may be setting in for the presidential spectaculars as Presidents overuse the ploy and public cynicism and indifference increase.

Yet the temptation to be diverted from the hard domestic tasks that yield little or no political dividend within the life of a single administration to the spotlights of the world stage that can deliver instant, if short-lived, popularity remains. Such foreign diversions are truly "presidential," though not in the sense in which the word is generally used. They epitomize the paradox of presidential power and impotence.

3

This book has been much concerned with the relationships between the presidency and those other institutions that might help the President to lead: with the cabinet, the federal bureaucracy, the White House staff, the media, the party, and, above all, with the Congress. The argument has been made that the presidency is neither too strong nor too weak but too isolated. The conclusion has been drawn that the presidency's relationships with these other institutions are not on the whole working well. Can they be improved? In the end, that will depend on the success or failure with which Presidents conduct another, even more fundamental relationship: with the American people. So the first question is: what do the American people want from their Presidents? And behind it there lurks an even more elusive question: in what direction do the American people want to go?

There is no need here to recite the elaborate job descriptions that used to be found in the textbooks. They can be reduced to one simple statement: the American people expect too much of their Presidents. They demand more from them than any man or woman is going to be able to give.

There is the sheer physical overload. From the cruel and inhuman punishment of the campaign, prolonged now over not less than eighteen months, the victor escapes into the even more fearsome severities of the White House. The routine of the White House has its compensations: power makes life more bearable for ambitious men. Yet for men who are also conscientious, the rhythm of work is unrelenting. Richard Nixon, silently scribbling on a yellow legal pad in his eyrie in the executive office building, or Jimmy Carter steadily checking boxes in his option papers before dawn, evoke the same pathos as the great emperor Charles V stolidly annotating the margins of reports from the governors of two continents in his cell in the monastery of the Escorial. Presidents can start their day with briefings before sunrise, and slog on with their reading long past midnight, and still fight a losing battle against the inrushing tide of information they really do need to know.

Then there is the emotional overload. The tendency has been to identify the nation with the presidency, and the presidency in turn with the President. As a result the man who happens to be President is laden with all the hopes, and fears, and frustrations, and aspirations of the nation.

He is also overburdened in terms of function. He is expected to do too many jobs at once; he cannot give proper attention to them all. He must simultaneously conduct the diplomacy of a superpower, put together separate coalitions to enact every piece of legislation required by a vast and complex society, manage the economy, command the armed forces, serve as a spiritual example and inspiration, respond to every emergency.

He would find it hard enough to do all these jobs satisfactorily even if he stood at the apex of an ordered and obedient government. As it is, he has to barter and haggle for everything he wants. Does the country need a Strategic Arms Limitation Treaty? A new mobile missile system? A national health insurance program? An energy policy? The President has neither scepter, nor marshal's baton, nor magic wand. He must go out into the Washington marketplace and trade for all of these things.

In the process, it is theoretically possible for him to acquire a usable surplus of political power. This is more likely to happen when the nation is felt to be in crisis. At such times there are things that so obviously need to be done that the President can convince his competitors for power to let him act. Franklin Roosevelt was in that lucky situation in 1933, and so was Lyndon Johnson from 1963 to 1965. If a President can trade at a profit, he will be freed from the debilitating preoccupation with mere survival. Other brokers in the market, seeing that he is in a position to reward or punish them, will spring forward with offers of help. The President will be freed to deal with some of the long-term problems all Presidents can see coming, but which, most of the time, they cannot afford to confront.

Unfortunately for Presidents, the country is not always in a period of perceived crisis. (Unfortunately for the country, the President nearly always is!) At other times, a President is likely to trade at a loss. All his efforts will then have to be concentrated on protecting his own position. He will consume his time in attempts to scrape together a few successes and a handful of allies. He will have to throw himself on the mercy of the modern presidency's court of ultimate appeal: popular support, as measured in the perpetual plebiscite of the opinion polls. He will be tempted to break the fundamental rule of sound banking and borrow short to lend long, that is, he will risk dangerous long-term consequences in pursuit of immediate gains. He will put much of his energy into trying to pull off spectacular successes in time to affect his own standing in the polls, his credibility in Washington, and his chances of reelection. Some of these bold strokes will come off. But overall the trend is likely to be downward, as long as the President is as isolated as he is today from institutional help.

The overloading of the presidency would be dangerous enough, in short, even if all the President's efforts could be spared for running the government. As it is, his first priority is survival. The danger is that, to a greater or lesser degree, depending on the President's personal integrity and the circumstances he is in, all other functions will be subordinated to his political needs.

The problem is not simply that of sheer overload in these different forms, however. It would take a political superman to do all the things Americans want their Presidents to do. There would be at least the possibility that a mere mortal might satisfy some of these demands, though, if only it were clear just what the people did want, or if the people agreed on what they want. Nothing could be less clear. The pattern of public opinion has rarely been more confused. Commentators correctly observe, for example, that people want to pay lower taxes. From this it is often concluded that a conservative tide is sweeping the nation. There is less evidence that people want lower Social Security benefits, poorer government services, smaller transfer payments to themselves or the social consequences of smaller payments to others, let alone skimping on national security. In fact, most people are neither "conservatives" nor "liberals." They want *both* lower taxes *and* better service from their government.

If there were a clear consensus, it would not matter whether it was liberal or conservative. A President could at least try to carry out its wishes. If there were solid support for a renewed attack on poverty and urban decay, or for better health care, a liberal President would not have to attain the millennium by the time of the midterm elections. He would only have to demonstrate clear progress in the direction endorsed by the majority. Alternatively, if there were truly a clear conservative consensus in the land, a conservative President would not have to take public policy back to the days of William McKinley overnight; regression, say, as far as the golden age of Herbert Hoover might be enough to ensure his reelection.

It is not like that. There is no clear consensus against which a President's achievement can be measured. He is the butt of all the citizens' grievances and the repository of all their hopes. All the interests look to him for protection and for favor. He could not satisfy them all, even if he possessed the omnipotence of God the Father, or if the system revolved with all the friction-free majesty of the eternal spheres. The reason is not hard to find. The things "the people" want are mutually inconsistent. They want lower taxes *and* higher benefits. They want to be sure of the supply of gasoline, *and* they do not want to pay higher prices for it. They want national security *and* disarmament. They do not want American boys to be sent abroad to be killed, *and* they want the United States to be respected and feared in Vietnam and Ethiopia and Iran.

The people, of course, are an abstraction that looks more like a fiction on closer inspection. The term includes stockbrokers and sharecroppers, sexists and feminists, whites and blacks, old and young and in between, Sun Belt and Snow Belt, Jews and Muslims, those who believe that a woman has an absolute right to an abortion, and also those who believe, with equally passionate intensity, that a fetus has the right to live.

There is nothing new about this diversity, of course, or about the demands the American people make on their Presidents, though the demands are perhaps becoming more insistent at the same time as they are getting harder to meet. Nor is there anything unique to the United States about it, though Americans are certainly not known for any preeminent propensity to keep quiet about their grievances or to settle for the second best.

There are, however, reasons why it is harder for an American President to cope with the maelstrom of incompatible demands from the citizens. And it may also be harder for him to meet those demands now than it was in the past.

To be modestly successful as the head of government in any of the Western European democracies (as success is measured in an imperfect world and a continent whose history has not taught its inhabitants to expect miracles!) you do not strive for consensus. Instead, you consciously kiss off close to half of the electorate, the half that did not vote for you. That is what the competition of ideological parties implies. Where executive power is based on a parliamentary majority, as it is in most other working democracies except the United States, the leader need only ensure the continuance of that majority. He or she may choose, as an electoral tactic, to aim for what is loosely called consensus by political journalists, in the sense that he or she may reckon that there are needed votes to be won near the center of the political spectrum. But equally he or she may decide to do nothing of the kind. Helmut Schmidt, a conspicuously successful West German head of government, has followed one tactic. Margaret Thatcher, in Britain, has practiced the other. In a parliamentary system with ideological parties, the executive leader strives to carry out as much as possible of the party's existing, agreed program.

This is utterly different from the strategy of a modern American President. He is free to pick his policies from all points of the ideological compass, with only the most perfunctory of nods to his party's traditional stance. The party's platform is a formality. The President's best course will be to mix in a variety of policies calculated to appeal to as many different groups of voters as possible, even at the risk of a little inconsistency around the edges. Because he has got to put his own coalition together, because party counts for so little, the President will go hunting where the ducks are: in the center.

That, at least, was how the system worked in the years of consensus. For most of the thirty years from 1933 to 1963, it worked fairly well. The modern presidency was well adapted to be the instrument of consensus. One of the reasons why it is harder to be a successful President now than it was is quite simply because consensus has largely evaporated. For a large part of the middle of the twentieth century, a particular cluster of assumptions and beliefs was intimately connected with the rise of the modern presidency. It began to form at the beginning of the century, in the days of Theodore Roosevelt and Woodrow Wilson, as it became clear to a growing number of Americans that the presidency was called upon to play a strong, interventionist role abroad, now that the United States had become a world power; at the same time that the urbanization, the industrialization, and the expansion of the nation, with their titanic consequences for American society, made it imperative that the presidency must intervene at home, too, and take responsibility for the health of both the economy and the society. These ideas were temporarily rejected during the normalcy years. But under the double impact of the Depression and the Second World War they triumphed. Consensus resulted from a kind of gigantic deal between liberals and conservatives: conservatives accepted the liberal contention that the government must intervene in the economy to secure prosperity, while liberals accepted the originally conservative insistence that government must be vigilant to safeguard national security against Communism and radicalism abroad. The consensus was also firmly based on the belief in infinitely receding new frontiers of economic growth. Out of the cornucopia of wealth that would be won from growth, social needs could be met and social tensions —including racial tensions—could be resolved without the conflict between competing classes that was the basis of the old politics.

For a variety of reasons, that consensus began to dissolve after the middle of the 1960s. It is usual to blame "Vietnam" and "Watergate." Other factors were just as important. The civil rights movement could remedy de jure segregation in the South; it could not cure de facto inequality in the Northern cities. The liberal reforms were disappointing. Some said they didn't work; others, that they were never given a proper chance to work. On either view, liberalism became discredited. Above all, economic growth, the motor that was to have powered the whole transformation of society, broke down. From the late 1960s on, it became plain that the promise of infinite growth without inflation was illusory. Conservationists asked whether it was even desirable. And from 1973 onward, the energy crisis made it plain that it was in any case not available. Once the promise of endless economic growth had been shattered, the intellectual foundations of consensus had been knocked away. Liberal thinkers had looked forward to the "fiscal dividend" by which government would distribute the proceeds of growth to presently conflicting cosharers in abundance. A new era seemed about to begin in which increasingly angry groups would be competing for increasingly scarce resources.

The foreign policy of the consensus years also had its origin in the confident assumptions of the historically brief period when the United States had no close rivals in the world. Already by the 1950s the Soviet Union had set out to challenge U.S. supremacy, but U.S. policy long continued to reflect assumptions formed between 1944 and 1949, when U.S. economic and military strength dwarfed all potential competitors. Many of modern Presidents' troubles flow from the fact that U.S. public opinion still looks back to that brief and now distant period as the norm.

Vietnam ended what might be called the innocent phase of the consensus for global containment. Richard Nixon and Henry Kissinger tried to re-create consensus behind a new policy that was more sophisticated and anything but innocent. It depended on elaborate efforts to deceive the American people about the prospective outcome of the war in Southeast Asia. Just as American responsibility there was to be subcontracted by a process of "Vietnamization," so in other regions of the world part of the responsibility for the stability of the status quo was to be delegated to a system of regional allies and surrogates, backed in the last resort with U.S. money and U.S. strategic forces. Many of the chosen surrogates—the Shah of Iran, the white regimes in southern Africa, President Park in South Korea, General Pinochet in Chile, and Anastasio Somoza in Nicaragua spring to mind, as do half a dozen assorted military governments elsewhere—were governments that made many Americans uneasy, not to say queasy. More to the point, in many places this hastily rigged structure came into conflict with the realities of a rapidly changing world. Nixon and Kissinger matched their uncompromising opposition to every kind of radical political change in the world with an unpromising attempt to reach an accommodation with the Soviet Union, the leader of the radical camp, which was to be now lured with offers of American grain and computers, now threatened with a new alliance between Washington and Peking. Not surprisingly, this system, at once so cynical and so naive, soon collapsed. Nixon's successors were left to grapple with the intractable complexities of a world that had never remotely corresponded to the cloudy nineteenth-century geopolitical constructs that won Henry Kissinger so much applause.

Long before that applause had died away, Jimmy Carter was confronted with a dilemma that would not go away merely because some other President, at a later date, might try to resolve it in a different way from Carter. Increasingly, public opinion resented the President's inability to make the world conform with American ideas of how it ought to be. The fall of Saigon, the tragedy of Kampuchea, Soviet and Cuban penetration in Africa, the Shah's fall, the extravagances of the Islamic revolution and the taking of American hostages in Iran, the failure of years of arms limitation talks to prevent the Soviet Union acquiring strategic superiority or something ominously close to it, Soviet power plays in Afghanistan and elsewhere, the inability of the United States to bring a settlement in the Middle East, above all the dependence of the U.S. economy on imported oil: all these separate humiliations and frustrations came together like so many illustrations of a single, ominous theme: the decline of American power.

From a babble of voices, a single response detached itself more and more clearly. It was a growl. It was telling any President, or any would-be President, that it would be dangerous to leave the American people much longer in impatient frustration at their inability to make their wishes felt in the world. The dilemma is this: what can the President—any conceivable President—*do* to meet this rising mood? Another President, to be sure, could easily follow very different policies from those Jimmy Carter has chosen. He could abrogate the search for arms limitation and build new strategic systems, maximize the leverage to be gained from U.S. economic power, demand that U.S. allies follow their leader, even send expeditionary forces to safeguard U.S. interests in Africa, Latin America, and the Middle East. That might be popular. It would certainly relieve a good deal of frustration. Would it really free him from the practical constraints on power that is limited and has declined, if only in comparison with the pinnacle of the postwar years? Conversely, if Jimmy Carter gained politically from the restraint with which he reacted to the problem posed by the U.S. hostages in Iran, there could be no certainty that public opinion would not whiplash later, and punish him for doing nothing when there was in truth nothing he could usefully do. How often recent Presidents must privately have echoed Lyndon Johnson's complaint: "The only power I have is nuclear, and I can't use that!"

Johnson was exaggerating. The President of the United States still has awesome power. Only in the terms that matter most to him, perhaps, is it utterly inadequate. It does not enable him to meet the expectations of the American people, for those expectations were formed at a time when the United States was virtually omnipotent. Public opinion cannot accept that this is no longer so and blames the President because he cannot turn back the waves.

The modern presidency was not designed by the two Roosevelts, by Wilson and Truman, for the task of lowering expectations either at home or abroad. It is not well adapted for that task. Yet expectations will have to be lowered.

There are some who are optimistic that the institution of the presidency can be made to meet the expectations that are heaped on it, if only the right man is elected to the White House, with the right mandate and the right policies, so that the political system will be galvanized once more by strong currents of personal leadership.

It is hard to share that optimism. For one thing, something more than mere charisma will be needed. That is why the system was so carefully built "not to promote efficiency," in Mr. Justice Louis Brandeis's words, "but to preclude the exercise of arbitrary power." If the analysis made in this book is even approximately correct, it is not likely that any imaginable charge of personal magnetism will overcome the institutional isolation of the presidency.

There is another reason for doubting that the problem of the presidency will be solved by the sheer quality of future Presidents' leadership. It has already been suggested that the crisis of the presidency is, in one aspect, only a part of a more general crisis of authority in Western societies. If there is a shortage of leadership, it is in part because people do not want to be led: they only want many things that only leadership can give them.

4

One of the reassuring aspects of a not wholly reassuring situation is that there is now widespread and growing agreement that the presidency is not performing as it should. No one would now write, I suppose, as such an eminent scholar and student of the presidency as James MacGregor Burns did only fifteen years ago, that the problems of the presidency are the problems of success. Most of those who have studied the presidency since then have come to the conclusion that the institution is badly in need of improvement in one way or another; most of them have also been ready with one or more suggestions for embarking on that process of improvement. Suggestions range from having several hundred White Houses to having none. Or at least Professor Burns has called for presidential offices in "several hundred regions" throughout the country, while Barbara Tuchman has asked, no doubt with her tongue some way into her historiographical cheek, "Shall we abolish the presidency?"

What follows, therefore, is no more than a sketch map of the mountain with some of the more popular lines of approach penciled in.

One group of reform proposals is aimed at the way the President is chosen. The most sweeping reform of the law on campaign finance in American history was enacted in the 1970s. At the beginning of the decade, the limits on campaign spending were tolerant and virtually unenforceable; by its end, the system had been radically transformed. Congress introduced partial financing with public money for the two major parties' candidates in the presidential primaries, and a flat grant for the candidates of the major parties in the presidential election itself. It also allowed almost the whole cost of the two parties' nominating conventions, hoopla and all, to be met from public money. Tighter control of campaign expenditure was hurried along by the realization of the sheer scale on which the Nixon people had broken both the letter and the spirit of existing law. Congress had been brutally reminded that restriction without enforcement was worse than useless. So part of the direct legacy of Watergate was an independent election commission to monitor campaign fundraising and expenditure and to investigate the detailed disclosure now required. One unforeseen result was the diversion of the tide of money available from special interests of every kind from presidential to congressional campaigns. Congress has so far shown no comparable zeal for limiting spending in congressional campaigns, though proposals for public financing of them are now before Congress. Over time, the changes in campaign finance can be expected to affect presidential campaigning. It can be argued, for example, that Kennedy would not have been nominated in 1960, or Nixon elected in 1968, under the law as it stands in 1980. Still, the influence of such changes is bound to be gradual. Further changes in the primary system would have a more abrupt effect.

Primaries, as we have seen, are now decisive in choosing presidential candidates (though other events, including caucuses in nonprimary states, affect primary results through media coverage). Many critics are not happy about this state of affairs.

Many hundreds of bills to reform the primary system have been introduced into Congress since the beginning of the century. The only one enacted since 1911 was the one that gave the District of Columbia a primary. Primary reform revives as an issue whenever there is a campaign in which the popular will appears to have been thwarted, as many felt it had been in the campaigns of 1912, 1952, and 1968. In each case, the proposition is doubtful; what certainly happened was that in each year minorities with passionately held convictions were defeated. Nonetheless, the failure of the McCarthy crusade and the death of Robert Kennedy in 1968 led to no fewer than thirty-five bills to reform the primaries being introduced into Congress in 1971 and 1972 alone.

There are two leading plans for reforming the long-drawn-out chaos of the present primary system: regional primaries and the single national primary.

Attempts have already been made to organize regional primaries without federal legislation. Oregon, Idaho, and Nevada held their primaries on the same day in 1976 in an attempt to organize a "Pacific Rim regional presidential primary"; Washington and California refused to join. Before the 1976 election there were also efforts to create a New England regional primary. Maine, Massachusetts, Rhode Island, and Vermont were willing to go along. The Granite State remained . . . adamant. It was so determined not to lose the kudos and revenue from holding the first of the primaries that the governor signed a bill allowing New Hampshire to change the date of its primary from March 2 and to hold it a week before that of any other state sneaky enough to try to edge New Hampshire out of the first place on the starting grid. The idea of a Dixie primary was put forward at the Southern Governors Conference in 1973 by the then governor of Georgia, one Jimmy Carter; nothing came of it.

The national primary has attracted even more support. Presidents Wilson and Truman were both adherents of it, and so was Gerald Ford before he became President. In February 1976 no fewer than 68 percent of respondents in a Gallup poll said they would prefer presidential candidates to be chosen at a single national primary, rather than by a nominating convention. A single primary, in which all Democrats and all Republicans would cast a single vote for the candidate of their choice on the same day might be less practical than it sounds. It might also be less "democratic" in some respects. It would tend to favor well-known candidates over unknowns and outsiders. It would tend to help incumbent Presidents to beat off challengers (which, of course, might in turn strengthen the presidency as an institution). It would very likely reduce media interest, since a single event would be less suitable for sustained reporting than the present prolonged epic. Some critics believe that under a national primary it would be more likely than it is under the present system that a candidate with strong support from one section of a party, but who was unacceptable to other groups, might be chosen if he won a plurality. On this view, the national primary might produce less moderate, centrist candidates than the existing system. It is a matter of opinion whether that would be an advantage or a disadvantage. Victory would be likely to go to the candidate with the most money, who could afford simultaneous media expenditure in every major market in the country, though this difficulty could perhaps be removed by legislation.

In spite of all its disadvantages, there is a lot to be said in favor of the single national primary. It would be swift, decisive, and beyond manipulation. It would do away with the "killing-match" character of the present series of elimination bouts, which have killed off some strong candidates recently, such as Edmund Muskie in 1972. This would preserve a wider freedom of choice. The winning of a national primary would not be within the grasp of wildcat raids by *condottieri* and their charismatic horde of followers. That might produce more experienced candidates. It would tend to revive party politics. It might also mean the end of government by campaign staff. If party leaders were to wheel and deal to preselect candidates ahead of the primary, the voters would always have the sanction of voting for the other party's candidate in the general election, or of "going fishing."

The national primary, in a word, could strike a happy balance between the element of party legitimation and the element of popular choice. In my opinion it is a promising reform and deserves a trial. The sad fact is, though, that however strong the arguments for a national primary, and even if two-thirds of the American people would still prefer it, as they did in 1976, their wish is not very likely to be granted. Few experts think Congress would enact the national primary, if only because, as Congressman Morris K. Udall (Democrat of Arizona) has put it: "The impetus to get something done only occurs in a year when you can't do anything about it." In election year, to alter the rules is inevitably to favor one candidate or another. Between election years, people have not so far shown enough enthusiasm for the national primary for it to be worth the while of congressmen and senators to overcome the natural inertial resistance to such a significant change. Perhaps another prolonged and messy primary campaign will generate that enthusiasm and overcome that resistance.

Many have sought to reform the primary by changing the President's term of office. Closely linked to that is the proposal to change the terms of congressmen and, in some versions, senators as well. Limiting the President to a single six-year term was discussed at the Constitutional Convention and proposed to Congress as a constitutional amendment as early as 1826. It has been reintroduced into Congress more than a hundred times since then, most recently in 1971, when both the Senate majority leader, Mike Mansfield (Democrat of Montana), and the venerable Senator George Aiken (Republican of Vermont) sponsored it jointly. As recently as February 1979 the then attorney general of the United States, Griffin Bell of Georgia, and a prominent Republican candidate for the presidency, John Connally of Texas, both came out for the six-year term, which was favored by former President Lyndon Johnson and by no fewer than nine other Presidents.

The case for a single six-year term is in part humanitarian: the burdens of the office are so heavy, it is argued, that no man should be asked to carry them for more than six years. A more convincing case for six years rests on the belief that too much of a President's time in the White House is taken up with working for his reelection. The President and his men are preoccupied with reelection, the argument goes, to the detriment of the national interest; reduce the proportion of the first term that is under the shadow of the coming election, and to that extent you free the President to concentrate on what ought to be his proper concerns. The White House is too preoccupied with reelection. But merely by removing the pressures of reelection, you do not necessarily remove the need or the temptation to be "political." If the image developed in these pages is accepted—that of a President reduced to trading for his political requirements because his ability to get them any other way is so restricted—then the six-year single term would not remove all the temptations to excessively "political" behavior. Indeed, another school of thought attacks the six-year proposal on the grounds that there is nothing wrong with the White House being political. George Reedy, for example, who also worked for Lyndon Johnson, dismisses this and indeed most other reform suggestions altogether, on the grounds that they are naive and fail to take account of existing "power relationships in society." The art of politics, says Reedy, is to reconcile these relationships with social needs. Any other approach must fail. Many other critics share his view. Only the constant need to take every political pressure into account, this counterargument goes, can ensure that the presidency will remain democratically responsive to what the people want. "Political," for many of this opinion, has become almost a synonym for "democratic."

An apparently similar proposal, actually motivated by quite different concerns, is the one to change the term of members of the House of Representatives from two years to four years. The object would be not only to free congressmen from the burden of almost constant campaigning, but also to phase congressional and presidential campaigns together. This, it is argued, would help to restore the lost link between President and Congress. If congressmen were always running for reelection with a President or a presidential candidate at the top of the ticket (instead of finding themselves in that situation only every other term), then, it is urged, they would be conscious of the President as their party leader and so feel a stronger obligation to defend his record and, even more important, to work to improve that record between campaigns. This, in turn—say the advocates of the four-year term for congressmen—would revive the frayed ties of party loyalty.

This would be a great object to achieve. It is not so clear that the proposal would actually accomplish it, however. The case has its weaknesses. The proposed reform would presumably only apply to congressmen of the President's own party, unless it is contended that the four-year term would create a wholly new leadership role for defeated presidential candidates. More serious, the proposal ignores all those recent social and political developments (social and geographical mobility, fading of ethnic and religious loyalties, decline of ideology, rise of television, etc., etc.) that have contributed to the weakening of parties. It fastens on a single peculiarity of the constitutional system (one, moreover, that was in place throughout the alleged heyday of party) and hopes, by changing that, to arrest the decline of party. Certainly it would not be likely to do the trick on its own. It might still be worth trying, in connection with a number of other measures seeking to revive the influence of party and the links of loyalty and cooperation between Presidents and members of their party in Congress. Unfortunately there is one rather cynical reason for doubting whether the four-year term for congressmen is likely to be adopted: senators are not likely to be in any great hurry to give their brethren in the House a free shy at their seats.

Nobody should expect too much from changes in the way Presidents are chosen. Such changes—a national primary, for example—might change the sort of men who get into the White House. And that might be to the good. It might also surround them in the White House with different kinds of men and women on their staff, making them less dependent in office on the bag carriers and traveling companions who have been been so prominent in the White House since 1960, and that would be even better.

But the intractable problems of the presidency have persisted whoever sat in the Oval Office. There is no reason to believe that changing the way the President is chosen, even if that in turn changes the men who get elected, will do anything to eliminate problems that have defeated the abilities of such different men as John Kennedy, Lyndon Johnson, and Richard Nixon. If the problems of the presidency are those of institutional isolation, then the solution must be to diminish that isolation. That must mean finding ways of reknitting the damaged relationships with bureaucracy, Congress, party, and media.

Some of the reforms intended to make the executive branch of the government *work* better, and to put the President more firmly in charge of the bureaucracy, do not perhaps go to the heart of the problem of the presidency. They would be just as helpful, or unhelpful, if the United States had some quite different form of government. Thus several political scientists have urged, for example, that the White House ought to be provided with better facilities for planning. Others have pointed out that the White House has proved better at starting new programs than at evaluating programs. There is a need for better evaluation both of proposed new programs and also of those that have been started. The same criticism can be leveled at other suggestions in themselves very reasonable. Some have recommended, for example, that the National Security Council ought to be abolished; others, that the Domestic Council ought to be revived. There are certainly many ways in which the machinery and the administrative performance of the White House could be improved. But the crucial goal of reform ought to be not to strengthen the White House bureaucracy, while leaving it to compete with the other bureaucracies of the executive department agencies and of Congress, but rather to break down the autonomy of the "iron triangles," to eliminate duplication (or triplication), and to restore to each part of the system—White House, departments, Congress—its proper place and function.

This, of course, will be easier said than done. The task will be possible if certain general principles are accepted. The first is that there is nothing inherently wrong or harmful about bureaucracy in itself. Americans are prone, and perhaps becoming more prone, to damn bureaucracy when they see it in the service of the government, while finding it perfectly acceptable in universities, hospitals, insurance companies, or the telephone system. The test ought to be how efficiently and economically a bureaucracy does the work it is supposed to do. The second great principle is that efficient and disciplined bureaucracies necessarily depend on subordination: not the subordination of one part of the bureaucracy to another, such as the subordination of the departments to the White House staff, but the subordination of both to what Woodrow Wilson called "a common service."

This in turn implies a third principle: that of definition. The respective roles of Congress, of the executive departments, and of the White House staff must be more clearly defined and distinguished. Congress, and the growing bureaucracies of the congressional committees, must be restricted to the consideration of legislation and the investigation of specific areas where legislation may be needed, and not allowed to interfere, as they so often do now, in what ought to be matters of routine administration. The departments must be entrusted with adequate authority for administration, and left to get on with it. The White House staff must serve as the President's eyes and ears, not as a parallel superbureaucracy moving in to second-guess those holding line responsibility when the President's interests are involved, then stepping back to leave confusion and demoralization behind as too often happens now.

Paradoxically, this process of defining and separating the roles of Congress, the White House staff, and the executive bureaucracy will be easier, not harder, if progress can be made in the direction of reducing division and competition between the legislative and executive branches of the government. The American constitutional tradition has always so firmly identified the idea of "checks and balances" with the separation of powers that it is difficult to distinguish between them. It may be time to recognize that, while the value of a system of checks and balances has been proved over and over again, and not least in the Watergate crisis, such safeguards do not logically or necessarily demand an impenetrable separation between the executive and the legislature.

This may seem shocking. But in fact the separation of powers has been breaking down in practice for a long time. The most striking example is the evolution of the President's legislative program, especially since FDR's presidency. That development, of course, was in the direction of giving the President more primacy in relation to Congress. But other recent developments, such as the "legislative veto" and the congressional budgetary system, have operated in the opposite direction. In these and other ways, Congress and the presidency are already being more closely knit together. There is a great deal of scope for developing this process.

Perhaps the most promising group of reforms is that which aims at strengthening the President by enabling him to share the burdens of his job. In its cruder form, this aim has led to suggestions that there should be one or more assistant Presidents, or a number of Vice Presidents with specific responsibilities of their own. Sometimes it is the President's ceremonial responsibilities that are to be hived off to an assistant or a deputy, sometimes the routine chores of managing the bureaucracy. Much of the presidency's ceremonial function has for years been performed by the President's family. Lady Bird Johnson was particularly conscientious in this regard, while Rosalynn Carter appears to have undertaken a significant role as an adviser, campaigner, and even political operative.

Many reforms speak wistfully of reviving and strengthening the cabinet (something most Presidents-elect say they mean to do, before they have acquired experience with a real, live cabinet!). The difficulty about strengthening the cabinet in the American system is that U.S. cabinet members have no independent stature or power base of their own. They are the President's creatures. He appoints them because they symbolize an intention he wants to convey or a block of support he wishes to retain. But they are only symbols not masters of those blocks of support. When they no longer serve the President's interests, they simply fade from the political stage and go back to their previous existence as lawyers, or deans of graduate schools, or labor leaders, or businessmen, or whatever else they were before the President tapped them. In a parliamentary system, in contrast, even the weakest, most obscure member of the cabinet is at the least an elected member of the legislature of some years' standing. The leading members of the cabinet are major political leaders in their own right, heavyweights roughly comparable to the two or three leading contenders for presidential nomination in the U.S. system. As such they generally represent important blocks of regional or interest group support, and each will be the guardian of some major strand of the party's ideological tradition. The result is that the leader listens to them in cabinet not because he thinks that pearls of counsel will fall from their lips, but because he has to; he cannot afford to alienate the blocks of support they represent.

Many reformers in the United States have proposed that the cabinet be strengthened. Stephen Hess, for example, has argued cogently for a more "collegial" presidency, one in which "Presidents rely on their cabinet officers as the principal source of advice and hold them personally responsible—in the British sense of the doctrine of ministerial responsibility—for the operations of the different sectors of government." Benjamin V. Cohen, who was one of FDR's brain trusters in the 1930s, suggested another variant in a 1974 lecture at the University of California: a small executive council of five to eight distinguished citizens, appointed by the President. It would have staff and the power to demand access to government records, plans, and information generally, to monitor and coordinate the activity of the government on the President's behalf, and also to advise him before he makes important decisions.

Such innovations, which on analysis amount to little more than attempts to enhance the authority of something not very different from the present cabinet, or from the "supercabinet" which Richard Nixon seems to have been thinking of introducing in his second term, might well be useful as far as they went. But they miss the point of the European parliamentary and cabinet system. That system, making all due allowance for the sins of omission and commission that can be charged to it since it grew up in the nineteenth century, has three very great advantages. First, it provides the executive leader with a council of genuinely independent advisers who share a broad body of principles with him, but are free to disagree within the limits of those principles. Second, it binds the executive and the legislature together in a way that provides the executive with organized democratic support, and at the same time involves the preponderant group in the legislature in responsibility for the executive's actions. Lastly, it provides for an automatic sanction. If the government goes so far wrong that it loses the confidence of the legislature, then it falls, with no need to prove impeachable offenses and consequently no messy, prolonged, or dangerous crisis.

That, at least, is the theory of the matter. In practice the European variants of the cabinet/parliamentary system have by no means always succeeded in avoiding prolonged and damaging crisis. At different times in the past thirty-five years—not to speak of earlier periods!—Britain, France, West Germany, and Italy all offer horrendous examples of the political system's failure to meet social needs. It would be a rash person who would urge the United States to imitate European models purely on the basis of how well they have performed. Still, if it were possible to adapt some elements of the European cabinet and parliamentary systems to American traditions and to the formal requirements of the U.S. Constitution, they might help to mitigate some of the most glaring weaknesses that now afflict the presidency. One idea that seems to me to have attractive advantages (as well as awkward disadvantages) would be for the President to be advised by a "supercabinet" or council, of the kind discussed above, but composed of leading figures in Congress. These could be either members of the official leadership or chairmen of important committees. Membership in this cabinet council could belong ex officio to specific officials such as the Speaker, the president pro tem of the Senate, the chairmen of the Senate Foreign Relations and Finance committees, and of House Rules and Ways and Means; or, better, the President could be free to choose his own cabinet council from among congressional leaders. This would save him from being embarrassed, and would save the council's work from being disrupted, by the unavoidable presence of one or more rivals or enemies. One obvious difficulty would arise where the President and the congressional leadership were of different parties. In that case, the purpose of the council would be best accomplished by its being chosen from ranking minority leaders in Congress.

That purpose would be something much more than the mere consultation that already takes place. It would, first, make available to the President advice from the most powerful and experienced elected politicians in Washington: a group of people far better qualified to advise him on the realities of power and politics in Washington than any recent presidential cabinet, and far less exposed to being browbeaten by Presidents or their aides, because it would be made up of men with an independent political base of their own in elective office. Second, these powerful figures in Congress would be involved in the framing of the President's legislative program. On the one hand, this would make the program more responsive to all the concerns that normally surface in congressional hearings and debate, and in good time; on the other, it would mean that major legislative proposals would arrive on the Hill with every likelihood of passage guaranteed by powerful sponsorship. This would not ensure that everything the President and his cabinet council wanted was railroaded through Congress. There would be every opportunity for other members of Congress to raise every reasonable question. It would mean that the President was not faced, as he is now, with the endless task of bolting together, on his own and out of his own resources, a brand-new coalition for every separate piece of legislation that he or the country needs. Third, and most important of all, such a cabinet council would be a step in the direction of closing the gap that has opened up between the presidential and congressional parties.

The most promising way of making the President a more effective leader in Congress lies in strengthening the ties of party so that more members of Congress feel impelled to support the President more often than is now the case. Many political scientists have agreed that it would be a good thing if the United States enjoyed "responsible party government"; that is, if Presidents and the members of their party were bound together by their joint commitment to a common program, duly presented to the voters at election time, and which they were jointly bound to carry out —at least in its main lines—once in office and to defend once they had enacted it. With this goal, reformers have urged that the national committees and their staffs should be strengthened, that Presidents and members of Congress alike should bind themselves to support the party platform, and that the parties should have the power to discipline elected officials who persistently opposed party policy by withholding party support. Most of the major parties of Western Europe have all or most of these characteristics. It would surely make for more effective government in the United States if American parties, too, had these powers. It would certainly strengthen the presidency as an institution if the President, as party leader, was normally in a position to demand support from members of Congress, as party leaders in other systems generally are on important issues.

The American President, however, has no such power. At the moment there seems slight chance that he will get it. If anything, the trends seem to be running the other way. "Once the President has won his battles and occupied the White House," writes the political scientist Richard M. Pious, "he finds no party structure to control, no party to unite." *No* party? Pious exaggerates, but only slightly. The Democratic party, for some years after 1972, was little more than a package of debts and a bundle of lawsuits. Jimmy Carter felt free to cold-shoulder it ostentatiously on his way to the White House. The Republican party adds up to even less: the memory of a once-great name, to be used or ignored by ambitious men as it suits their purpose.

It will not be easy to reverse these trends and to breathe new life into the political party, one of the oldest and most valuable American contributions to the technique of democratic politics. But it will surely be worth the effort. Only if the President is rearmed with the support that comes from party leadership can he be freed from dangerous reliance on personal popularity courted by means of the media and registered by the opinion polls. Isolated from the discipline of party, the President is like a barbarian chief, wholly dependent on his personal charisma and at the mercy of any defeat that strips him of that fickle, magical authority. As the legitimate leader of a structured and responsible party, he is enabled, like the general of civilized armies, not only to bring far greater power to bear, but also to survive temporary setbacks and personal shortcomings. Party is the mechanism which can steadily and rationally transform democratic choice into action. It can transform fragile popularity into legitimate authority.

The revival of party, a reworking of the relationship between President and Congress on a cooperative not a competitive basis, a bold reform of the federal bureaucracy founded on clear definitions of role and purpose: these are some of the strategic innovations that promise to relieve the President's isolation. Forty years ago, the Brownlow committee wrote that the President needs help. It would be truer to say today that he needs friends: institutional friends and partners in the operation of a system where too often today he has only rivals and competitors.

Sound strategies are needed if wars are to be won. But actual victory comes from an accumulation of small tactical successes in the places chosen by strategy. The presidency will be revived not by a few grand strokes of constitutional change but by the accumulation of small improvements at the right points in the system. There are some things a President can do on his own authority, for example by executive order or simply by changing his own informal practice in such matters as whom he consults about what. There are other reforms that require statutory authority from Congress. Then any truly radical changes in the ground rules of the system—such as any substantial division in the authority of the presidency of the kind that would be needed for any move in the direction of a plural presidency—would take a constitutional amendment. Reforms will be needed at all three levels.

In practice, though, all projects for the reform of the presidency bump up against a frustrating dilemma. If they can be easily undertaken, the chances are that they will not do much good. If they are bold enough to improve the odds now so heavily stacked against the President, then they are unfortunately not very likely to happen. The chances must be little better than minimal of organizing a two-thirds majority in Congress, and then of procuring ratification from three-quarters of the States, for a constitutional amendment radically to reform the presidency.

It is right that this should be so, for while there is a strong consensus, at least among those with personal experience of the working of the system, that the presidency as an institution does not work as well as it should, there is as yet no consensus on what ought to be done or even on what is the most serious problem to put right. Is it that the presidency needs to be made into a more effective instrument of government? Or is it to safeguard the system against the manifest dangers of an overmighty presidency? Which is the greater threat: the man on the white horse or the white mouse in the White House?

In short, if we shop aimlessly in the great supermarket of proposals that have been put forward for reforming the presidency, we will find ourselves back in no time at our starting point, the paradox of presidential power: is the President too weak? Or is he too strong?

I have contended that he is neither too weak nor too strong, but trapped in a more subtle and complex malfunction of the system which can best be summarized that he is too isolated, too cut off both from the "real nation" and from complementary sources of democratic authority that could make him more effective with no risk of any dangerous monopoly of power.

If this truth is accepted, a strategic decision will have been taken. A standard will have been set against which specific reform proposals can be tested. The possibility of an effective consensus of political will will have returned; the strategic direction for tactical advance will have been chosen. The task will be to reduce the President's isolation. New links will have to be forged, old links reforged, and new relationships knit together to carry the drive of presidential leadership through Congress and the government to the country and the people, and to carry back popular assent and authority. Then optimism will be possible, for the American system—so apparently rigid in its constitutional arrangements to unperceptive eyes—is a living thing, and so can adapt flexibly and with surprising speed to new dangers. That is why it has lasted so well. All that remains to be said is that there is no time to be lost, for—to quote one of the oldest poems in our language, "The Lay of the Battle of Maldon":

> Thought shall be the harder,
> Heart the keener,
> Mood shall be the more,
> As our might lessens.

Notes

Notes to Chapter One

Page 13. "The tragedy of the presidency, he concluded, was the impotence of the President." The view is attributed to Roosevelt by Arthur M. Schlesinger, Jr. (*The Age of Roosevelt,* vol. 2, *The Coming of the New Deal,* pp. 512–13), but surely correctly.

Page 14. The quotation from Richard Neustadt is taken from a magazine article: "Size-up of Kennedy in the White House," *U.S. News and World Report,* July 16, 1962.

Page 14. The Johnson quotation is taken from Hugh Sidey, *A Very Personal Presidency* (1968), p. 260.

Page 16. Personal observation of the East Room over many years was checked and supplemented by *The White House: An Historic Guide,* issued by the White House Historical Association, esp. pp. 34–37.

Page 17 ff. The following passage owes a great deal to Ms. Wexler, who briefed me and also arranged for me to attend the hospital administrators' reception.

Page 24 ff. I accompanied the President on his trip to North Carolina and South Carolina on September 22, 1978. During the whole of September and October 1978, I spent as much time as possible in the White House, interviewing a large number of aides at many levels. I had previously worked as a reporter in the White House for one news organization or another during the Kennedy, Johnson, Nixon, and Ford administrations, and interviewed many aides of all those four Presidents. In addition, while preparing a special ninety-minute documentary on the presidency for the Independent Television Network in Britain in 1976, I interviewed some two dozen former White House aides to Presidents from Truman to Ford.

Page 30. The Reston column, undated in my files, was written in April 1978.

Page 31. The quotation comes from Harry McPherson, *A Political Education,* p. 268.

Page 31. Kessel sets out his analysis of the several "calendars" which a President must work with in John H. Kessel, *The Domestic Presidency,* pp. 9–11.

Page 32. Cronin identifies his source more precisely as "a high policy aide during Nixon's first term." Thomas E. Cronin, *The State of the Presidency,* p. 184.

Page 32. Stephen Hess, *Organizing the Presidency,* pp. 16–25.

Page 33. For Presidents' steadily declining popularity, except for Eisenhower, see John E. Mueller, *War, Presidents and Public Opinion,* e.g., p. 267. Mueller lists four variables that predict presidential popularity. They are: (1) a "coalition of minorities" variable that means the trend of presidential popularity will be downward; (2) a "rally-round-the-flag" variable which anticipates that international crises and similar phenomena will give the President a short-term boost in popularity; (3) an economic slump variable, with negative effects; (4) a war variable, also with negative effects.

Page 36. On the similarity of Kennedy's and Nixon's policies for Cuba, see my *America in Our Time*, p. 73. Kennedy's policy is analyzed (and defended) in Schlesinger, *A Thousand Days;* Nixon's position is exposed in his autobiographical *Six Crises* (1962).

Page 37. Edward Jay Epstein's *Legend: The Secret World of Lee Harvey Oswald* contains an intriguing discussion of Oswald's links to the secret worlds of intelligence agencies and organized crime. On balance, with regard to Oswald's motivation, while accepting Epstein's and the other evidence of Oswald's contacts with covert action and the secret struggle with Cuba, I prefer the interpretation of Priscilla Johnson McMillan (*Marina and Lee* [1977]), which stresses Oswald's fascination with Kennedy's success and glamour.

Page 37. I am indebted to my friend and colleague Bruce Page for first pointing out to me the relevance of Weber's concept of charisma to presidential campaigning. See Lewis Chester, Bruce Page, and Godfrey Hodgson, *An American Melodrama*, pp. 307–10. See also below in Chapter III, pp. 115–18.

Page 38. It was not uncommon in Washington in 1963–64 to hear half-serious suggestions that Lyndon Johnson might have been responsible for the assassination. What is far more relevant is that Johnson, Lady Bird Johnson, and many of Johnson's aides felt that the fact that the assassination had taken place in Texas aggravated Johnson's problem in establishing the legitimacy of his presidency. See, for example, Harry McPherson, *A Political Education*, p. 213, "There would be perilous suspicions." And cf. William Manchester's description of the relationship between the Kennedy and Johnson aides immediately after the assassination: "it was undeniably very, very sick." *The Death of a President* (1967), p. 385.

Page 38. Johnson discusses the problem of a President's need to establish his "right to govern" very lucidly in his memoirs: Lyndon Baines Johnson, *The Vantage Point*, p. 18.

Page 40. The prosecutor of Calley, Captain Aubrey Daniel, wrote a letter of protest to President Nixon, saying, "You have subjected the judicial system of this country to the criticism that it is subject to political influence." Jonathan Schell, *The Time of Illusion*, p. 148.

Page 41. Nixon's speechwriter, Raymond Price, is a good example of the tendency to identify "Watergate" only with relatively "trivial" incidents, thus exculpating Nixon of more serious transgressions. Raymond Price, *With Nixon*, pp. 360–69: "None of this, even if true, excuses the White House . . . The break-ins and the bugging did take place." Yes, and so did far more serious infringements of constitutional law and practice, as the House Judiciary Committee formally determined, though Price and similar authors ignore or minimize the fact.

NOTES TO CHAPTER TWO

Page 50 ff. In my assessment of President Franklin D. Roosevelt, I have followed the standard biographers, especially James MacGregor Burns, *Roosevelt: The Lion and the Fox* and *Roosevelt: Soldier of Freedom;* and Arthur M. Schlesinger, Jr., *The Age of Roosevelt.* I also learned a great deal from Samuel Rosenman, *Working with Roosevelt,* and from the book Judge Rosenman wrote in collaboration with his wife Dorothy, and which she finished, *Presidential Style.*

Page 51 ff. For the history of the constitutional relationship between presidential power and congressional prerogatives, I relied heavily on E. S. Corwin, *The President: Office and Powers;* Raoul Berger, "The Presidential Monopoly of Foreign Relations," *Michigan Law Review,* November 1972; Louis Fisher, *President and Congress;* Louis Henkin, *Foreign Affairs and the Constitution;* and Arthur M. Schlesinger, Jr., *The Imperial Presidency.*

Page 51 ff. The quotations from Thaddeus Stevens, Wilson, and Bryce are all taken from Corwin, *op. cit.,* pp. 28–33.

Page 52. The two books that chart the change in Woodrow Wilson's views are his *Congressional Government,* first published in 1885, and *Constitutional Government in the United States,* first published in 1908.

Page 53. Theodore Roosevelt's skill in dealing with the press is analyzed in Elmer E. Cornwell, Jr., *Presidential Leadership of Public Opinion,* pp. 13–26 and *passim.* See also Henry Fairlie, "The Press Secretary," *The New Republic,* March 18, 1978.

Page 53. The quotation from TR when governor of New York is taken from Edmund Morris, *The Rise of Theodore Roosevelt,* p. 690, citing Theodore Roosevelt, *Autobiography,* p. 290.

Page 54. As evidence that William Howard Taft's view of the presidency was not as supine as has sometimes been suggested, see the speech he gave at Columbia University, which is published in W. H. Taft, *Our Chief Magistrate and His Powers,* p. 53, and quoted in Richard M. Pious, *The American Presidency,* p. 49.

Page 55. The quotation from Bertrand H. Snell was taken from Burns, *Roosevelt: The Lion and the Fox,* p. 167.

Page 60. Benjamin C. Bradlee, *Conversations with Kennedy,* p. 193.

Page 62. The aide was Charles Taussig, quoted in Schlesinger, *The Age of Roosevelt,* vol. 2, *The Coming of the New Deal,* p. 539.

Page 63 ff. On Roosevelt's public relations technique, see Rosenman, *Presidential Style,* pp. 328–35, and Cornwell, *op. cit.*

Page 66. The remark by Roosevelt to his wife is taken from Samuel and Dorothy Rosenman, *Presidential Style,* p. 358. In full, what FDR said was, "First things come first, and I cannot alienate certain votes I need for measures that are more important for the moment by pushing any measure that would entail a fight."

Page 67. The magical adieu of Mr. Valiant-for-Truth will be found at p.

397 of John Bunyan's *The Pilgrim's Progress* in the Oxford Standard Authors edition.

Page 69. The 1960 orthodoxy about the presidency is well, and scathingly, described in William G. Andrews, "The President, Congress and Constitutional Theory" in Aaron Wildavsky, ed., *The Presidency,* pp. 24–42. Andrews is unkind enough to suggest that the new doctrine of the presidency was influenced by ideological prejudice and even personal self-serving. "One handy explanation that deserves consideration," he wrote, "is that the constitutional theory consensus of the 1960 writers sprang from their partisan political consensus . . . Most of the presidency glorifiers had in common the experience of service in the executive branch of the national government during the administration of Roosevelt and Truman but not under any of the Republican presidents."

Page 70. For the idea that the concept of "President of all the people" can be traced back even beyond Theodore Roosevelt, see Marcus Cunliffe, *American Presidents and the Presidency,* p. 191: "He [i.e., TR] and Wilson knew that it was an ancient assertion of presidential prerogative, relied on to the full by Jackson and Lincoln."

Page 70. Truman's remark was made in a speech on his seventieth birthday in Washington, quoted in Louis Koenig, ed., *The Truman Administration* (1956), p. 17.

Page 70. The Finer remark is unkindly quoted by Andrews, *op. cit.,* p. 25.

Page 70. The Lane passage comes from Robert E. Lane, *Political Ideology,* 1962, pp. 148–49, quoted in James MacGregor Burns, *Presidential Government,* p. 106.

Page 71. The first quotation from Rossiter comes from *Constitutional Dictatorship* (1948), p. 314; the passage about the "magnificent lion" comes from Clinton Rossiter, *The American Presidency,* pp. 72–73.

Page 72. The Rossiter quotation comes from *ibid.,* p. 261.

Page 73. The quotations from Rossiter, Koenig, and Tugwell are taken from Andrews, *op. cit.,* p. 26.

Page 74. Wildavsky's "The Two Presidencies" article first appeared in *Trans-action* 4, no. 2 (December 1966). It was reprinted in Wildavsky, ed., *The Presidency,* p. 448.

Page 74. Rexford G. Tugwell, "The President and the Historian, a Review Essay," *Political Science Quarterly,* June 1971. Cf. Andrews, *op. cit.,* p. 28.

Page 75. The anecdote about the Harvard professors was told by Michael Kinsley in the *Harvard Crimson* and reprinted in *The Washington Monthly,* July 1970.

Page 76. Califano, *A Presidential Nation,* p. 326.

Page 77. Hughes, in Washington Journalism Center and Charles Roberts, eds., *Has the President Too Much Power?* p. 17.

Page 77. George E. Reedy, *The Twilight of the Presidency,* p. 9; Burnham, "American Politics in the 1970s," in W. N. Chambers and W. D. Burnham, eds., *The American Party System* (rev. ed., 1975); Hutchins, "Presidential Autocracy in America," in Cronin and Tugwell, eds., *The Presidency Reappraised,* p. 134; Reedy, *op. cit.,* p. 168.

Page 78. Cronin, *The State of the Presidency,* p. 290; Schlesinger, *The Imperial Presidency,* p. x.

Page 79. Benjamin V. Cohen, "Presidential Responsibility and American Democracy," Royer Lecture, University of California, Berkeley, May 23, 1974, discussed in Cronin, *The State of the Presidency,* pp. 267–68; Pious, "Is Presidential Power Poisonous?" *Political Science Quarterly* 89, no. 3 (Fall 1974); Wildavsky, "The Past and Future Presidency," *The Public Interest,* no. 41 (Fall 1975).

Notes to Chapter Three

The ideas in this chapter are derived, first, from watching the White House at work over eighteen years, and second, from interviews with present and former White House staff over the same period, especially those I did in connection with the British Independent Television program on the presidency in 1976. I am also grateful to friends who have worked in the White House for the insight they have given me into the problems of working there. I must cite three names among many: Daniel Patrick Moynihan, now senator from New York; Harry McPherson, now practicing law in Washington; George Reedy, now dean of the journalism school at Marquette University. One specific interview, with James L. Sundquist of the Brookings Institution, guided several of the lines of thought in this chapter.

On the domestic executive bureaucracy and the White House staff, I found the following books specially useful: Thomas E. Cronin, *The State of the Presidency,* which besides many valuable insights contains the results of interviews the author conducted with fifty White House staffers in 1970–72; Hugh Heclo, *A Government of Strangers;* John H. Kessel, *The Domestic Presidency;* Richard P. Nathan, *The PlotThat Failed: Nixon and the Administrative Presidency;* Stephen J. Wayne, *The Legislative Presidency;* and the contributions by Heclo and Fred I. Greenstein, particularly, in *The New American Political System,* edited by Anthony King.

Page 82 ff. My attention was first drawn to the case of the Forest Service by a reference in Schlesinger, *The Coming of the New Deal,* pp. 329–38, which by coincidence fell under my eye when I had just read an article by Elizabeth Drew, which explained that the service was at risk in the Carter reorganization, in *The New Yorker,* February 27, 1978. I found the articles by Rochelle L. Stanfield in *National Journal* very helpful. (*National Journal,* "Reorganization Plans in Trouble," January 20, 1979, "Carter Scales Down Reorganization Plans," March 10, 1979, and "The Reorganization Effort's Sputtering Climax," June 2, 1979.)

Page 85. "One of Carter's aides," quoted by Elizabeth Drew, *The New Yorker,* February 27, 1978.

Page 86. Richard P. Nathan, *The Plot That Failed,* p. 40.

Page 87. Douglass Cater used the phrase "iron triangle" in his book *Power in Washington* (1965). Otis L. Graham has shown that the phenomenon itself dates back at least as far as Franklin Roosevelt's administration; Otis L. Graham, Jr., "The Planning Ideal and American Reality: The 1930s," in Stanley Elkins and Eric McKitrick, eds., *The Hofstadter Aegis: A Memorial* (1974). Paul Weaver has tried to invalidate the concept, but he appears to think that it applies primarily to regulatory agencies; this is surely too restrictive: Paul H. Weaver, "Regulation, Social Policy and Class Conflict," *The Public Interest* 50 (Winter 1978).

Page 87. A good example of a microtriangle is the intricate relationship between S. Dillon Ripley of the Smithsonian Institution; Joseph H. Hirschhorn, the uranium magnate and sculpture collector whom Ripley persuaded to give his treasures to the Smithsonian; and various baffled congressional subcommittees which tried to trace the commitments of public money involved. This relationship is wittily described in Karl E. Meyer, *The Art Museum* (1979). It is the only one example among legion, however.

Page 87. Heclo, *A Government of Strangers*, pp. 200–201.

Page 88. Kermit Gordon, "Reflections on Spending," in J. D. Montgomery and A. Smithies, eds., *Public Policy*, vol. 15 (1966).

Page 88. Harry McPherson, *A Political Education*, pp. 224–25.

Page 89. Stephen P. Strickland has tellingly described the three-cornered relationship among the National Institutes of Health, the medical research lobbyists Albert and Mary Lasker, and Congressman Frank Keefe of Wisconsin, chairman of the relevant appropriations subcommittee, in his book *Politics, Science and Dread Disease* (1972).

Page 89. There is an excellent outline of the TFX/F-111 affair in Congressional Quarterly Service, *Congress and the Nation, 1965–1968*, vol. 2. (1969), pp. 875–78.

Page 90. The anonymous quotation comes from *ibid.*, p. 877.

Page 91. Reedy, *The Twilight of the Presidency*, p. 21. "The concept of the overburdened president represents one of the insidious forces which serve to separate the chief executive from the real universe of living breathing troubled human beings," Reedy wrote. "It is the basis for encouraging his most outrageous expressions, for pampering his most childish tantrums, for fostering his most arrogant actions."

Page 92. The Roosevelt quotation comes from Marriner Eccles, *Beckoning Frontiers* (1951), p. 336.

Page 92. Truman's remark to David Brinkley is cited in Cronin, *The State of the Presidency*, p. 18.

Page 92. Eisenhower's amazement at Kennedy's unawareness of the limits on presidential power was recorded in his memoirs, Dwight D. Eisenhower, *The White House Years*, vol. 2, *Waging Peace: 1956–1961*, p. 713.

Page 92. Doris Kearns, *Lyndon Johnson and the American Dream*, p. 305.

Page 93. Nixon's comment to Ehrlichman was recorded in an Oval Office tape of April 17, 1973, published in the *Washington Star-News* of July 20, 1974, and cited by Richard P. Nathan, *The Plot That Failed,* p. 69.

Page 93. The Carter directive and its results are reported in "Carter Issues an Order . . ." *National Journal,* July 14, 1979.

Page 93. Graham T. Allison, *Essence of Decision: Explaining the Cuban Missile Crisis* (1971).

Page 93. Morton H. Halperin, with the assistance of Priscilla Clapp and Arnold Kanter, *Bureaucratic Politics and Foreign Policy* (1974).

Page 95. Cf. Thomas F. Tout, Chapters in the *Administrative History of Medieval England* (1933; reprint, 1967).

Page 96. On the spoils system and "reform," see, for example, Matthew Josephson, *The Politicos* (1938).

Page 97. Samuel H. Beer, "In Search of a New Public Philosophy," in Anthony King, ed., *The New American Political System,* pp. 10, 20. See also Frederick C. Mosher, *Recent Trends in Governmental Finances in the United States* (1961), p. 13.

Page 97. For the nongrowth of the federal bureaucracy, see Hugh Heclo in Anthony King, ed., *The New American Political System,* p. 95.

Page 97. For the Willis plan, see Heclo, *A Government of Strangers,* pp. 72, 74.

Page 97 ff. Heclo, *op. cit.,* pp. 69–70.

Page 98. For Harold D. Smith, see Fred I. Greenstein, "Change and Continuity in the Modern Presidency," in Anthony King, ed., *The New American Political System.* Greenstein cites a Princeton Ph.D. thesis by Larry Berman, "The Evolution of a Presidential Staff Agency . . . on the Bureau of the Budget." Smith's papers are in the FDR library at Hyde Park, New York.

Page 99. Author's interview with James L. Sundquist, October 1978.

Page 99. Heclo, *op. cit.,* p. 74.

Page 100. For Grant's establishment, see James MacGregor Burns, *Presidential Government,* p. 54. For the interesting fact that Lincoln opened his own mail, see Stephen J. Wayne, *The Legislative Presidency,* p. 30.

Page 100. On the size of the White House staff, see Cronin, *The State of the Presidency,* p. 119; Heclo, *Studying the Presidency* (1977), p. 37; Wayne, *The Legislative Presidency,* pp. 220–21; etc.

Page 100. For the Brownlow report, see Nathan, *The Plot That Failed,* p. 87.

Page 102. Cited in Nelson W. Polsby, ed., *The Modern Presidency,* p. 112.

Page 103. Califano, *A Presidential Nation,* p. 251.

Page 103. Interview with Moyers by Hugh Sidey, "The White House Staff vs. the Cabinet," *The Washington Monthly,* February 1969.

Page 103. Wildavsky, "The Past and Future Presidency," *The Public Interest,* 10th anniversary issue, no. 41 (Fall 1975), p. 68.

Page 104. John Newhouse, *Cold Dawn: The Story of SALT,* p. 146.

Page 104. Author's interview with Donald McHenry, 1975.

Page 105. For the Ash Council, see Nathan, *The Plot That Failed,* p.

59. See also Dom Bonafede, "The Ash Council Would Be Proud," *National Journal,* June 9, 1979.

Page 107. The observer was Hugh Heclo, "OMB and the Presidency," *The Public Interest,* no. 38 (Winter 1975).

Page 107. Nathan, *op. cit.*

Page 108. Elizabeth Drew, *The New Yorker,* February 27, 1978.

Page 109. Quoted by Dom Bonafede, "A Day in the Life of a Cabinet Secretary," *National Journal,* May 12, 1979.

Page 110. Dean Acheson, *President at the Creation,* p. xxx, cited in Polsby, ed., *The Modern Presidency,* p. 55.

Page 110. Wildavsky, "The Past and Future Presidency," *The Public Interest,* 10th anniversary issue, no. 41 (Fall 1975), p. 67.

Page 110. J. Edward Day, *My Appointed Round,* pp. 96–98, quoted by Thomas E. Cronin, *The State of the Presidency,* p. 185.

Page 110. Kearns, *Lyndon Johnson and the American Dream,* p. 253.

Page 111. *Ibid.,* p. 255.

Page 111. Dom Bonafede, *National Journal,* "The Collapse of Cabinet Government?" April 22, 1978.

Page 112. Richard B. Cheney, quoted by Richard Cohen, *National Journal,* "Carter: the Forgotten Man in Congress," June 2, 1979.

Page 113. *The New York Times,* June 18, 1956, cited in Polsby, ed., *The Modern Presidency,* p. 113.

Page 115. Robert C. Wood, "When Government Works," *The Public Interest,* no. 18 (Winter 1970).

Page 115. On Max Weber I consulted S. N. Eisenstadt, ed., *Max Weber on Charisma and Institution Building,* 1968; J. T. Eldridge, ed., *Max Weber,* 1971; H. H. Gerth and C. Wright Mills, eds., *From Max Weber: Essays in Sociology,* 1946; Reinhard Bendix, *Max Weber: An Intellectual Portrait, 1959.*

Page 117. "He [Kennedy] guessed that J. Edward Day, the postmaster general, might have what he called 'a Hughes-type book' in him." The reference is to Emmet John Hughes, *The Ordeal of Power,* about the Eisenhower White House. Benjamin C. Bradlee, *Conversations with Kennedy,* p. 158.

Page 117. J. Edward Day, *My Appointed Round,* pp. 96–98, cited in Cronin, *The State of the Presidency,* p. 185.

NOTES TO CHAPTER FOUR

Page 119. Mr. Justice Brandeis's dissenting opinion in *Myers* v. *United States,* 272 U.S. 52. See also Louis Fisher, *President and Congress,* p. 3.

Page 119. Wilson's remark is quoted in Rosenman, *Presidential Style,* p. 166.

Page 119. Senator Long's perhaps jesting comment is cited by Harvey C. Mansfield, Sr., "The Dispersion of Authority in Congress," in Mansfield, ed., *Congress Against the President.*

Page 120. My account of the Carter administration's efforts at civil service reform is based on interviews with White House and congressional committee staff, checked against coverage in *Congressional Quarterly* and *National Journal.*

Page 126. That "celebrated, cultivated, underrated nobleman" appears in W. S. Gilbert and Sir Arthur Sullivan's *The Gondoliers.* "In enterprise of martial kind, / When there was any fighting, / He led his regiment from behind, / He found it less exciting."

Page 128. Doris Kearns, *Lyndon Johnson and the American Dream,* p. 226.

Page 129. For Truman's program being the first comprehensive presidential package of legislation, Wayne, *The Legislative Presidency,* p. 105.

Page 129. For Eisenhower's refusal, Wayne, *op. cit.,* p. 105.

Page 130. For the wartime Office of Legislation and Liaison and Persons' and Harlow's background, Richard M. Pious, *The American Presidency,* p. 187.

Page 130. For the President as legislative leader in general, see John F. Manley, "Presidential Power and White House Lobbying," *Political Science Quarterly,* Summer 1978.

Page 130. Harlow's recollection was given in an interview with Stephen J. Wayne, *The Legislative Presidency,* p. 145.

Page 131. The political scientist was John F. Manley, *op. cit.* See also Pious, *The American Presidency,* p. 179; Cronin, *The State of the Presidency,* p. 87.

Page 132. Pious, *op. cit.,* p. 87. He comments: "It isn't often that a President wins passage of a bill he really wants in exactly the form he wants it."

Page 135. For the growth of congressional staff, see Heclo, *A Government of Strangers,* p. 59; and Harrison W. Fox, Jr., and Susan Webb Hammond, "The Growth of Congressional Staffs," in Harvey C. Mansfield, Sr., ed., *Congress Against the President.* Also Fox and Hammond, *Congressional Staffs,* pp. 12–21.

Page 137. Congressman Brademas also put his thoughts on the changes that have occurred in Congress in a speech at the American embassy in London on July 6, 1978, printed in the *Congressional Record,* August 2, 1978.

Page 138. On the decline of patronage, see Eric L. Davis, "Legislative Liaison in the Carter Administration," *Political Science Quarterly,* Summer 1979, to whom I am indebted for the Chicago example and quotation.

Page 140. On the history of the DSG and on reform generally, see Norman J. Ornstein and David Rohde, "Political Parties and Congressional Reform," in Jeff Fishel, ed., *Parties and Elections in an Anti-Party Age.*

Page 143. On committee reform in the Senate, see Judith H. Parris, "The Senate Reorganizes Its Committees, 1977," *Political Science Quarterly,* Summer 1979.

Page 144. On the advantages of incumbency, see Richard E. Cohen, "Incumbents in Congress," *National Journal,* September 23, 1978.

Page 144. The quotation from Congressman Vander Jagt comes from the Cohen article cited above.

Page 144. The Harrington quotation is taken from Dennis Farney, "A Congressman Takes His Leave," *Wall Street Journal,* September 21, 1978.

Page 145. On Congress, the Constitution, and foreign policy, see E. S. Corwin, *The President: Office and Powers;* Louis Fisher, *President and Congress;* Louis Henkin, *Foreign Affairs and the Constitution;* and Arthur M. Schlesinger, Jr., *The Imperial Presidency.*

Page 145. That the framers deliberately divided responsibility was the opinion of the great constitutional scholar Alpheus T. Mason, given in his testimony to the 1971 hearings of the Senate Foreign Relations Committee.

Page 146. For the debate between Hamilton and Madison, see Fisher, *op. cit.,* p. 33.

Page 146. For a fierce attack on the doctrine of presidential monopoly of power in the foreign affairs, see Raoul Berger, "The Presidential Monopoly of Foreign Relations," *Michigan Law Review,* November 1972. "Something of the wonder that suffuses a child upon learning that a mighty oak sprang from a tiny acorn," Berger wrote, "fills one who peers behind the tapestry of conventional learning and beholds how meager are the sources of presidential claims to monopolistic control of foreign relations."

Page 146. For the number of times Presidents have ordered the use of armed force abroad and the number of declarations of war, see Louis Fisher, *President and Congress,* p. 177, quoting the Library of Congress's 1970 compilation. For the number of treaties and executive agreements, see Fisher, *op. cit.,* p. 45.

Page 146. For the tariff, see Congressional Quarterly Staff, *Powers of Congress* (1976), pp. 122–23.

Page 147. On Mr. Justice Sutherland and *U.S.* v. *Curtiss-Wright,* see Fisher, *op. cit.,* pp. 64–65; Henkin, *op. cit.,* pp. 19–28; Schlesinger, *op. cit.,* pp. 100–104; Berger, *op. cit.,* p. 28.

Page 147. For the "Great Debate," see Congressional Quarterly Staff, *Powers of Congress* (1976), p. 87.

Page 147. The Bricker amendment was a constitutional amendment introduced by Senator John W. Bricker (Rep., Ohio) in 1953. It provided that "a treaty which denies or abridges any right enumerated in this Constitution shall not be of any force or effect," and also that no treaty should "permit any foreign power or any international organization to supervise, control or adjudicate rights of citizens of the United States." On February 26, 1953, the amendment failed by only one vote. Congressional Quarterly Service, *Congress and the Nation, 1945–1964,* vol. 1 (1965), pp. 111–12.

Page 148. As late as 1970, a State Department official, asked on what authority U.S. pilots were flying combat missions in Laos, replied, "They are there under the executive authority of the President." Fisher, *op. cit.,* p. 200.

Page 149. On the congressional actions leading to the War Powers Act, see Fisher, *op. cit.;* Schlesinger, *op. cit.;* and Congressional Quarterly Staff, *Powers of Congress* (1976). For a highly critical account, see Thomas F. Eagleton, *War and Presidential Power.*

Page 151. Schlesinger, *op. cit.,* pp. 331–76, is a detailed account of "the secrecy system" which I have largely followed.

Page 152. For the ABM debate, see Fisher, *op. cit.,* pp. 212–24; Congressional Quarterly Service, *Congress and the Nation, 1969–1972,* vol. 3 (1973), pp. 196–97.

Page 154. On the legislative veto, see Heclo, *A Government of Strangers;* Fisher, *President and Congress,* pp. 82–84; Samuel C. Patterson, "The Semi-Sovereign Congress," in Anthony King, ed., *The New American Political System;* House of Representatives Committee on International Relations, *Congress and Foreign Policy,* 1976.

Page 155. On the congressional budget process, see Allen Schick, "The Battle of the Budget," in Harvey C. Mansfield, Sr., *Congress Against the President;* and Harvey G. Zeidenstein, "The Reassertion of Congressional Power: New Curbs on the President," *Political Science Quarterly,* Fall 1978.

Page 157. On *Train* v. *City of New York,* see Schick, *op. cit.,* pp. 61–66.

Notes to Chapter Five

Page 161. The epigraph is taken from a speech President Truman gave in Washington on March 24, 1946, printed by Louis W. Koenig, ed., *The Truman Administration* (1956), pp. 250–51.

Page 161. The traveler was Victor Jacquemont, quoted in Philip Woodruffe, *The Men Who Ruled India,* vol. 1, The Founders (1953), p. 233.

Page 161. In general this chapter owes a good deal to David S. Broder, *The Party's Over;* John S. Saloma III and Frederick H. Sontag, *Parties;* Jeff Fishel, ed., *Parties and Elections in an Anti-Party Age;* and to Austin Ranney, "The Political Parties: Reform and Decline," in Anthony King, ed., *The New American Political System.*

Page 161. The point about Nixon and McGovern both minimizing party ties in 1972 comes from John G. Stewart, *One Last Chance,* p. 29.

Page 162. Koenig, *op. cit.,* p. 241.

Page 163. For the Camp David guests, see *Newsweek,* July 23, 1979. And cf. Elizabeth Drew, *The New Yorker,* August 27, 1979, p. 80.

Page 163. For an original and penetrating critique of the received view about parties in America, see Walter Dean Burnham, "The End of American Party Politics," *Trans-action,* December 1969. "It is open to ask whether the United States any longer possesses" parties, says Anthony King, the British political scientist. "Presidential politics," writes Austin Ranney of the American Enterprise Institute, "have become . . . something closely approaching a no-party system." "We do not have political parties in the contemporary sense of that term as it is understood elsewhere in the Western world," says Walter Dean Burnham.

Page 166. Marcus A. Hanna (1837–1904), Cleveland coal and iron entrepreneur, who was elected senator from Ohio in 1897. He was chairman of the Republican National Committee and McKinley's campaign manager and adviser, especially about patronage and politics.

Page 167. I owe much of my knowledge of California Republican politics to conversations with men such as Stu Spencer, Lyn Nofziger, and Caspar Weinberger, and also to the tuition of my friend Frederick G. Dutton, a California Democrat who knows his opponents.

Page 169. See, for example, Penn Kimball, *Bobby Kennedy and the New Politics* (1968); Lewis Chester, Bruce Page, and Godfrey Hodgson, *An American Melodrama,* pp. 375–401, in which we argued that "there were actually two brands of New Politics on view in 1968," and that "the new politicians were successful in exactly the proportion that they learned to play the old game."

Page 171. Kennedy's speech is quoted in Broder, *The Party's Over,* p. 34.

Page 173. David Halberstam, *The Powers That Be,* p. xxx.

Page 174. James Q. Wilson's phrase is quoted in Jeane J. Kirkpatrick, *The New Presidential Elite,* p. 9.

Page 175. Kirkpatrick, *ibid.,* p. 9.

Page 179. For similar descriptions of the lobbyists in action, see Tad Szulc, *Saturday Review,* March 3, 1979; and Dennis Farney, *Wall Street Journal,* September 21, 1979.

Page 179. On the lobby generally, see Congressional Quarterly Staff, *The Washington Lobby* (1974); and Congressional Quarterly Service, *Congress and the Nation,* vols. 1–4 (1965, 1969, 1973, and 1977); see their indexes under "Lobbies and Lobbying."

Page 180. For a good general account of PACs, see Ward Sinclair, "96th Congress: Where Money Begets Power," *Washington Post,* September 23, 1979.

Page 180. Cf. a comment by Congressman Eckhardt in his newsletter for constituents, Summer 1978: "The 95th Congress has been good to a commercial priesthood that takes its tithe from the consumer dollar without affording goods or services of commensurate value."

Page 180. Interview with Senator John Culver, October 1978. And cf. his speech to Wisconsin Democratic State Convention, June 1978.

Page 180. There was an interesting argument in the *Washington Post* about single-issue pressure groups in early 1979. David S. Broder wrote an article on January 7, 1979, "Let 100 Single Issue Groups Bloom," arguing the need "to reinvent political parties." This drew a fierce rejoinder from Paul Wieck, "The Trouble with the Parties," *Washington Post,* February 4, 1979: "I do not believe Americans will put our political process back into the strait-jacket of tightly controlled party faithful, with rigid discipline which so many 'grassroots people' of every cause struggled to overcome."

Page 182. Congressman Fowler's remark was quoted by Mary Russell in *Washington Post,* June 4, 1979.

NOTES TO CHAPTER SIX

Page 183. Eisenhower's remark is quoted in William J. Small, *Political Power and the Press* (1972), pp. 90–91. Johnson's outburst is quoted in David Halberstam, *The Powers That Be,* p. 6.

Page 183. Three indispensable general works on the media and presidential politics are Erik Barnouw, *The Image Empire,* the third volume of Professor Barnouw's magisterial history of broadcasting in the United States; Elmer E. Cornwell, Jr., *Presidential Leadership of Public Opinion;* and Newton N. Minow, John Bartlow Martin, and Lee M. Mitchell, *Presidential Television.* Of the many recent books about television and the media in general, I found William J. Small, *Political Power and the Press* (1972) consistently useful. Two excellent recent articles are Alan P. Balutis, "The Presidency and the Press . . ." *Presidential Studies Quarterly,* Fall 1977, and Michael Baruch Grossman and Martha Joynt Kumar, "The White House and the News Media: the Phases of Their Relationship," *Political Science Quarterly,* Spring 1979. A careful list of occasions when press coverage can be shown to have affected presidential policy is to be found in William J. Lanouette, *National Journal,* "The 'Power' of the Press Corps," June 2, 1979.

Page 183. Joseph A. Califano, Jr., *A Presidential Nation,* p. 103.

Page 185. Pointing out that a lot had happened since Cornwell measured coverage in *The New York Times* and the *Providence Journal* from 1885 to 1957, Alan P. Balutis measured coverage in *The New York Times* and his local paper, the *Buffalo Evening News,* from 1958 to 1977. He found (1) "a marked dominance of presidential news in contrast to a noticeable decline of congressional news," and (2) "some relationship . . . between the amount of news about a President and his standing in the opinion polls."

Page 185. Cf. Minow, Martin, and Mitchell, *Presidential Television,* p. 110.

Page 186. FDR's remarks about radio are taken from Leila A. Sussman, "FDR and the White House Mail," *Public Opinion Quarterly,* no. 20 (Spring 1956).

Page 186. For Kennedy's article, see Cornwell, *Presidential Leadership of Public Opinion,* pp. 278–79.

Page 186. The Halberstam comment comes from *The Powers That Be,* p. 328.

Page 186. For Truman's speech and Jack Gould's comment, Cornwell, *op. cit.,* p. 266.

Page 187. Nixon's Checkers speech was made to a viewing audience of twenty-five million in mid-September 1952. It was, comment Minow, Martin, and Mitchell, "perhaps the most brilliant use that had ever been made of the mass media." *Presidential Television,* pp. 49–50.

Page 187. Salinger, *With Kennedy* (1966), p. 83.

Page 188. *The New Yorker*'s comment was in an unsigned editorial early in 1973.

Page 188. For Johnson and the Dominican Republic, see Small, *op. cit.,* p. 118.

Page 189. Nixon's reservations were quoted by Earl Mazo, *Richard Nixon* (1959), p. 299.

Page 190. For Ford's audience, Pious, *The American Presidency,* pp. 196–97.

Page 191. The Harris study is quoted in Minow, Martin, and Mitchell, *Presidential Television,* p. 19.

Page 191. For Gallup ratings expressed as a graph from 1945 to 1975, see Cronin, *The State of the Presidency,* pp. 110–111. Cf. Pious, *The American Presidency,* p. 200.

Page 195. The anecdote about Agnew and Cronkite comes from Small, *op. cit.,* p. 137.

Page 195. Price's charges can be found in his book *With Nixon,* pp. 175–91.

Page 195. Ron Nessen is quoted in Philip Shabecoff, "Appraising Presidential Power: The Ford Presidency," in Thomas E. Cronin and Rexford G. Tugwell, eds., *The Presidency Reappraised,* p. 33.

Page 198. On the extent of TV viewing, see Minow, Martin, and Mitchell's summary of the evidence, *Presidential Television,* pp. 5–6.

Page 200. Kennedy's remark is quoted in Schlesinger, *A Thousand Days,* p. 476.

Page 200. Emmet John Hughes told this anecdote at a Washington conference in October 1973. The proceedings were published as a book, Charles Roberts, ed., *Has the President Too Much Power?* p. 23.

Page 204. On Paley, Murrow, and Stanton, see Halberstam, *The Powers That Be,* pp. 134–57; Barnouw, *The Image Empire,* pp. 40–56; Robert Metz, *CBS: Reflections in a Bloodshot Eye,* pp. 108–10, 279–92.

Page 206. Reedy, *The Twilight of the Presidency,* p. 117.

Page 206. Grossman and Kumar, "The White House and the News Media: the Phases of Their Relationship," *Political Science Quarterly,* Spring 1979. I find their thesis very persuasive.

Page 207. Dom Bonafede, "Thank You, Mr. President," *National Journal,* August 11, 1979, p. 1336.

NOTES TO CHAPTER SEVEN

Page 209. Henry Jones Ford, *The Rise and Growth of American Politics,* p. xxx.

Page 209. James Bryce, *The American Commonwealth,* 3rd ed. rev., vol. 1, p. 187.

Page 209. Arthur M. Schlesinger, Jr., *The Imperial Presidency,* p. 254.

Page 212. Philip L. Graham quoted in Maurice Klain, "Politics—Still a Dirty Word," *Antioch Review,* Winter 1955–56.

Page 213. V. O. Key is quoted by F. Rhodes Cook, "National Conventions and Delegate Selection: an Overview," in Jeff Fishel, ed., *Parties and Elections in an Anti-Party Age,* p. 199.

Page 213. For the Stevenson and Truman opinions, *ibid.,* p. 200.

Page 213. For the number of primaries, see F. Rhodes Cook, *op. cit.,* p. 196. The number for 1964 includes a presidential preference poll taken by the Texas Republican party. For the proportion of delegates chosen in primaries, *ibid.,* p. 189.

Page 215. For an analysis of those available to become presidential candidates, see William R. Keech and Donald R. Matthews, "Patterns in the Presidential Nominating Process," in Fishel, ed., *Parties and Elections in an Anti-Party Age,* pp. 203–16.

Page 216. For the "paradox of voting," see Garry Wills, *Confessions of a Conservative* (1979), pp. 106–16.

Page 218. David S. Broder, *Washington Post,* May 22, 1979.

Page 218. James Fallows, "The Passionless Presidency, II," *Atlantic Monthly,* June 1979, p. 77.

Page 218. James MacGregor Burns, *Presidential Government,* p. 168. Emphasis in the original.

Page 219. For John Ehrlichman and Norm McCullough, John H. Kessel, *The Domestic Presidency,* p. 85.

Page 219. Carter speech in Martin Schram, *Running for President: A Journal of the Carter Campaign,* pp. 235–36.

Page 220. Edward Walsh, "Carter Looking to '80, Revives His Style of '76," *Washington Post,* July 31, 1979.

Page 220. Editorial introduction to James MacGregor Burns, "Jimmy Carter's Strategy for 1980," *Atlantic Monthly,* March 1979.

Page 220. David S. Broder, "Betting on the Budget," *Washington Post,* January 31, 1979.

Page 220. Terence Smith, *The New York Times,* January 28, 1979.

Page 221. Elizabeth Drew, *The New Yorker,* February 27, 1978.

Page 221. Harry McPherson, *A Political Education,* p. 268.

Page 221. Drew, *The New Yorker,* February 27, 1978, on cargo preference. On the politics of reorganization generally, see for example, Rochelle L. Stanfield, "Reorganization Plans in Trouble," *National Journal,* January 20, 1979, pp. 84 ff.

Page 222. Lewis Chester, Bruce Page, and Godfrey Hodgson, *An American Melodrama,* p. 446.

Page 228. Thomas E. Cronin, *The State of the Presidency,* pp. 12–13.

Page 228. Bob Woodward and Carl Bernstein, *The Final Days,* pp. 224–25.

Page 229. David Halberstam, *The Powers That Be,* p. 447.

Page 229. For the *Mayagüez* episode, I relied on contemporary coverage in the *Washington Post, The New York Times,* and *Congressional Quarterly;* William Shawcross, *Sideshow* (1979), pp. 433–35; Roger Morris, "What to Make of *Mayagüez,*" *The New Republic,* June 14, 1975; John Osborne, "Afterthoughts," *The New Republic,* June 28, 1975; Richard Rovere, *The New Yorker,* May 17, 1975.

Page 231. James Fallows, "The Passionless Presidency," *Atlantic Monthly,* May 1979, p. 40.

Page 232. Boorstin coined the phrase "pseudo-events" in his book, Daniel J. Boorstin, *The Image: A Guide to Pseudo-Events in America* (1961).

Page 233. For an account of the Nixon trip to China and how media coverage was manipulated, see Newton N. Minow, John Bartlow Martin, and Lee M. Mitchell, *Presidential Television,* pp. 4, 41–42, 66–68.

Page 234. Martin Schram, "It Will Make Him Look Presidential," *Washington Post,* March 27, 1979.

Page 236. Nancy Collins and Robert G. Kaiser, *Washington Post,* May 4, 1977.

Page 247. The whole second half of Stephen Hess's *Organizing the Presidency,* pp. 143–218, is given over to discussing ways in which the presidency could be made more effective by making it more "collegial," an approach with which I am in skeptical sympathy. For a systematic discussion of reform proposals, see also Thomas E. Cronin, *The State of the Presidency,* pp. 262–87. These two writers offer two of the most comprehensive handbooks to what is now a voluminous literature of presidential reform.

Page 247. For Burns's "several hundred" regional presidential agencies, see his *Uncommon Sense,* p. 132.

Page 247. For Barbara Tuchman's suggestion, cf. Tuchman, "Shall We Abolish the Presidency?" *The New York Times,* February 13, 1973. Incidentally this article was written remarkably early in the Watergate process.

Page 247. A handy guide to reform of campaign finance is in Congressional Quarterly Service, *Congress and the Nation, 1972–1976,* vol. 4 (1977), pp. 1001–2.

Page 248. For the history of proposals for regional primaries, a national primary, and other primary reform proposals, see F. Rhodes Cook, "National Conventions and Delegate Selection: An Overview," in Fishel, ed., *Parties and Elections in an Anti-Party Age,* pp 200–202.

Page 250. On the six-year term, see Joseph A. Califano, Jr., *A Presidential Nation,* p. 296; David Broder, *Washington Post,* February 11, 1979; and cf. George E. Reedy, *The Twilight of the Presidency,* pp. 137–38.

Page 251. On the four-year term for congressmen, see Marcus Cunliffe, *American Presidents and the Presidency,* p. 272.

Page 253. Wilson's remark was made in his address to a joint session of Congress in April 1913. Rosenman, *Presidential Style,* p. 166.

Page 255. Hess, *Organizing the Presidency,* p. 154.

Page 255. Benjamin V. Cohen, "Presidential Responsibility and American Democracy," Royer Lecture, University of California, Berkeley, May 23, 1974, quoted in Cronin, *The State of the Presidency,* pp. 267–68.

Page 258. Pious, *The American Presidency,* p. 141.

Page 260. The lines from the end of the "Lay of the Battle of Maldon" are one of the three epigraphs to Arnold J. Toynbee's vast *Study of History,* first published five years before the beginning of the Second World War. The other two were briefer but no less prophetic. "Work . . . while it is day," from the Gospel according to John, 9:4; and from the sixth book of Virgil's *Aeneid,* line 539: "Nox ruit, Aenea": "Night rushes on us, Aeneas."

Bibliography

Aaron, Henry J. *Politics and the Professors*. Brookings Institution, 1978.
Allison, Graham T. *Essence of Decision: Explaining the Cuban Missile Crisis*. Little, Brown, 1971.
Bagdikian, Ben H. *The Effete Conspiracy*. Harper & Row, 1972.
Balutis, Alan P. "The Presidency and the Press: the Expanding Presidential Image." *Presidential Studies Quarterly* 7, no. 4 (Fall 1977).
Barber, James David. *The Presidential Character*. Prentice-Hall, 1972.
———, ed. *Race for the Presidency: The Media and the Nominating Process*. Prentice-Hall, 1978.
Barnouw, Erik. *A History of Broadcasting in the United States*. Vol. 3, *The Image Empire*. Oxford University Press, 1970.
Beale, Howard K. *Theodore Roosevelt and America's Rise to World Power*. The Johns Hopkins Press, 1956.
Bendix, Reinhard. *Max Weber: An Intellectual Portrait*. Doubleday, 1960.
Bennet, Douglas J., Jr. "Congress in Foreign Policy: Who Needs It!" *Foreign Affairs*, Fall 1978.
Berger, Raoul. *Impeachment: the Constitutional Problems*. Harvard University Press, 1973.
———. "The Presidential Monopoly of Foreign Relations." *Michigan Law Review*, November 1972.
Bickel, Alexander M. *The New Age of Political Reform*. Harper & Row, 1968.
Bradlee, Benjamin C. *Conversations with Kennedy*. Norton, 1975.
Broder, David S. "Let 100 Single-Issue Groups Bloom." *Washington Post*, January 7, 1979.
———. *The Party's Over: The Failure of Politics in America*. Harper & Row, 1972.
Burnham, Walter Dean. "The End of American Party Politics." *Transaction*, December 1969.
Burns, James MacGregor. *The Deadlock of Democracy*. Prentice-Hall, 1963.
———. *Presidential Government*. Houghton Mifflin, 1965.
———. *Roosevelt: The Lion and the Fox*. Harcourt, Brace & World, 1956.
———. *Roosevelt: Soldier of Freedom*. Harcourt, Brace, 1971.
Califano, Joseph A., Jr. *A Presidential Nation*. Norton, 1977.
Chester, Lewis; Page, Bruce; and Hodgson, Godfrey. *An American Melodrama*, Viking, 1969.
Cornwell, Elmer E., Jr. *Presidential Leadership of Public Opinion*. Indiana University Press, 1965.

Corwin, E. S. *The President: Office and Powers.* New York University Press, 1940.

Cronin, Thomas E. *The State of the Presidency.* Little, Brown, 1975.

———. U.S. House of Representatives Select Committee on Committees, vol. 2 pt. 3, "The Swelling of the Presidency and Its Impact on Congress," 1973.

———, and Greenberg, Sanford D., eds. *The Presidential Advisory System.* Harper & Row, 1969.

———, and Tugwell, Rexford G., eds. *The Presidency Reappraised.* Praeger, 1977.

Crotty, William J. *Decision for the Democrats: Reforming the Party Structure.* Johns Hopkins Press, 1978.

Crouse, Timothy. *The Boys on the Bus.* Random House, 1972.

Cunliffe, Marcus. *American Presidents and the Presidency.* McGraw-Hill, 1972.

Davis, Eric L. "Legislative Liaison in the Carter Administration." *Political Science Quarterly* 94, no. 2 (Summer 1979).

Dean, John. *Blind Ambition.* Simon and Schuster, 1976.

Destler, I. M. *Presidents, Bureaucrats and Foreign Policy.* Princeton University Press, 1972.

Diamond, Robert A., ed. *Powers of Congress.* Congressional Quarterly, 1976.

Dolce, Philip C., and Skau, George H., eds. *Power and the Presidency.* Scribner's, 1976.

Donovan, Robert J. *Conflict and Crisis: the Presidency of Harry S. Truman.* Norton, 1977.

———. *Eisenhower: The Inside Story.* Harper, 1956.

Drew, Elizabeth. "Constituencies." *The New Yorker,* January 15, 1979.

———. "Engagement with the Special Interest State." *The New Yorker,* February 27, 1978.

Eagleton, Thomas F. *War and Presidential Power: A Chronicle of Congressional Surrender.* Liveright, 1974.

Eisenhower, Dwight D. *Mandate for Change.* Doubleday, 1963.

Eisenstadt, S. N., ed. *Max Weber: On Charisma and Institution Building.* University of Chicago Press, 1968.

Etzioni, Amitai. "The Domestic Carter: Avoiding Interest Groups." *Current,* February 1979.

Evans, Rowland, Jr., and Novak, Robert D. *Nixon in the White House.* Random House, 1971.

Fairlie, Henry. *The Kennedy Promise.* Doubleday, 1973.

Fallows, James. "The Passionless Presidency." *Atlantic Monthly,* May and June 1979.

Fenno, Richard F. *The President's Cabinet.* Vintage, 1959.

Finer, Herman. *The Presidency: Crisis and Regeneration.* University of Chicago Press, 1960.

Fishel, Jeff, ed. *Parties and Elections in an Anti-Party Age: American Politics and the Crisis of Confidence.* Indiana University Press, 1978.

Fisher, Louis. *President and Congress.* The Free Press, 1972.

Fox, Harrison W., Jr., and Hammond, Susan Webb. *Congressional Staffs: The Invisible Force in American Lawmaking.* The Free Press, 1977.

Geyelin, Philip L. *Lyndon Johnson and the World.* Praeger, 1966.

Grossman, Michael Baruch, and Kumar, Martha Joynt. "The White House and the News Media: the Phases of Their Relationship." *Political Science Quarterly* 94, no. 1 (Spring 1979).

Halberstam, David. *The Powers That Be.* Knopf, 1979.

Halperin, Morton H. with the assistance of Priscilla Clapp and Arnold Kanter. *Bureaucratic Politics and Foreign Policy.* Brookings Institution, 1974.

Hardin, Charles M. *Presidential Power and Accountability: Towards a New Constitution.* University of Chicago Press, 1974.

Heclo, Hugh. *A Government of Strangers: Executive Politics in Washington.* Brookings Institution, 1977.

Henkin, Louis. *Foreign Affairs and the Constitution.* Foundation Press, 1972.

Hess, Robert D., and Easton, David. "The Child's Changing Image of the Presidency." *Public Opinion Quarterly* 24 (Winter 1960).

Hess, Stephen. *Organizing the Presidency.* Brookings Institution, 1976.

———. *The Presidential Campaign.* Rev. ed. Brookings Institution, 1978.

Hodgson, Godfrey. *America in Our Time.* Doubleday, 1976.

———. *Congress and American Foreign Policy.* Royal Institute of International Affairs, 1979.

Hughes, Barry B. *The Domestic Content of American Foreign Policy.* Freeman, 1978.

Hughes, Emmet John. *The Living Presidency.* Coward, McCann and Geoghegan, 1973.

———. *The Ordeal of Power.* Atheneum, 1975.

———. "The Presidency vs. Jimmy Carter." *Fortune,* December 4, 1978.

Hyman, Sidney. *The American President.* Harper, 1954.

James, Marquis. *Andrew Jackson: Portrait of a President.* Bobbs-Merrill, 1937.

Jaworski, Leon. *The Right and the Power.* Reader's Digest, 1976.

Johnson, Lyndon Baines. *The Vantage Point: Perspectives of the Presidency, 1963–1969.* Holt, Rinehart & Winston, 1971.

Kearns, Doris. *Lyndon Johnson and the American Dream.* Harper & Row, 1976.

Keech, William R. *Winner Take All,* the Report of the Twentieth Century Fund Task Force on Reform of the Presidential Election Process. Holmes & Meier, 1978.

Keogh, James. *President Nixon and the Press*. Funk & Wagnalls, 1972.

Kessel, John H. *The Domestic Presidency: Decision-making in the White House*. Wadsworth, 1975.

King, Anthony, ed. *The New American Political System*. American Enterprise Institute, 1978.

Kirkpatrick, Jeane J. *The New Presidential Elite: Men and Women in National Politics*. Russell Sage Foundation and the Twentieth Century Fund, 1976.

Koenig, Louis. *The Chief Executive*. Harper & Row, 1968.

Ladd, Everett Carll, Jr. "The Candidates and the State of the Presidency." *Fortune*, December 3, 1979.

Laski, Harold. *The American Presidency*. Grosset & Dunlap, 1940.

Leubsdorf, Carl P. "Winging It with Jimmy." *Columbia Journalism Review*, July/August 1978.

MacNeil, Robert. *The People Machine*. Harper & Row, 1968.

McPherson, Harry C. *A Political Education*. Little, Brown, 1972.

Maisel, Louis, and Cooper, Joseph, eds. *The Impact of the Electoral Process*. Sage Electoral Studies Yearbook, vol. 3. Sage Publications, 1977.

———, and Sacks, Paul M., eds. *The Future of Political Parties*. Sage Electoral Studies Yearbook, vol. 2. Sage Publications, 1975.

Manley, John F. "Presidential Power and White House Lobbying." *Political Science Quarterly* 91, no. 2 (Summer 1978).

Mann, Thomas E. *Unsafe at Any Margin: Interpreting Congressional Elections*. American Enterprise Institute, 1978.

Mansfield, Harvey C., Sr. *Congress Against the President*. Praeger, 1975.

May, Ernest R. *Imperial Democracy: The Emergence of America as a Great Power*. Harcourt, Brace & World, 1961.

Metz, Robert. *CBS: Reflections in a Bloodshot Eye*. New American Library, 1975.

Minow, Newton N., Martin, John Bartlow; and Mitchell, Lee M. *Presidential Television: A Twentieth Century Fund Report*. Basic Books, 1973.

Morris, Edmund. *The Rise of Theodore Roosevelt*. Coward, McCann & Geoghegan, 1979.

Moynihan, Daniel Patrick. *Maximum Feasible Misunderstanding*. The Free Press, 1969.

———. *The Politics of a Guaranteed Income*. Random House, 1973.

Mueller, John E. *War, Presidents and Public Opinion*. John Wiley, 1973.

Nathan, Richard P. "The Administrative Presidency." *The Public Interest*, Summer 1976.

———. *The Plot That Failed: Nixon and the Administrative Presidency*. John Wiley, 1975.

Neustadt, Richard E. *Presidential Power: The Politics of Leadership.* John Wiley, 1960.

Newhouse, John. *Cold Dawn: The Story of SALT*. Holt, Rinehart & Winston, 1973.

The New York Times. *The White House Transcripts: The Full Text of the "Submission of Recorded Presidential Conversations to the Committee on the Judiciary of the House of Representatives by President Richard Nixon."* Viking, 1974.

Nie, Norman H.; Verba, Sidney; and Petrocik, John R. *The Changing American Voter.* Harvard University Press, 1976.

Ornstein, Norman J. and Elder, Shirley. *Interest Groups, Lobbying and Policymaking.* Congressional Quarterly, 1978.

Osborne, John. *The Nixon Watch* (an annual series). Liveright, 1971.

Parris, Judith H. "The Senate Reorganizes Its Committees, 1977." *Political Science Quarterly* 94, no. 2 (Summer 1979).

Pious, Richard M. *The American Presidency.* Basic Books, 1979.

———. "Is Presidential Power Poisonous?" *Political Science Quarterly* 89, no. 3 (Fall 1974).

Polsby, Nelson W., ed. *The Modern Presidency.* Random House, 1973.

Price, Raymond K. *With Nixon.* Viking, 1977.

The Public Interest passim, esp. no. 41 (Fall 1975), 10th anniversary issue.

Reedy, George E. *The Twilight of the Presidency.* New American Library, 1970.

Reston, James. *The Artillery of the Press.* Harper & Row, 1966.

Robinson, Michael J. "Television and American Politics." *The Public Interest,* Summer 1977.

Rosenman, Samuel. *Working with Roosevelt.* Harper & Row, 1952.

———, and Rosenman, Dorothy. *Presidential Style.* Harper & Row, 1976.

Rossiter, Clinton. *The American Presidency.* Harcourt, Brace & World, 1956.

Safire, William. *Before the Fall: An Inside View of the Pre-Watergate White House.* Doubleday, 1975.

Saloma, John S., III, and Sontag, Frederick H. *Parties: The Real Opportunity for Effective Citizen Politics.* Knopf, 1972.

Sandburg, Carl. *Abraham Lincoln.* 6 vols. Harcourt, Brace, 1926–39.

Schachner, Nathan. *Thomas Jefferson.* 1 vol. ed. Thomas Yoseloff, 1957.

Schell, Jonathan. *The Time of Illusion: An Historical and Reflective Account of the Nixon Era.* Random House, 1975.

Schlesinger, Arthur M., Jr. *The Age of Roosevelt.* 3 vols. Houghton Mifflin, 1957, 1958, 1960.

———. *The Imperial Presidency.* Houghton Mifflin, 1973.

———. *Robert Kennedy and His Times.* Houghton Mifflin, 1978.

———. *A Thousand Days: John F. Kennedy in the White House*. Houghton Mifflin, 1965.
Schram, Martin. *Running for President: A Journal of the Carter Campaign*. Pocket Books, 1977.
Sinclair, Ward. "96th Congress: Where Money Begets Power." *Washington Post*, September 23, 1979.
Senate Select Committee on Presidential Campaign Activities. *The Watergate Hearings: Break-in and Cover-up: Proceedings*. Edited by The New York Times Staff and R. W. Apple, Jr. Viking, 1973.
Siracusa, Joseph M., ed. *The American Diplomatic Revolution: A Documentary History of the Cold War, 1941–1947*. Kennikat, 1977.
Sorauf, Frank J. *Political Parties in the American System*. Little, Brown, 1964.
Sorensen, Theodore C. *Decision-making in the White House*. Columbia University Press, 1963.
———. *Kennedy*. Harper & Row, 1965.
———. *Watchmen in the Night: Presidential Accountability After Watergate*. MIT Press, 1975.
Stewart, John G. *One Last Chance: The Democratic Party, 1974–76*. Praeger, 1974.
Strum, Philippa. *Presidential Power and American Democracy*. Goodyear Publishing, 1979.
Talbot, Strobe. *Endgame: The Inside Story of SALT II*. Harper & Row, 1979.
Thomas, Norman C. and Baade, Hans W., eds. *The Institutionalized Presidency*, Oceana, 1972.
"Towards a More Responsible Two-Party System: A Report of the Committee on Political Parties, American Political Science Association." *American Political Science Review*, Supplement, vol. 44, no. 3, pt. 2 (September 1950).
Warren, Sidney, ed. *The American President*. Prentice-Hall, 1967.
Washington Journalism Center, and Roberts, Charles, eds. *Has the President Too Much Power?* Harper Magazine Press, 1974.
Wayne, Stephen J. *The Legislative Presidency*. Harper & Row, 1978.
Weiner, Sanford A. and Wildavsky, Aaron. "The Prophylactic Presidency." *The Public Interest*, no. 52 (Summer 1978).
White, Theodore H. *The Making of the President 1960*. Atheneum, 1961.
———. *The Making of the President 1964*. Atheneum, 1965.
———. *The Making of the President 1968*. Atheneum, 1969.
———. *The Making of the President 1972*. Atheneum, 1973.
Wicker, Tom. *JFK and LBJ*. Morrow, 1968.
Wieck, Paul R. "The Trouble with the Parties." *Washington Post*, February 4, 1979.
Wildavsky, Aaron. "The Past and Future Presidency." *The Public Interest*, no. 41 (Fall 1975), 10th anniversary issue.

———, ed. *The Presidency*. Little, Brown, 1969. Contains Wildavsky's own seminal essay, "The Two Presidencies."

Wilson, Woodrow. *Congressional Government*. Houghton Mifflin, 1885. Reprint. Meridian Books, 1956.

———. *Constitutional Government in the United States*. 1908. Reprint. Columbia University Press, 1961.

Winfrey, Lee. "Television Techniques: The 1976 Presidential Election." *Nieman Reports* 30, no. 3 (Autumn 1976).

Wise, David. *The Politics of Lying*. Random House, 1973.

Witcover, Jules. *Marathon: The Pursuit of the Presidency, 1972–1976*. Viking, 1977.

Wood, Robert C. "When Government Works." *The Public Interest*, no. 18 (Winter 1970).

Woodward, Bob, and Bernstein, Carl. *The Final Days*. Simon and Schuster, 1976.

Young, James S. "The Troubled Presidency." *The New York Times*, December 6 and 7, 1978.

Zeidenstein, Harvey G. "The Reassertion of Congressional Power: New Curbs on the President." *Political Science Quarterly* 91, no. 3 (Fall 1978).

Index